Critical Psychology, which has been developing in Germany for over twenty years, constitutes a radical critique and reconstruction of scientific psychology from a dialectical and historical-materialistic point of view. Its aim is to provide a firmer foundation than presently exists for a psychology that is methodologically sound, practically relevant, and theoretically determinate. This book makes the work available for the first time to an English-speaking audience.

Critical Psychology

Critical Psychology

Contributions to an Historical Science of the Subject

Edited by

CHARLES W. TOLMAN

Department of Psychology,
University of Victoria

WOLFGANG MAIERS

Psychological Institute,
Faculty of Philosophy and Social Sciences,
Free University of Berlin

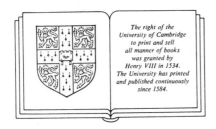

The right of the
University of Cambridge
to print and sell
all manner of books
was granted by
Henry VIII in 1534.
The University has printed
and published continuously
since 1584.

CAMBRIDGE UNIVERSITY PRESS

Cambridge

New York   Port Chester   Melbourne   Sydney

Published by the Press Syndicate of the University of Cambridge
The Pitt Building, Trumpington Street, Cambridge CB2 1RP
40 West 20th Street, New York, NY 10011, USA
10 Stamford Road, Oakleigh, Melbourne 3166, Australia

First published 1991

Printed in the United States of America

Library of Congress Cataloging-in-Publication Data
Critical psychology : contributions to an historical science of the
subject / edited by Charles W. Tolman and Wolfgang Maiers.
p.   cm.
Chiefly essays translated from German.
Includes bibliographical references and index.
ISBN 0–521–39344–2
1. Critical psychology. I. Tolman, Charles W. II. Maiers, Wolfgang
BF39.9.C75   1991
150.19 – dc20   90-48290
                                                 CIP

British Cataloguing in Publication Data
Critical psychology : contributions to an historical science of the subject.
1. Psychology. Applications of dialetics
I. Tolman, Charles W. II. Maiers, Wolfgang
100.1
ISBN 0-521-39344-2

Contents

v

Preface

Books like this frequently have innocent beginnings. The editors were among those who gathered in Plymouth, U.K., from 30 August to 2 September 1985, for the founding conference of the International Society for Theoretical Psychology. Michael Hyland, the principal organizer of the conference, had thoughtfully arranged an evening of relaxation and sightseeing aboard an excursion boat that took us some distance up the River Tamar. It was just what we needed after two days of vigorous debate over matters that could arouse only those keenly interested in the "just right" conceptualization of psychological phenomena. For the most part, however, although the seriousness abated, the discussions continued. We (C. T. and W. M.) found ourselves regretting the general lack of acquaintance among our English-speaking colleagues with the work of the German Critical Psychologists.

"Someone ought to translate a collection of key articles," one of us said.

"Yes," the other replied, "that's a good idea."

"It's a fairly straightforward task."

"Yes, with a little effort we could have the thing together by next spring."

Almost five years later we are getting the manuscript off to the publisher. It has been five years of translating text that was often extremely difficult. It was a job that was assumed "on the side," to be squeezed into the all-too-infrequent spaces between normal teaching and administrative and research obligations. For a time our project even had to compete with the urgencies associated with the preparation of an *Habilitationsschrift*. During this period of gestation, some of the ideas, issues, and analyses have been overtaken by more recent developments in Critical Psychology, but all of the pieces chosen for inclusion continue to provide clear examples of characteristic concepts, methods, and applications. We understand the present volume to be only the beginning of Critical Psychology in English and hope that it will stimulate the interest needed to motivate the translation or direct publication in English of more recent developments, particularly those in the areas of the psychology of

vii

women, racism and xenophobia, multidisciplinary therapeutic practice, and learning.

It has been a long and difficult path, one that could not have been traveled successfully without the assistance and support of many people. We have both been sustained in numerous visible and invisible ways by our respective institutions. The University of Victoria gave us a grant for translation assistance. Although most of the translation work was done by the first editor, very useful initial translations were provided by Frigga Haug for Chapter 12, by Ole Dreier for Chapter 10, and by John Garner for Chapters 6, 7, and 8. Renate Eulig-Tolman, without whose moral support some of the translations would never have been completed, read much of the English text and made valuable suggestions for improvement.

We have received much needed encouragement from numerous colleagues in many countries. Among these we wish especially to acknowledge the support of Jean Lave, who played a significant part in the successful completion of our innocently undertaken project.

The project began in the atmosphere of discussion created by the newly founded International Society for Theoretical Psychology. We feel very strongly that this book is ultimately a product of that atmosphere and therefore constitutes some measure of proof for the value of such enterprises.

To those named here and many left unnamed we are much indebted and acknowledge that debt here with sincere gratitude.

Charles W. Tolman *Wolfgang Maiers*

Acknowledgments

Chapter 1 was written for this volume.

Chapter 2 originally appeared as "Problemgeschichte der Kritischen Psychologie" in N. Kruse and M. Ramme (Eds.), *Hamburger Ringvorlesung Kritische Psychologie. Wissenschaftskritik, Kategorien, Anwendungsgebiete* (pp. 13–36), Hamburg: ergebnisse, 1988, and is included here with permission of the publisher.

Chapter 3 originally appeared as "Zum Verhältnis zwischen gesamtgesellschaftlichem Prozess und individuellem Lebensprozess" in *Konsequent. Diskussions – Sonderband "Streitbarer Materialismus"* (pp. 29–40), West Berlin: Zeitungsdienst Berlin, 1984, and is included here with permission of the publisher.

Chapter 4 originally appeared as "Selbsterfahrung und wissenschaftliche Objektivität" in K.-H. Braun and K. Holzamp (eds.), *Subjektivität als Problem psychologischer Methodik. 3. Internationaler Kongress Kritische Psychologie, Marburg 1984* (pp. 17–37), Frankfurt/M.: Campus, 1985, and is included here with permission of the publisher.

Chapter 5 originally appeared as "Die Bedeutung der Freudschen Psychoanalyse für die marxistisch fundierte Psychologie," *Forum Kritische Psychologie*, 1984, *13*, 15–30, and is included here with permission of the publisher.

Chapters 6 and 7 originally appeared as "Erkenntnis, Emotionalität, Handlungsfähigkeit," *Forum Kritische Psychologie*, 1978, *3*, 13–90, and are included here with permission of the publisher.

Chapter 8 originally appeared as " 'Persönlichkeit' – Selbstverwirklichung in gesellschaftlichen Freiräumen oder gesamtgesellschaftliche Verantwortungsübernahme des Subjekts" in H. Flessner, K. Hühne, H. Jung, A. Leisewitz, K. Maase, J. Reusch, and B. Wilhelmer (Eds.), *Marxistische Persönlichkeitstheorie. Internationale Beiträge* (pp. 69–92), Frankfurt/M.: Institut für

ix

marxistische Studien und Forschung, 1986, and is included here with permission of the publisher.

Chapters 9 and 10 were written for this volume.

Chapter 11 originally appeared as "Spiel und Ontogenese. Zur Diskussion ausgewählter marxistisch begründeter und psychoanalytischer Ansätze" in H. Flessner, K. Hühne, H. Jung, A. Leisewitz, K. Maase, J. Reusch, and B. Wilhelmer (Eds.), *Marxistische Persönlichkeitstheorie. Internationale Beiträge* (pp. 203–226), Frankfurt/M.: Institut für marxistische Studien und Forschung, 1986, and is included here with permission of the publisher.

Chapter 12 originally appeared as "Zeit der Privatisierungen? Verarbeitungen gesellschaftlicher Umbrüche in Arbeit and Lebensweise," *Das Argument,* 1986, *156,* 174–190, and is included here with permission of the publisher.

Contributors

Karl-Heinz Braun
Fachbereich Sozialwesen
Fachhochschule Fulda
Fulda, Germany

Ole Dreier
Psykologisk Laboratorium
Universitet Koebenhavn
Koebenhavn, Denmark

Frigga Haug
Hochschule für Wirtschaft and Politik
Hamburg, Germany

Klaus Holzkamp
Psychologisches Institut
Fachbereich Philosophie und
  Sozialwissenschaften I
Freie Universität Berlin
Berlin, Germany

Ute Holzkamp-Osterkamp
Psychologisches Institut
Fachbereich Philosophie und
  Sozialwissenschaften I
Freie Universität Berlin
Berlin, Germany

Wolfgang Maiers
Psychologisches Institut
Fachbereich Philosophie und
  Sozialwissenschaften I
Freie Universität Berlin
Berlin, Germany

Morus Markard
Psychologisches Institut
Fachbereich Philosophie und
  Sozialwissenschaften I
Freie Universität Berlin
Berlin, Germany

Charles W. Tolman
Department of Psychology
University of Victoria
Victoria, British Columbia, Canada

Critical Psychology

1 Critical Psychology: An Overview

Charles W. Tolman

To one degree or another a state of crisis has existed in psychology from the beginning of its existence as a separate scientific discipline in the second half of the nineteenth century. The result has been a fairly continuous flow of "crisis literature," sometimes ebbing, sometimes flooding, but always there.

For reasons that are not hard to understand, the crisis has always been of such a nature as to reflect the *relevance* of psychological theory and/or practice. This is a consequence of the historical character of the discipline. No original formulation of the psychological object of investigation or of methodology can be expected to have been utterly correct and unproblematic. The problem remains the same today as in 1918 when R. S. Woodworth observed the "curious fact" about psychology, that "it is uncertain, or seems so, as to its proper line of study" (Woodworth, 1918: 20). It is certainly a sign of immaturity but, Woodworth maintained, is less serious than it at first appears. Such is the way sciences develop. Their history is one of ever more precisely identifying and approximating their "proper line of study," including its appropriate methods.

Relevance comes into the picture as a criterion for recognizing that a "line of study" or its methods have ceased to move us ahead or are moving us in the wrong direction. It serves the same function as "satisfaction" in William James's theory of truth. The ordinary correspondence theory of truth was abstract. It described only part of the picture if it did not inform us about how we recognize correspondence or its absence or why it ought to be important to us.

The experimental method was introduced into psychology by Fechner, Wundt, and others because the more traditional speculative methods of the philosophers were not yielding the reliable knowledge that was relevant to the felt intellectual and practical needs of the time. The behaviorist revolt was even more obviously focused on relevance. Knowledge of mental contents was, for Watson and his followers, simply not relevant to the practical needs "both for general social control and growth and for individual happiness"

1

(Watson, 1924: 8). Gestalt psychology, too, came upon the scene as a protest against the stagnant and false "lines of study" associated with both "structuralism" and behaviorism. The focus of their attack was the irrelevance of the elemental analysis, whether it was of mental contents or of stimulus and response. These analyses did not, as they should, begin and end in the "world as we find it" (Köhler, 1947: 3).

The list of examples is a long and familiar one. The lesson to be extracted is clear: Psychology makes historical progress, that is, expands its command of relevant knowledge, through periodic protests aimed at some aspect of residual irrelevance in the mainstream "line of study" and its methods. These protests almost always begin outside the mainstream. Insofar as a fair and scientific spirit guides their reception, they become tested and, it is hoped, to the extent they actually put us back on course, become absorbed in time into the mainstream to become themselves the object of future protest and correction.

Of course, not every protest is "on track." Many come to nothing for reasons that are clearer in the cooler aftermath than in the heat of debate. Those that do make an impact vary considerably in their profundity. Gestalt psychology eventually but effectively put an end to the more simplistic forms of associationism that had dominated psychological thought for at least two centuries. Behaviorism was quicker in putting an end to an exclusive emphasis on mental contents and introspective methods. The ecological theory of perception (Gibson, 1979) will take much longer time to supplant the traditional representational theories inherited from ancient Greece, but, if successful, its effects will be pervasive. Less profound, but successful, protests are harder to identify because they appear to belong to the everyday existence of science. Failures, the grander ones at least, are easier to identify. After a considerable flurry of radical claims, humanistic psychology has left little discernible impact on mainstream subject matter or methods in psychology.

Critical Psychology as Protest

The scientific activity that has become known in Europe as Critical Psychology began as a protest against mainstream "bourgeois" psychology. Its complaints originated in the ideological critique of a psychology that had aligned itself with one segment of the population against another (as exemplified in the well-known Hawthorne experiments). It emerged as the pro–scientific psychology branch of the critique, opposed to those who claimed that a scientific psychology could do nothing other than serve dominant interests and thus could never, in principle, be relevant to the interests of ordinary people. Those who were to become known as Critical Psychologists argued that although psychological knowledge and practice would always be tied to interests, these interests were not necessarily those of the ruling classes. It was possible, they maintained, to organize scientifically, theoretically, and politically a psychology that served the genuine interests of working people.

What makes the Critical Psychological protest different from those of behaviorism, Gestalt psychology, and most others that are familiar to us is its strongly political nature. Its protest was first and foremost a political one and might well have evaporated into the ether as far as organized psychology was concerned if this political protest had not been soon translated into one that was scientific, that is, theoretical and methodological. That the proponents of Critical Psychology did this, and successfully it appears, makes it historically unique in Western psychology, which has experienced many purely political protests, as well as the numerous and well known purely theoretical and methodological ones. It is the successful combination of these forms of protest that is new and interesting. I have called the combination successful for two reasons. First, it has succeeded in sustaining its political point in psychological discussions in West Germany and elsewhere in Europe. That is, its opponents have had difficulty rejecting its position out of hand as being "merely" political, so even those who have rejected the position have been forced to do so for other reasons. Second, and related to the first, it has succeeded in showing how the political concerns are translated into recognizable theoretical and methodological terms. Critics have found it difficult to avoid the recognition that even "purely" theoretical and methodological matters are in the last analysis also political (without implying any simple relativism at all).

Irrelevance and Indeterminacy in Bourgeois Psychology

In the theoretical and methodological debates of English-language psychologists the prevailing position against which protests are made is normally characterized as "mainstream." The Critical Psychologists insist that although their target may very well be mainstream, the label tends to hide its political nature. During the protest-filled sixties the position was often politicized by calling it the "establishment." Critical Psychologists would be sympathetic to this but would object that it does not go far enough. The mainstream is guided by the interests of the establishment, but the nature of the latter must be specified. In a capitalist society the establishment is capital. In Western "democracies" this is manifested in the nearly invariable sacrifice of individual freedoms for the freedom of capital. Consider the fish-processing plant on the coast that is to be closed because it is unprofitable. It is being shut down not because there are no more fish or because people no longer eat fish or because the workers in the plant no longer need work. No, the plant is closed because the capital that owns it has found a more profitable outlet, perhaps by moving its operations to the Third World, where labor is cheaper. Such a movement by capital is, of course, facilitated by provincial, federal, and international laws that are promulgated by people who are themselves capitalists or who have unimpeachable records as supporters of the interests of capital. Why do we have such strict laws regulating strikes by workers, when strikes by capital are openly and devoutly supported by our governments? There is no need here for a lesson in capitalist political economy. The point is simply to remind ourselves that the establishment is not simply those in power; it is specifically the power of capital.

Now if the establishment is the power of capital and the mainstreams of the social sciences are guided and influenced by it, then we are fully justified in distinguishing these mainstreams as bourgeois. There is ample evidence, again, of the bourgeois nature of social scientific theory and method. One particularly well-known study of this was the book *The Servants of Power* by Loren Baritz (1960). Baritz concluded his study with the following paragraph:

Over the years, through hundreds and hundreds of experiments, social scientists have come close to a true science of behavior. They are now beginning to learn how to control conduct. Put this power – genuine, stark, irrevocable power – into the hands of America's managers, and the work that social scientists have done, and will do, assumes implications vaster and more fearful than anything previously hinted. (p. 210)

It must not be concluded that the problem is simply one of an essentially neutral social science being misused by unscrupulous individuals. The science, both theoretically and methodologically, is pervaded by the bourgeois attitude. It is not hard, for instance, to read the work of John B. Watson and be led to the conclusion that his whole scheme was from the start intended to respond to Veblen's advice:

It is not a question of what ought to be done, but of what is the course laid out by business principles; the discretion rests with the business men, not with the moralists, and the business men's discretion is bounded by the exigencies of business enterprise. (1904, quoted in Baritz, 1960: xiii)

It was, of course, the "exigencies of business enterprise" that demanded a view of the worker as a nonthinking, nonfeeling machine that could be selected and trained solely according to the interests of the employer. The same exigencies urged the definition of psychology's mission as "prediction and control," with engineering efficiency, which included the understanding of psychological subject matter in terms of independent and dependent variables.

The point should not be belabored. It will be dealt with again in the chapters that follow. When Critical Psychologists speak of bourgeois psychology, they are pointing to a very real phenomenon, one that practicing psychologists should be aware of. It is an insistence on the recognition of the societal embeddedness of social science, that is, that the "ideas of the ruling class are in every epoch the ruling ideas" (Marx & Engels, 1846/1970a: 64). Without conscious acknowledgment, and resistance where necessary, the priorities contained in these ideas will necessarily be blindly reproduced in the ideas of organized science, that is, in theory and method. Critical Psychologists insist, however, that psychology need not be bourgeois in this way; there is also a possibility of its being critical.

It should also be noted that "bourgeois" cannot be reduced to "mainstream" for the simple reason that many positions in social science and particularly in psychology have been clearly bourgeois but never mainstream. Abraham Maslow's theory of self-actualization is but one example.

Critical Psychology's insistence on using the category "bourgeois" implies a critical stance toward it. In adopting this critical stance, which is now not critical merely of particular ways of thinking about and doing psychology, but also of the societal arrangements in which psychology is practiced, Critical Psychology openly embraces a kind of partisanship (*Parteilichkeit*) that has traditionally been considered inappropriate in science. Science is a societal practice and has to do with societal existence; as such, it cannot be value-free. Its very existence presupposes its societal value. The point of Critical Psychology's partisanship is to make its societal value as conscious as possible. This partisanship can be expressed in class terms: It takes the side of the working classes. But more immediately important, it takes the side of the individual human subject.

Why should partisanship for the individual human subject be necessary? This question brings us back to the topic of *relevance*. The problem is not so much that psychology has been irrelevant in any absolute sense. Even the mechanistic stimulus–response behaviorism of Watson was relevant to somebody's interests, namely those of capital and its managers. This, the Critical Psychologists maintain, proves to be the case for all of Western psychology's nomothetic psychology. A psychology that deals with averages in the hopes of achieving generality through abstraction can never become relevant to the particular individual. But this is precisely what happens with our insistence on the measurement and statistical treatment of independent and dependent variables. This is altogether more suited to capital's need to manipulate the masses than to shedding light on the experience or problems of individuals.

But what about that aspect of our psychological practice that concerns itself specifically with the measurement of individual differences? We need only reflect on whose interests have been served by all the attention to IQ to see that the answer is no different here.

The conclusion of Critical Psychology is that while mainstream bourgeois psychology may well have accumulated genuine knowledge about human psychological functioning, the depth of this knowledge and its relevance to real human needs will remain seriously limited as long as the experiences of historically and societally situated concrete individuals are ignored. It has, in short, not taken the standpoint of the subject into account, even in its more idiographic forms. Bourgeois psychology has, on the whole, tended in fact to deny subjectivity in the interest of an ostensible objectivity. Critical Psychology is concerned, then, with identifying the reasons for these and related deficiencies and developing strategies for overcoming them.

The irrelevancy of bourgeois psychological knowledge is linked to another problem, one that forms the second prong of the Critical Psychological critique. This is the indeterminacy of psychological theory. The difficulty is that any number of apparently different theories may be held by different people at any one time about what is presumed to be the same subject matter, and there appears to be no way of resolving the differences. On the one hand, a large number of psychologists seem to have accepted this as a natural state of affairs. It is rationalized in terms of the presumptiousness of overarching theory. "The age of grand theory is past," they say. "It was never anything but vain hope." As an alternative, these psychologists assign virtue to "pluralism" and rail against the "dogmatism" of those who still seek to overcome it.

Critical Psychologists, on the other hand, maintain that if psychology is to become truly relevant to the existence of concrete individuals, indeterminacy must be overcome, not in any dogmatic way, such as by forcing compliance to a uniform doctrine, but by identifying its causes and principled solutions. In short, the attitude is that indeterminacy is not a natural state of affairs, but the product of a particular constellation of historically conditioned approaches to the subject matter and methods of psychology, approaches that, once again, can be identified as bourgeois.

The project of Critical Psychology is thus a radical one: It seeks to get at the roots of irrelevancy and indeterminacy and to discover the scientifically principled methodological and theoretical means for producing a reformed psychology that is both relevant and determinate. The extent of what they have in mind is reflected in their claim to be developing an entirely new *paradigm* for scientific psychology.

Critical Psychology's Levels of Analysis

The Critical Psychological project is carried out on a broad front, embracing specifically four levels of analysis: the philosophical, the societal-theoretical, and two levels of strictly psychological inquiry, the categorial and the special theoretical.

At the *philosophical level,* Critical Psychology is dialectical materialist. The choice is not an arbitrary one. Consider determinacy. At the very least a realist epistemology is required to resolve this problem. All subjective idealisms and relativisms are themselves thoroughly indeterminate and thus can only undermine systematic efforts to solve the problem. The objective forms of idealism (for example, Platonism, Thomism) are more promising but depend in the last instance on a dogmatic acceptance of their fundamental abstraction (the "good," divine will, and so forth). They therefore merely provide means of putting off indeterminacy, not of resolving it in any scientifically acceptable way. Traditional empiricism or positivism, while nominally realist, is made problematic by its sensationism. If taken seriously and consistently it leads necessarily to skepticism (vide Hume) and/or phenomenalism (vide Mach), which are better seen as varying forms or manifestations of the problem, rather than as its solution.

Only materialisms have claimed to be consistently realist, which undoubtedly accounts for their having been the philosophies of scientific choice from the time of Bacon onward, but, here again, problems arise. Traditional materialism carries with it an enormous amount of metaphysical baggage, such as elementalism, associationism, identity of essence and appearance, and mechanical determinism, to name only a few of its problematic contents that may create more serious difficulties than the one its realism promises to solve.

Dialectical materialism retains the realist epistemology and dumps most of the troublesome metaphysical baggage. Its weak ontological position, which leaves the details of reality to discoveries by science, has led some to suggest that it should not be called materialism at all, but given a more neutral label less identified with its rigid ancestors. For better or for worse, however, it has become known as materialism, and any attempt to change that here and now would only create more confusion than already exists. Cornforth described the "teachings" of materialism as follows:

1. The world is by its very nature material; everything which exists comes into being on the basis of material causes, arises and develops in accordance with the laws of the motion of matter.
2. Matter is objective reality existing outside and independent of the mind; far from the mental existing in separation from the material, everything mental or spiritual is a product of material processes.
3. The world and its laws are knowable, and while much in the material world may not be known there is no unknowable sphere of reality which lies outside the material world. (Cornforth, 1975: 25, altered slightly but not substantively.)

An important aspect of dialectical materialist epistemology that is often overlooked in discussions like this is its rejection of the traditional indirect realist or representationalist theory of perception. The replacement theory is not a naive but a direct realism. Implicit in the writings of Marx and Engels, this theory was first articulated by Lenin (Goldstick, 1980) and anticipates, at least in broad outline, the version that is current in psychology, namely the ecological theory of perception (Gibson, 1979). The adoption of this theory by itself overcomes one important source of theoretical indeterminacy, the presumed lack of access to objects in themselves. Direct realism is a theory that specifically accounts for that access, rather than denying it outright. Furthermore, unlike naive realism, this theory does not imply a neglect of the specifically human capacity for meaning in perception. Rather, it attempts to give a more adequate account of meaning based on the direct access to or reflection of objects (for example, Leontyev, 1971: 180–185).

The dialectical side of dialectical materialism is also important. Dialectics is essentially a movement away from a static and toward a dynamic worldview, from an additive and accretive model of reality to one that is processual and developmental. Hegel's intent was to bring our thinking about the world into closer agreement with it. It is less a set of ontological assumptions about reality than a method for grasping it, as it were, on the run. The most important features of materialist dialectics were summarized by Lenin:

In the first place, in order really to know an object we must embrace, study, all its sides, all connections and "mediations." We shall never achieve this completely, but the demand for all-sidedness is a safeguard against mistakes and rigidity. Secondly, dialectical logic demands that we take an object in its development, its "self-movement" (as Hegel sometimes put it), in its changes. . . . Thirdly, the whole of human experience should enter the full "definition" of an object as a criterion of the truth and as a practical index of the object's connection with what man requires. Fourthly, dialectical logic teaches that "there is no abstract truth, truth is always concrete," as the late Plekhanov was fond of saying after Hegel. . . . (Quoted in Selsam and Martel, 1963: 116)

The bearing of this on the problems of indeterminacy and irrelevance will become clear in what follows. As we shall see, an important source of both is psychology's customary method of forming concepts (categories) through a static procedure of definition whose results can only be abstract. A dialectical approach to the matter, following a more developmental method yields concepts (categories) that are both more concrete, thus more relevant to individual cases, and more determinate.

At the *societal theoretical level,* Critical Psychology adopts the Marxist position of historical materialism. This, too, is not an arbitrary choice. Once dialectical materialism is adopted on such principles as I have tried to indicate and attention is turned to human phenomena, it follows that these phenomena must be viewed historically as the outcome of a material process of development. This means much more than simply taking history and society somehow into account. The phenomena of psychological interest must be seen as being inherently historical-societal. Some implications of this will be presented in later sections. Two implications of general importance can be mentioned, however, at this point.

The first has to do with the way in which the subject of psychological functioning is viewed. Bourgeois mainstream psychology has tended to treat the subject abstractly, as "human being in general," or even as "organism in general." It has been understood as desirable to achieve the broadest possible generality of laws, and this has usually been achieved through abstraction. Watson's laws of recency and frequency in the acquisition of habits, for example, or Thorndike's "law of effect" were intended to apply to virtually all organisms at all times. They contain no recognition that important qualitative differences might attach to the subject's being human as opposed to animal, working class as opposed to bourgeois, hunter-gatherer as opposed to factory worker, and so forth. One prominent expression of this focus on the abstract "organism in general" is found in the well-known 1956 paper by Skinner in which he displays three cumulative records in graph. They all look the same. He tells the reader that one was from a pigeon, one from a rat, and one from a monkey: "[W]hich is which? It doesn't matter" (Skinner, 1956). Given his experimental conditions, humans produce identical curves; that also appears not to matter. Skinner here is virtually confessing that his theory is blind to differences that most of us would regard as very important. The end result is a psychological theory that pertains to the abstract organism. It cannot be expected to make much sense of the concrete individual human experience.

This abstract ahistorical-asocietal approach to psychology, which typifies mainstream bourgeois psychology, is linked by Critical Psychologists to its methodological concentration on "variables" (for which reason they speak of it as variable psychology). On the one hand, to treat every psychological problem as one of identifying variables and their relations is to commit oneself from the start to an abstract understanding of the subject matter. Beginning thus with an abstraction, the variable, it is little wonder that psychology has relevance problems. On the other hand, even those more "contextualist" theories that insist on the importance of culture treat it as a collection of variables that can, where necessary or just convenient, be held or rendered constant. The essentially historical and societal nature of psychological phenomena cannot be grasped in this way.

A second general implication of historical materialism is that a recognition of the historical and societal embeddedness, not just of the subject matter, but of scientific theory and practice, is a minimal requirement for overcoming the blind reproduction of dominant societal priorities. The earlier discussion of the use of the term *bourgeois* was one such result of taking historical materialism seriously.

The *categorial level* of analysis is the one that has recently occupied Critical Psychologists the most. Indeed, they often claim that their most important contributions to psychology in general have, until now, been at this level.

Although as a result of this work they have provided psychology with a number of new and reworked categories (basic concepts), some of which we shall examine presently, it is most important that they have devised a new *method* for generating or forming categories. And the most important feature of this new method is that it provides means of verifying or falsifying categories, which have a status similar to that of theories. This is the basis for their solution to the problem of indeterminacy. The method follows from historical materialism. Most simply put, it derives from the maxim that a thing is best understood as to what it is by examining how it got that way. Thus the categories of the psychical (psychological phenomena) are best identified and defined by an examination of their phylogeny, history, and ontogeny. The method is called historical-empirical: "empirical" to emphasize its scientific (as opposed to speculative) nature; "historical" to distinguish its reconstructive character from the "actual-empirical" methods of ordinary scientific practice (observation, experimentation, measurement, and so forth). The method necessarily turns to other historical sciences for its material – anthropology, history, paleontology, ethology, and so on.

To appreciate this new approach to categories correctly, some results of which will be the focus of the next section of this chapter, we need to be reminded of where our traditional categories come from. These have mostly been taken over as labels from everyday language (learning, motivation, emotion, cognition, intelligence, and so forth) and then assigned definitions motivated largely by the need to arrive at some kind of working consensus among scientists. It is seldom clear where these definitions come from, frequently lending them a rather obvious arbitrariness. It is therefore common that many often incompatible definitions exist side by side in the discipline, leaving the newcomer with the task of choosing the one that seems to suit momentary needs. Operational definitions and construct validity provide fully institutionalized and sanctified examples of this procedure.

It should be noted that psychologists have been satisfied with categories derived in this manner because of the widespread belief – the heritage of our positivist and phenomenalist origins – that concepts like motivation cannot be specified in any other way. There appears to be no way of finally resolving just *what* motivation really is. The concept is taken as one of convenience only. Scientists who have agreed to agree that it is x cannot go "wrong," because there is, in the last instance, no "right." Such a view of things is, of course, plainly relativistic and leads necessarily to conceptual and theoretical indeterminacy in psychology.

Critical Psychologists do not maintain a priori that the categories of mainstream bourgeois psychology must, owing to their origin, be false. It is unquestionably the case that much of what we say about emotion, learning, motivation, and so forth, is correct. The present methods, however, do not allow us to say exactly what is correct about a concept, or why. In other words, the present methods leave the categories indeterminate. They offer, however, as good a place as any for a start. Critical Psychologists call them "preconcepts." The historical-empirical method, then, undertakes to assess their value against the evidence of phylogenetic and historical development. The end result may be a "new" or "rehabilitated" concept of, say, motivation, the preconcept may prove to be so totally corrupt as to need discarding ("attitude" comes close to this), or the process may reveal the need for new categories ("action potence").

The *specific theoretical level* is the one of detailed theories about learning, human development, and so on, that level at which ordinary scientific explanation of phenomena takes place. This is the least developed level in Critical Psychology, but work is going on, and there is every reason to believe that it will eventually prove as successful as the work on the categorial level.

The Categorial Reconstruction of Psychology's Object

The general approach of the categorial reconstruction of psychology's object is "genetic" in the broadest sense of the term, that is, developmental, focusing on the genesis of psychical functions and structures. As such, it is modeled after the reconstruction of taxonomy resulting from the theory of evolution. Just as the definitions of plant and animal species become more accurate and scientifically useful when they are made with regard to phylogenetic relationships, so, too, should the psychological categories resulting from such an analysis be more accurate and useful. The logic governing the development of psychical functions is much the same, generally speaking, as that governing structural taxonomy. It is assumed, for example, that on the whole more generalized forms precede more specialized ones. Consciousness, consequently, is more likely to have developed from sensibility than vice versa. Likewise a generalized adaptive modifiability must precede the kind of learning that in higher species becomes essential to the full development of the individual.

The first stage of the analysis is to identify the development, the qualitative leap, that marks the transition from prepsychical to psychical organisms. Prepsychical living forms are generally described as "irritable"; that is, they can respond with appropriate movements or secretions to relevant aspects of their environments. Such organisms evolve to a psychical stage when, owing to conditions of food scarcity and development of locomotion that is at first undirected, they begin to respond to properties that are relevant only because they assist in orienting the organism to other properties that are relevant. An example would be a simple organism that is able to move relative to light in order to find food. This ability to utilize mediating properties or signals is called sensibility and is regarded as the most generalized form of the psychical from which all other forms developed.

Out of the barest form of sensibility arise more complex types of orientation, first to gradients, then to separated properties, and so on to increasingly differentiated reflection of the surrounding world. Holzkamp sees the most rudimentary capacity for analysis and synthesis developing here, as well as equally rudimentary capacity for meaning. The latter also begins to differentiate what is significant for reproduction and what is significant for maintenance of the individual living system. The analysis continues through the differentiation of emotion as a means of assessing environmental conditions in terms of the organism's internal condition, a rudimentary form of motivation, to the development of communication and social structures.

The next major development is that of individual learning and development. This occurs in two stages. First comes the appearance of "subsidiary" learning, in which learning plays an increasingly important role in the organism's life but is not yet essential to its development. In the second stage learning is increasingly linked to the organism's developmental possibilities. Motivation begins to become differentiated from emotion at this level, and the stage is set for a reversal of the dominance of fixed action patterns over learned ones in the animal's overall adaptive strategy. This prepares the way for the development of the specifically human level of development at which the results of the categorial analysis are seen most clearly.

The development of motivation here serves well to illustrate the "genetic reconstruction" of the categories, the principal ones here being orientation, emotion, and motivation. Rudimentary orientation occurs in animals prior to the stage of individual learning and development. At this stage, however, emotion develops as a means of the organism's appraisal of its environment against the "yardstick" of its own internal state. This, together with curiosity and exploratory behavior, becomes a necessary precondition for orientation. It is out of this precondition for orientation that motivation develops as an anticipatory component of emotion. What becomes anticipated is the emotional valence of objects, to which the animal now demonstrates preferential behavior. Action takes on an obvious goal orientation, which becomes supraindividual and forms the basis for more complex social behavior and organization.

It is important here that the categories are thus rederived in such a way as to yield an "organically" unified account of the animal psyche.

The Specifically Human Psyche

Generally speaking what is specific to human existence is its societal nature. This is qualitatively different from the merely social existence of the higher (and some lower) animals in ways I hope to make clear in the paragraphs that follow.

Societal existence is achieved in two major steps. The first begins with the use of tools. Of course, many animals use tools, with the higher primates displaying the most humanlike behavior in this regard. It is also well known from laboratory experiments that their capacity to use instruments is generally greater than observations in natural settings suggest. There are even instances of "tool making" in primates, or at least of some rudimentary preparation of the instrument for its intended use. Again, laboratory experiments have revealed astonishing capabilities in this regard. What distinguishes the human from other animals is the preparation of tools independent of the object for which they are intended. This includes the keeping of tools for future eventualities. When this first happened among our prehominid ancestors, the Critical Psychologists maintain, the first great step was taken toward the distinctly human mode of existence. They call it an ends–means inversion. The tool, that which mediates our relationships with the material world around us, now becomes not merely a means, but an end in itself. Unlike animals, we deliberately set about the design and manufacture of tools.

The psychological implications of this "inversion" are incomparably profound. The encouragement it gives to the development of abstract thinking and language is obvious. The maker of a tool as an end in itself must be able to represent to him- or herself mentally the object with which it is to be used. The tool itself must represent the idea of its use. Having meaning invested in a portable object and given the social conditions of its manufacture and use, the invention of more portable symbols, such as words, seems a quite natural result.

Of course, none of this would have occurred without the social context of its development. And it is in this social context that some of the most far-reaching effects were felt. Although there must already have been social differentiation based on function such as we now see in many primate social groupings, these differentiations would now take on an entirely new quality based on a social division of labor. This begins with the separation of the deliberate making of a tool from its use. The individual who makes it now need no longer be the one who uses it, and vice versa. The important feature of this new differentiation is that it now begins to be based on some kind of deliberate social arrangement among individuals and not on characteristics determined directly by the organism's biology. While biologically determined features may have remained important for a very long time, it is obvious that as the tools are made more and more effective and the success of their applications depends more and more on their design, the biological characteristics of the user become less relevant (we need merely think of modern machines that can be operated by the mere push of buttons). When the lives of individuals become more determined by such social arrangements than by biology, the second major step in hominization occurs. Critical Psychologists speak of this step as a change in dominance (*Dominanzwechsel*) from the biological to the *societal,* which now, because it is dominant, is qualitatively distinct from what is called social in other animals.

When this second step is accomplished, the specifically human form of existence is achieved. Its distinctive characteristic is what Critical Psychologists call – rather awkwardly, I'm afraid – societal mediatedness (*gesamtgesellschaftliche Vermitteltheit*). What this means is that, whereas the individual prehuman animal's link to its world is a relatively direct one, the human's is a mediated one. The most obvious mediator is the tool itself. We do not operate directly upon objects in our world as do animals with their teeth and claws. We use a knife, a hammer, or a bulldozer. What's more, these tool mediators are normally not made by their users but by others. Thus even our use of tools itself is mediated by others. But most of our needs are not satisfied even by our use of tools. If we want food, we go to a restaurant or to a grocery store. Individuals produce for themselves by participating in the social arrangements we call society. It is in fact society that mediates each individual's relationship to the material world, which is no longer "natural" in the strict sense of the word. Furthermore, our effectiveness in dealing with the world is no longer governed by natural, biologically determined abilities. It is governed rather by the stage of our society's development and the effectiveness with which we have individually and collectively appropriated the skills necessary for participation in societal existence. There is, in short, very little that we do that is natural, very little that is not governed exclusively by the society that we are born into and the places that we as individual subjects occupy within it. The aspects of existence that we call psychical are thoroughly penetrated and determined by societal existence. A psychology that fails to make the essential distinction between societal and presocietal (that is, social) existence has no hope of capturing what is important here. Categories of psychology like learning, emotion, motivation, and cognition cannot fail to be significantly altered by the fact of our existence's societal mediatedness.

The first implication of this recognition is the utter falsity of any simple stimulus–response, or even stimulus–organism–response, scheme that implies an unmediated link to environmental conditions. Humans have always proved troublesome for such theories, which have traditionally necessitated the construction of abnormally impoverished laboratory situations for even moderately successful testing. The reason that humans are troublesome in this way is that there are very few unequivocal objective relationships between the individual's behavior and its environmental conditions, whether these be material or societal. The human's relationship to the environment is almost always mediated (certainly *always* so, when it is humanly important). The most important mediation category is *meaning*. We do not respond to things as such, but to what we make them out to be, and that is never unequivocal. Unlike other animals, our societal existence ensures that we live in a world of meanings and not of bare physical things. When presented with a hammer, we find it extraordinarily difficult to see it as anything but a hammer. We pick it up in the correct way and find it awkward to make any movements with it except those that express its normal use. A chimpanzee will behave quite otherwise. (It is interesting how we have denigratingly referred to this typically human characteristic as "stimulus error" and "functional fixedness." Do we really mean to suggest that chimpanzees are likely to be more "creative" because they lack the latter characteristic?) The typically human relationship to the world that mediation and particularly meaning create is referred to by Critical Psychologists as a *possibility relation*. What the world presents to me is a set or range of possibilities. It is these that determine what I do, not things directly.

Meaning mediates the individual's relationship to the world of objects, but more important is the mediation it provides with society at large. In this connection Critical Psychologists differentiate between meaning and meaning structures. The meaning structures make up the societal context within which the individual acts and lives. These represent the totality of all actions that must, on average, be carried out by individuals if the society is to survive. They therefore represent the necessities of society. The meanings of the individual are determined by the societal meaning structures and define the position of the individual with respect to the societal whole. These are felt as subjective necessities and represent the individual's possibilities of action within society. Although the subjective necessities for any given individual may be quite different from those of others, they form the basis for the consciousness of oneself as a "center of intentionality" and the consciousness of others as equivalent centers.

The Reconstruction of Needs: Action Potence

This new societally mediated relationship between the individual and the world of objects and other people requires a thorough reevaluation of even the most basic, seemingly biological, categories. For example, an animal's need is a biological deficit that it overcomes by its own behavior directed in some appropriate way toward the object of the need. When it is hungry, it forages, finds the food it requires, and consumes it. Humans, however, have no such unmediated relationship to the objects of their needs. Between the human needing food and the food itself lies a very complex set of societal relations, a complicated division of labor involving the production and distribution of food, along with a myriad of other cultural attitudes and practices. In modern capitalist society, with its advanced state of technological development, it is safe to say that the societal capacity to produce and distribute food far outstrips the need for it. Yet even in the most advanced capitalist countries, not to mention the Third World countries they exploit, there are hungry people. The hunger of these people is not like that of animals, a simple biological deficit. Far more, it represents a defect in the societal fabric. Further, it cannot be satisfied in the same way that the animal's hunger is satisfied. Human hunger is not satisfied by the mere availability and consumption of food. This presumes a nonmediated nature in the relationship between the individual and the world.

From the framework of the societal mediatedness of distinctly human existence, it can be seen that human needs are transformed by it such that they do not refer directly to the objects that we need so much as to our capacity to participate in the mediating societal arrangements by which the consumable objects are produced and distributed. The Critical Psychologists call this having control over (*Verfügung über*) the conditions of production. It is not at all uncommon to hear that needy people in our society or others say that what they need is not a handout but an opportunity to earn a living. According to our present analysis, this is a quite precise expression of the peculiarly human nature of needs.

This understanding of needs is linked to two other basic concepts of Critical Psychology, one of which is already familiar. This is the idea of *possibility relationship*. The problem of, say, hunger lies not in the availability of food as such but in the possibility relationships that exist for single individuals or a group within society. It is precisely because our relationship to the world is characterized by societally mediated possibility relationships that our needs are qualitatively different from those of other animals. The second concept is that of *subjective situation (Befindlichkeit)*. This is the subjective side of the individual's objective relationship to the world. It is the individual's assessment of the quality of his or her existence and is directly related to his or her control over the conditions in which the objects of needs are produced. Two important implications follow from this analysis of needs and subjective situation.

The first implication yields one of Critical Psychology's most central categories, action potence (*Handlungsfähigkeit*). This is the focal category that embraces everything that has been said up to now. It reflects the need for psychology to consider the individual's ability to do the things that he or she feels are necessary to satisfy his or her needs, that is, to ensure an acceptable quality of life. It has a subjective side, which is how one feels about oneself and one's relations with the world. It has an objective side in the actual possibilities for need satisfaction through cooperative effort with other members of society. Action potence is what mediates individual reproduction and societal reproduction.

The second implication has to do with the way in which human action is grounded. Again reflecting the mediated nature of human existence, human action is grounded subjectively in meaning that reflects the individual's objective possibility relationship with the world and society. Subjective grounds for action (*subjektive Handlungsgründe*), then, is what we are looking for when we want the immediate explanation of behavior. Critical Psychologists note that the objective societal conditions provide only "premises" for individual behavior, not causes. Thus the "independent variable" approach to human behavior typical of mainstream bourgeois psychology is wrong on two counts. First, it does not take subjective grounds for action into account. In fact, experimental designs are often explicitly intended to eliminate such subjective grounds. Second, the concept of "variable" is altogether too abstract. Real understanding of human action can only come from an analysis of the concrete societal situation of the individual. A very different methodological approach is needed for this.

Action Potence in Capitalist Society

It should be obvious from the above discussion that action potence is not likely to have exactly the same character for everyone in a society distinguished by class divisions, exploitation, and uneven distribution of wealth and power. Whatever overall possibilities are contained in such a society, they will be more restricted for some than for others. The owners of the capital invested in a fish-processing plant will likely never have to worry about how to feed themselves or their families. This is, however, an ever-constant worry for many of the workers in the plant. No decision of an individual worker can affect the owner's control over the means of need satisfaction. Yet whatever control the worker possesses is entirely subject to the decisions, even whims, of the owner. Liberal democracy has from time to time taken measures to ensure the worker against this imbalance (though only on the basis of immediacy, never on the basis of mediacy), but little real progress has been made in the past century, nor, owing to the very structure of capitalist society, is much more likely to occur. Owners are still moving capital, with the blessings of governments, to suit their needs. Workers are still being laid off and they and their families are still being forced onto the dole, which creates a state of immediacy in which one literally cannot be fully human.

But action potence is not just something that one has in some particular quantity, nor is it a quantity that accounts for differences among individuals. It is more important as an analytic category, a means of revealing the *way* in which individuals relate to their possibilities. With respect to the possibilities given to us in society, we all have two basic options. The first, in some ways the most obvious, is to take the possibilities offered and make the best of them. But the very fact of history illustrates that this is not the only or the best option. If the general quality of life has advanced historically at all beyond that of our early hominid ancestors, it can only be because individuals have sought to go beyond the limits of existing possibilities; that is, they have sought to extend their possibilities. This is the case both absolutely, where the new possibility sought is one that never existed for anyone before, and, what is far more often the case, relatively, where individuals seek to gain for themselves more of the possibilities that already exist in society.

These two options are designated by Critical Psychologists as *restrictive action potence*, characterized by its utilizing of possibilities, and *generalized action potence*, characterized by the extending of possibilities.

Expressed as strategies, these options each contain important contradictions that will have implications for other psychical functions. The restrictive strategy appears to be the easiest to adopt for the short run. It means getting along with the "authorities" and generally receiving the benefits of the "good citizen." In the long run, however, it means helping to consolidate an unsatisfactory situation that can be the source of much unhappiness and misery, both for oneself and one's family. The rationalizations, displacements, and repressions required by such a strategy are often recognized as signs of mental disturbance.

The generalized strategy responds to the real possibility of extending possibilities, thereby overcoming the irritations in one's subjective situation and achieving an objectively better quality of existence. But it also contains a very high risk of offending those who monopolize the wealth and power and whose interests existing arrangements are designed to protect. The consequences of this cannot be lightly taken.

Whichever strategy is taken in a particular instance, a subjective framework of action (*Handlungsrahmen*) will result in terms of which the action taken will seem to be grounded and understandable. But however understandable action is within the restrictive framework, no matter how much more "ideologically available" it is, the end result is that people become their own enemies. What's more, it runs counter to the very process by which we became human in the first place. Objectively, then, the generalized option is "healthier." The conditions under which it becomes feasible therefore are important to both individuals and to society.

Critical Psychologists insist that we understand the alternative forms of action potence as "analytical categories." They are not intended to provide the basis of classifying persons, personality traits, or situations. They are intended as tools for analyzing the complexities of our situations in the world, to see more clearly the opportunities and restrictions in our lives and the possible ways of our consciously relating to them. They are there to help us better understand the mediated nature of our existence.

Implications for Cognition, Emotion, and Motivation

The restrictive and generalized forms of action potence are associated with different forms of *cognition*. The former is characterized by what Critical Psychologists call interpretive thinking (*Deuten*), the latter by comprehensive thinking (*Begreifen*). Interpretive thinking is marked by its failure to reflect the societal mediatedness of existence. It therefore also fails to reflect the fact that the individual has the options to utilize or to extend existing possibilities. Both the nature of the restrictions and the potential for extension of possibilities are said to be "bracketed off" by this form of thinking. When the restrictions are experienced, as they inevitably are, they are interpreted as functions of the immediate surroundings. The person may blame his or her poverty or unemployment without comprehending its societal nature. The resulting unhappiness may be blamed on neighbors, fellow workers, spouse, parents, or children or on a lack of material goods. The wider context remains incomprehensible. A common result of this way of cognizing one's life situation is to blame one's own deficiencies. The resulting action may then be aimed at "improving" oneself. Societal conditions are personalized and psychologized. Whatever solution is taken, it inevitably turns out to be one that contributes to the affirmation and consolidation of the distortions in societal mediation that are the real cause of the problem. This provides the ground on which societal conditions are blindly reproduced in the individual.

Bourgeois psychology, in both its mainstream and its "radical" forms, tends to contribute to this blind reproduction by assuming this form of relating to the world to be universal. An irony here is that insofar as interpretative thinking is widespread and encouraged in capitalist society (it makes good consumers!), bourgeois psychology, despite its blindness, will be an accurate reflection of societal reality. The problem with bourgeois psychology, then, is not that it is a false reflection of reality, but that it takes the reality that it reflects to be the universal one: It fails, in short, to reflect the real *possibilities* of the individual under societal mediation.

Comprehensive thinking does not so much replace interpretive thinking as sublate it (*aufheben*). We do in fact live in our immediate life situation. The point is not to live beyond it, but to *comprehend* it within the societal and historical context. This means, basically, understanding one's own situation, possibilities, and actions in much the terms that we have already discussed. If psychotherapy or other psychological help must therefore involve some sort of education with respect to these matters, it is apparent that psychological practice cannot fail to be partisan and political.

The critical psychological categorial reconstruction of *emotion* revealed it as an essential component of the knowing processes. It orients knowledge by appraising environmental factors. It tells us when knowledge is adequate and when it is inadequate. Contrary to the traditional view, it is an adjunct to cognition, not its opponent. A person operating in the restrictive mode of action potence will obviously understand his or her own emotion differently than someone operating in the generalized mode. The restrictive aspect of emotion is called emotional inwardness (*emotionale Innerlichkeit*).

The basic problem here is that actions under restrictive action potence are bound to be ineffective in dealing with the real aspects of problems. This means that while it is cognitively functional it leads to emotional uneasiness and feelings of inadequacy. That is, when it is most effective cognitively, it creates the greatest problems emotionally. The result of this contradiction is that emotion becomes severed from the environmental conditions that it is appraising. This is then felt as the traditional separation of emotion and thought in which emotion appears to have the effect of interfering with thinking. This interference is then interpreted as having inner origins; it becomes an "emotional problem" that appears to require treatment independent of the environmental conditions. The commonest example is the treatment of anxiety with tranquilizing drugs.

In the generalized mode of action potence emotion is seen for what it is. It becomes *intersubjective emotional engagement*. Attention is then directed at correcting the offending circumstances and increasing, rather than decreasing, the individual's control over the conditions relevant to need satisfaction. Emotion becomes an ally rather than an enemy. Obviously, the therapeutic application of this principle will be a good deal more complex than mere admonishment.

Motivation, according to the categorial reconstruction, is an anticipation of emotion or, more precisely, the anticipation of the emotional valence of the outcome of an action. As such it must reflect the societally mediated nature of action, that is, the way in which goals are attained only in cooperation with others. It cannot be understood without a recognition, in short, of the supraindividual nature of the goals of individual actions and of the mutual interdependence of individuals and society at large. The raised emotional valence or security, and thus the heightened quality of life, that motivation anticipates is one that the individual shares with other members of society. The only contradiction that exists here lies in the risks that genuinely motivated action incurs in capitalist society.

Critical Psychologists identify three prerequisites for motivated action. First, there must be a real connection between the individual's contribution to the maintenance of society and the securing of his or her own existence. Second, this connection must be adequately represented in societal forms of thought. Third, the individual must be able to understand this connection. This is a very tall order and obviously applies only to the generalized form of action potence. The more common restrictive form appears differently.

Strictly speaking, according to this analysis, action in the restrictive mode is not motivated. This does not mean, however, that no action occurs. The alternative to motivated action is not inaction, but *acting under inner compulsion*. Because the person operating in the restrictive mode has bracketed off his or her connection with the societal mediation processes, it becomes impossible to tell whether an action serves the general and thus the individual interest or the interests of particular others (for example, those of capital). In the latter case there are two consequences. First, the results will not be such as to increase the individual's control over relevant conditions. They are more likely to consolidate the individual's oppression. Second, in order to maintain the subjective functionality of his or her own restrictive action potence, the real compulsory character of the action must be suppressed and the compulsion internalized. Its actual character then becomes an "unconscious" aspect of the person's motivation.

Implications for Research Practice

Such a radically different approach to the problems of scientific psychology will necessarily have profound methodological implications. Some of these will be dealt with in the chapters that follow. I wish to call attention here only to some of the broader implications for the practice of psychological research.

Some aspects of bourgeois mainstream methodology to which Critical Psychologists object are worth mentioning. We have touched on some of these already. One of these was the objection to the way in which the societal and historical contexts of psychical processes are ignored. The result of this, as we have seen, is the blind reproduction – and therefore justification – in psychological theory of oppressive societal relations. One aspect of this is the way in which individuals are abstracted, with the result that the subject of psychological investigation becomes the abstract-isolated individual, stripped of all societal and historical concreteness. But there is some truth to this abstract-isolated individual. It is the real person acting under restrictive action potence. The unreflected categories and theories of such a psychology serve to affirm the "naturalness" and "necessity" of this condition. The psychology, when applied, necessarily becomes a psychology of control and justification. Because of the abstraction involved, for example, in the insistance that what is

relevant can only be expressed as quantitative variables to be statistically anal-
ysed, there is not the least hope that any concrete individual will see himself
or herself in the theories. Even where a person has directly contributed "data"
to a psychological investigation, there will be no self-recognition in the results, let alone any illumination of his or her own concrete subjective situation. What was donated was an abstraction to begin with. Whatever concrete
individuality might have remained in the donation was then removed as "error
variance." Critical Psychologists agree that this is not the best way of practicing science.

It should be clear from what has been said above that Critical Psychology's
every move is guided by the intention to overcome abstractness and isolation
and to restore concreteness to our knowledge of psychical functioning. This
has meant first and foremost taking the societal and historical context seriously, seeing the individual *in relation*. The categories then become more than
mere descriptors to be fitted into an abstract theory. They become tools for the
analysis of the individual subjective situation, not merely for the psychologist,
but for the subject as well. Furthermore, seeing partisanship not as something
to be suspended for the sake of objectivity, but as an essential prerequisite for
genuinely objective knowledge, there remains no need to "deceive" subjects.
Indeed, the ideal research situation is one in which the subject sees the research problem as his or her own problem and is enlisted as coresearcher in
the project. This is essentially how Critical Psychologists are now proceeding
with their current emphasis on the development of the "actual empirical"
level of investigation. In its explicit partisanship for the concrete subject, Critical Psychology seeks to become a psychology that is not merely *about* people
but a psychology that truly is *for* people. This is what Critical Psychologists
mean when they speak of the possibilities of psychology as a *subject science*.

2 Critical Psychology: Historical Background and Task

Wolfgang Maiers

1

Critical Psychology is a politically engaged, Marxist, scientific position that is critical of traditional psychology. An introductory sketch of the historical background and program of such a position is made somewhat problematic by the fact that it can be approached and assessed from a number of different scientific and political points of view. I shall simplify matters for myself here by limiting my scope to the "internal scientific" aspects and focusing on just one question: How does Critical Psychology make good the claim that in deriving its concepts and categories, it is being critical both of bourgeois science and of the societal context to which it refers?

I shall have to leave out many details of how Critical Psychology found its origins in the student movement's critique of psychology in the late 1960s, even though an account of these events would aid an understanding of many of our current ideas and pursuits.

A more comprehensive analysis would have to take into account the fact that Critical Psychology has been only one of several attempts to apply the "leftist" critique of science and ideology to an area of knowledge. To avoid confusion, it would be desirable to include a description of the immediate prehistory of Critical Psychology in the initial project of a "critical-emancipatory psychology." This would show how the demand to overcome the dominant psychology's "science of control" point of view and to do away with the practical and theoretical denial of the subject in an independent development of science and professional practice led to alternative approaches. One group of these was the "materialist psychology of action" (for example, M. Stadler) and other adoptions of the Soviet Marxist tradition in psychology (for example, G. Feuser or W. Jantzen; see also Hildebrand-Nilshon and Rückriem, 1988). Another group turned to a social-theoretically reflective psychoanalysis (as in the "critical theory of the subject" of A. Lorenzer, K. Horn, P. Brückner, and others). It is important to remember

23

that these options for a "critical psychology" were vigorously and constantly debated in the political movements of students and scientists at the psychological institutes in West Berlin and West Germany (and in some circles are still being debated) (see *Kritische Psychologie*, 1970; Mattes, 1985; Staeuble, 1985).

A more comprehensive treatment of our topic would remind us that a key event in determining contrasting critical positions with respect to psychology was the Congress of Critical and Oppositional Psychologists held in Hanover in May 1969. It was only a minority that took the view that an understanding of the psychical mechanisms mediating political dominance could aid in orienting the collective emancipation of human individuality. The majority took the contrasting view that it was illusory to think that psychology could have theoretical and practical significance for the processes of revolutionary change. It was not their concern to reverse the function of psychology, but to expose and subvert it as an instrument of domination. The course taken by this split ought to be reconstructed.

At the same time we would have to describe, in all their self-critical transformations, the attempts that were made to link active social criticism with an alternative professional practice by formulating theoretical conceptions of "antiauthoritarian" and "compensatory" education and putting them to practical test in the "children's shops" or "pupils' campaign" or in work with peripheral groups. Especially important here was the Schülerladen Rote Freiheit [a location where pupils could meet after school, be looked after, and so forth], supported by members of the Psychological Institute of the Free University of Berlin (cf. Autorenkollektiv, 1971).

We would have to describe how the means and standards of the critique of science and society changed by moving away from the "critical theory" of the Frankfurt School and adopting more directly "classical" Marxist philosophical and social-theoretical positions. This "paradigm change," described as the "socialist turn" in the student movement, was related to critical theory's lack of practical political orientation, as compared with the intensification of the political struggles in both the student and the workers' movements (for example, the September strike of 1969).

It was in such theoretical and practical contexts that the standpoint of Critical Psychology became gradually clarified as an individual-scientific orientation in the tradition of dialectical and historical materialism, on the one hand, and the discipline of psychology, on the other. It is this particular position that distinguishes Critical Psychology (regardless of otherwise common features) from other approaches in the student movement's critique of psychology. We cannot go further into this here (see Maiers and Markard, 1977; Mattes, 1985.)[1]

2

We won't get away entirely, however, without reminiscences. Historically, our approach to a critical psychological concept formation has taken place along with a clarification of the interconnections among truth claims, knowledge-guiding interests, and the function of scientific research in society, and it remains systematically bound to such a clarification. That clarification was placed onto the agenda of the student movement under the rubric "crisis of relevance" or "dominance character" of the social sciences.

The fact that psychological knowledge and practice supported interests of political-ideological, economic, military/police dominance was obvious (cf. Baritz, 1960). From a liberal point of view, shared by most members of the discipline in those days, this demonstrated the deplorable state of the professional-ethical attitudes of some colleagues but was not seen as a problem beyond that. It was consistent with the official doctrine of value-free science that science had do with the knowledge of objective things or events, not with decisions about values. Scientific results as such were understood as neutral with respect to their use for this or that societal purpose. Individual scientists, admittedly, could not be released entirely from concern for a socially responsible use of the results of their work.

The representation of basic research as disinterested – as expressed at the time by the Berlin psychologist Hans Hörmann at the memorial service for Benno Ohnesorg[2] – was tailor-made for the critical arguments against the nomothetic-analytic conception of empirical social science presented by Adorno and Habermas in their so-called positivism debate with Popper and Albert (Adorno et al., 1969).

There followed in the fall of 1968 an article, "On the Problem of the Relevance of Psychological Research for Practice" (Holzkamp, 1972b), the first of a series of scientific contributions, with which Klaus Holzkamp, ordinarius at the Psychological Institute and recognized experimental psychologist and methodologist, began his connection with and intervention in the science critique of the student movement.

These articles represented the development of Holzkamp's attempts to link an understanding of the relationship between science and society taken from Critical Theory and its brand of Marxism with the constructivist logic of science as an immanent critique of traditional psychological research practice, in this way to lay a philosophical-scientific foundation for a "critical-emancipatory psychology."[3]

In *Theorie und Experiment* (1964) or *Wissenschaft als Handlung* (1968) Holzkamp presented a critique of psychological experimentation aimed at the lack of binding criteria for evaluating the meaningfulness of experimental designs and their empirical results for the theoretical proposition in question or for evaluating the differences in results often obtained in experimental replications. It was an expression of the fundamental weaknesses of the leading idea of a strictly empirical approach to the formation and assessment of theories, weaknesses that even critical rationalist fallibilism could not consistently overcome, that these problems could not be solved with the usual procedures for improving methods. Rather, following Dingler and May, they required a constructivist (action-) logic of research as a practical realization of theory.

In the "Relevance" article Holzkamp, following the lines of a critical theory of society, focused the constructivistic explanation of the theoretical and empirical disintegration of nomothetic-experimental psychology on the problem of the practical meaninglessness of psychology. He introduced the notion of "external relevance" as a criterion, defined in terms of societal-practical knowledge interests, for the value of scientific research. For him this had primacy over the usual formal scientific criteria, such as verifiability of hypotheses, degree of integration with superordinate theories, and internal relevance, that is, representativeness of empirical propositions for theoretical ones. Following Habermas (1968) Holzkamp distinguished between mere "technical" relevance and the "emancipatory" relevance of psychological research that contributes to individuals' understanding their societal dependencies, thus helping to create the prerequisites for people's liberating themselves and improving their circumstances. This and the subsequent contributions, "The Retreat of the Modern Theory of Science" (1972c) and "The Critical-Emancipatory Turn of Constructivism" (1972d), opened a theoretical and methodological debate with the Critical Rationalists. Their objections were surely encouraged by the contradictions and problematic implications of Holzkamp's attempt to link the constructivistic logic of science with neo-Marxist social criticism. (Holzkamp assessed his own treatises as "the manifestation of a critical turn in scientific orientation" [1972a: 7]).

Today, we can see that the problems arose out of the untenable epistemology of constructivism, with its agnostic aschewal of truth claims. On the other side, the critical theory suffered from its denunciation of scientific-analytic forms of knowledge and their positivistic expression alike as a "logic of dominance." (cf. Furth, 1980).

Nevertheless, with this synthesis and in the course of the debates around it, very important steps were taken with respect to philosophy, social theory, scientific methodology, and the formation of categories – first approaches to the current Critical Psychological definitions of the means and goals of scientific research and practice pertaining to the subject.

Everywhere that constructivism was used as a methodological critique of the conception and practice of mainstream psychology, Holzkamp's arguments, while aiming at a philosophy of science (*Wissenschaftstheorie*), gave content to the predominant critique of ideology. They specified how in its particulars traditional psychological theory affirmed the political-ideological apparatus of bourgeois society by turning the objective societal miseries and contradictions into individual psychological inadequacies and naturally occurring conflicts. An analysis of the "organismic anthropology" inherent in psychology belongs here, that is, the theoretical reduction of individuals, who live in historically created class relations that can be altered by people as subjects of their own history, to organisms, who adjust themselves to a natural and unchangeable "environment." Holzkamp also showed how the experimental method in psychology immunizes against empirical data that prove resistant to such a nativistic tendency (Holzkamp, 1972b). In a similar vein he criticized the "reversal of the concreteness and abstractness of human relations," that is, the mistaking, through a psychological mode of thinking called introjection, of an isolated individuality abstracted from all its societal and historical determinants for an empirically concrete fact (1972d).

The object and especially the methods of critical-emancipatory psychology remained, however, for the most part negatively defined. Insofar as the critique of function led to positive alternatives, these were strongly flavored by the antiauthoritarian utopia of a society freed of all social pressures and marked by the dominance-free discourse of its members. Science would have to subordinate itself to the purposes of such a society. Without a radical examination extending to the epistemological foundations of traditional psychology, the demand for psychology to provide knowledge relevant for a critical-emancipatory practice was reduced to a voluntaristic call for psychologists to refrain from working for the interests of profit and power and to place the positive knowledge of their discipline "in the service of social progress."

Not least, these foundational weaknesses in the critical proposals regarding the "relevance" problem invited from positivists the accusation that the critical-emancipatory conception was just "instrumentalism with an ideological basis" (Albert, 1971: 22), and we were reminded of the strict neutrality of psychological research regarding extrascientific commitments that would "dogmatically" pervert the usual scientific standards. In this countercritique, however, the fact was deliberately "overlooked" that, insofar as the Critical Psychologists in fact carried on their analyses in an ideologically critical way, they based their judgments about the societal relevance of psychological theory on the insight gained from the critique of positivism, that the people are caught in a circle (to be dialectically resolved): In relating cognitively to societal reality, they are always a part of that which is to be known. At the basis was therefore the recognition of an objective interconnection between the scientific and professional institutions of psychology – together with the individuals who comprise them – and a societal totality that is in no way neutral with regard to social antagonisms. Knowledge directed at or determined by this cannot *eo ipso* be indifferent. In this critical dimension, the idea that the partisanship of the subject of knowledge, either progressive or reactionary, was reducible to a free subjective decision (decisionism) was avoided from the start. To ignore this while making the charge of instrumentalism can only mean that the countercritics, themselves prejudiced by the positivistic fiction of an interest-free, impartial, and "pure" science, could only understand the internal connection of knowledge and interests as an external linkage and could therefore only understand the objectively based partisanship of the subjects of knowledge in decisionistic terms.

I shall skip over some rather tedious attempts at orientation and move directly to the "second stage" in the development of the Critical Psychological critique of psychology. This was characterized by a critique based on the Marxist analysis of capitalist political economy. Only on this basis did the critique of positivism acquire the necessary edge. Marx's *Capital* (1867/1969b) explains concretely and historically how it is that human consciousness – as conscious being in ultimately economically determined forms of societal practice – occurs in contradictory, objective forms of thought that correspond to the contradictory movements of societal practice and are structured by them. In this sense, in "Conventionalism and Constructivism" (1972f) and " 'Critical Rationalism' as Blind Criticalism" (1972e), Holzkamp marked out the boundary of an immanent argumentation in terms of a supposedly suprahistorical logic of science, which he then (self-)critically ascribed equally to constructivism, logical empiricism, and critical rationalism. What became clear in principle was the interdependence of societal relevance, interest-relatedness, and the knowledge content of science, and thus also that between subjective partisanship and objective partiality. The partisanship of scientists does not come from a "progressively" motivated selection of preexisting themes or from a subsequent decision in favor of emancipatory interests or movements; it is based on the objective partiality of the science they represent – as a function of the truth content of the knowledge that their instruments allow them to achieve of the internal structure and laws of motion of their object of investigation. (Science in bourgeois society only conflicts with the objective interests of capital and is accordant with the emancipatory interests of the exploited class when – fulfilling its specific knowledge role, characterized by a division of labor – it contributes to the elucidation of the historically transitory mechanism of this society and its objective potential for development. A lack of critical relevance in social or human science is therefore an expression of (1) its biased view that societal reality is something existing outside the scientist that can be approached unaffectedly, from any "external standpoint," and (2) epistemological, methodological, and conceptual blindness with respect to contexts and contradictions (cf. Holzkamp, 1972g: 282ff).

3

The implications for a critique of psychology can be summarized as follows: In its predominant objectivistic direction, psychology has misapprehended the activity and subjectivity of concrete human beings living in historically determined societal conditions as the behavior or experience of abstract individuals standing opposed to and determined by an environment (which itself is misunderstood in naturalistic and ahistorical terms). This misjudgment was not just a theoretical inadequacy stemming from the implicit adoption of an erroneous epistemological postulate of immediacy that need simply be given up. Rather, just like its subjectivistic inversion, which hypostatizes individuals as ultimate empirical units of analysis whose forms of living are explained by indwelling essential powers, it is an expression of "necessarily false consciousness." This consciousness, which arises spontaneously from the all-embracing forms of motion of the capitalist mode of production and which reifies them, reflects the actual inverted relations on the surface of bourgeois society: the privateness of individuals isolated from one another, whose societal relations appear in the form of natural relations among things.

Insofar as psychology fails in the fundamental definition of its object to penetrate this societal inversion, it will remain prejudiced – like the everyday theory of which it is the scientifically stylized version – by the bourgeois ideology of the nonsocietal nature of human beings and the natural immutability of their life circumstances. It is precisely in this sense of constituting a "psychological illusion" (Wolf, 1976) that psychology is characterized as bourgeois.

What was gained by this finding? Given the insight into the material-societal reality of "objective forms of thought," we have been able to identify insurmountable barriers to knowledge from the point of view and in the ideological forms of bourgeois society. At the same time, we have managed to characterize the substantive nature and relevance of bourgeois psychological theory formation in an abstract and general way. In a way, too, the direction of its conceptual negation could also be anticipated. The theory- and method-critical revelations of the inversions contained in traditional psychology, however, added nothing essentially or concretely new to the critique of ideology based on the model of Marx's "Critique of Political Economy" (1867/1969b) but only reaffirmed its judgment on the concrete material provided by the various psychological modes of thinking. The heterogeneity of their nature – their specific limitations hidden in the form of general mystifications, their criticisms of each other, their different societal usefulness – could not be judged in a positive light (Holzkamp, 1976/1978; Maiers, 1979).

Other efforts at the same level of knowledge critique were made to reconstruct the origins, developmental conditions, and objective purposes of psychology as a part of the scientific division of labor from the point of view of historical materialism. Such "analyses of constitution (or genesis) and function" were expected to help us gain a realistic evaluation of the possibilities of progressive research and professional practice within the objective reproductive relations of bourgeois society (see *Psychologie als historische Wissenschaft* [Psychology as historical science], 1972). However, these, too, offered no sufficient basis for a differential critique of psychology, especially not where this critique went beyond the institutional or professional aspects of psychology to deal with the characteristics of the content and methods of its basic scientific research.

The global reproach that bourgeois psychology systematically missed the human-societal specificity of its object could only be substantiated by "rising" from the abstraction of a psychology to the concrete reality of its various approaches, whether mainstream, nomothetic-functionalistic psychology, or peripheral streams like hermeneutic-psychoanalytic, phenomenological, and so on. What was needed was to carry out the critique on particular categorial definitions of differing kinds of theoretical formations and to dispute their claims to be empirically verified.

This third level of critique was decisive in the turn toward Critical Psychology as a positive science. To show how, it will be necessary to leap ahead of my description of its development and say something, at least roughly, about our present view of the situation in traditional psychology.

4

To begin with, we understand categories to mean those basic concepts that define a theory's objective reference. They determine which dimensions, aspects, and so on, can be extracted from prescientific reality so as to become the object of "psychological" investigation – and therefore, too, which dimensions, aspects, and so on, are ignored, thus remaining invisible for psychological research, regardless of the more specialized theories and methods it may employ.

We can make this clear with an example. The model of conditionality that we have already mentioned represents a categorial choice. According to it, the person–world connection is conceptually cut off from those determinants that characterize the objective constitution of the individual life world beyond what is immediately experienced. Societal relations appear, for instance, as a "socioeconomic factor," "conditions of social reinforcement," or something of that sort, to be studied in terms of their effects on the ways in which individual lives express themselves. These ways are then understood as results of situational conditions. Individuals appear in this model as channels through which external influences, even when refracted by the prism of individual life experiences (which are, of course, themselves effects of such influences), are lawfully transformed into behaviors and experiences.

Taking account of societal relations in this manner does not alter the ahistoricity of the hypothetical universal links between conditions and effects assumed in a particular theory. Corresponding to this categorial framework is the methodological principle of nomothetic-functionalist psychology, according to which hypotheses are tested empirically as functional connections between independent and dependent variables, preferably in experimental-statistical analyses. Built into the research logic of this "variable scheme" is the postulate of behaviorism that only stimulus conditions and externally recordable responses are intersubjectively accessible. The necessary, though hardly realizable, practical consequence of this is that the unavoidable subjectivity of what is being investigated must become the main disturbing factor to be brought under control.

This is the scheme underlying the crude mechanistic S–R approach. Assuming subjectivism to be inherent in the "subjective," it adopted a radical standpoint of external observation and tried to purge mentalistic vocabulary from the psychological language for all time (cf. the programmatically eloquent title of Max Meyer's 1921 book: *Psychology of the Other One*). As we know, it proved impossible to adhere consistently to such a point of view.

J. B. Watson, for example, constantly maneuvered theoretically between a strictly physicalistic, stimulus–response conceptualization and the use of terms like "subjectively meaningful situation," and "act." In the 1920s this led E. C. Tolman to define psychological stimuli and responses exclusively at the molar level and to fill the "inner space" between these "peripheral" events with hypothetical mediating states or events. As his devastating (self-) critique of the neobehavioristic categorial and methodological scheme of "intervening variables" demonstrated (cf. Koch, 1959), near the end of his life Tolman appears to have become aware of the antinomous nature of his strictly operationistic cryptophenomenology: Insofar as independent empirical characteristics could be ascribed to "inner space," their content could not be known, according to the assumption of intersubjective inaccessibility; yet insofar as these characteristics are viewed as totally excludable (as epiphenomena) from the observables, then nothing need be known of them ... (under such premises, Skinner's critique of methodological behaviorism was undeniably correct!).

In view of the ubiquitous methodology of the functional analysis of variables, it cannot be claimed that modern mainstream psychology – no matter how "cognitive leaning" its theories may have become – has taken any practical account of Tolman's insights into the failings of both assumptions. If theories today are understood in terms of reflective, conscious action, and so on, but then are tested according to the variable scheme, a tacit category error is committed that is just as tacitly reversed in the interpretation of the findings thus gained. What follows from this for the objectivity of such theory testing deserves more discussion than we can give it here. The basic research logic of modern variable psychology has been criticized by various alternative approaches (1) categorially, for its quasi-behavioristic elimination of subjectivity and the subjective quality of human action, and (2) methodologically, for its advocacy of experimental-statistical analysis (together with its empiricistic observability criterion, its rules for operationalization and/or measurement, and its logical scheme for [causal] explanation and prediction) as the royal road to psychological knowledge, and so on.

The "one-sidedness" and "immediacy bias" of this reduction of the person–world connection to a deterministic model in terms of conditioned behavior are not overcome by gearing to meaningful action if meanings as grounds for action are moved into the subject (even if it is allowed that the meanings are constituted through reciprocal interpretation in the "interaction" of subjects). What is happening here is a kind of categorial determination of the object in which meanings are psychologized, while the psychical, robbed of its objective relation to the world, is privatized as a mere inwardness. (Even in the interpersonal mode of constituting meaning in symbolic interactionism the ultimate source of meaning remains the privacy of the psyche.) The irony here, we might add, is that both the call for a psychology of the subject and the objectivistic denial of subjectivity are based on the same subjectivistic conception of the "privacy" of consciousness.

Historically viewed, this is not surprising. The change from introspectionism to functionalism and behaviorism took place under a clandestine introspectionist assumption about consciousness. It was the hypostatization of consciousness given as the individual experience of the first-person singular that allowed the "subjective" to appear scientifically inaccessible, that is, removed from any claims of objectification and generalization, and thus disavowed the "psychical" as a scientific object. The same assumption explains why oppositional positions like humanistic psychology sought to declare the subjective immediately amenable to scientific treatment by sacrificing rigorous claims to generalization and objectification.

It must be emphasized that it is such psychological categorizations of the person–world relation, in all their specific theoretical variations, that must be brought into the critique so that their relative contribution to knowledge can be given a detailed and differential assessment. This is also necessary because otherwise we can't answer the objection that, in spite of everything, so-called bourgeois psychology has made progress in developing its research programs and has accumulated a growing, solid store of explained phenomena and well-established conceptions.

5

What about the claimed solidity of traditional psychological knowledge? It has become characteristic of our discipline that different theories, each equally empirically confirmed according to prevailing standards, exist side by side. We are pointing here to more than a mere multiplicity of theories. Rather, they make universal claims about identical objects on the basis of incompatible (or at least mutually problematic) concepts, and we are in no position to be able to decide which of the theories is tenable and which ought to be rejected. (A comparable situation would exist in physics if there were a half dozen permanently competing theories about the free fall of objects.) One consequence of this is that the historical sequence of basic theoretical conceptions in psychology has the appearance of a sequence of "fads," without any recognized grounds for the replacement of one by another and without leading to a qualitative deepening of our knowledge (such that both questions and answers that are at any particular time out of style remain latent as unresolved, and then eventually recur). In the course of a theory's development a point of conceptual consolidation is never reached such that (as in physics) the power of newer theories relative to older ones can be unequivocally assessed, and older concepts can be conclusively rejected, while others retain limited validity, thus providing a basis for further theoretical development. I refer here to Hilgard (1970) and Moscovici (1972), to mention only two, as witnesses to this description of the current state of affairs. With his "epistemopathology," Koch (for example, 1959) has documented the fact that such "negative knowledge" is not limited to the areas of learning and social psychology. The warning voices of a few reknowned representatives of our discipline should not, however, be allowed to conceal the fact that in traditional psychology the full implications of the problem have remained largely underestimated. Holzkamp addressed this problem already in his constructivist work on the problem of obtaining a semantic correspondence between the determinants of theoretical and empirical propositions (1964), although at that time without insight into its deeper implications, let alone its solution. But in an article in 1977 he had something to say about both; there, in turning critically to the positive studies of Critical Psychology, he characterized the situation as the "scientific indeterminacy" of conventional psychological theorizing. This, in his judgment, was based on the fact that traditional psychology has, to a large extent, left the origin of its categories undetermined. The basic concepts, out of which are formed the theoretically generalized assumptions about the interconnections of empirical events, are presupposed as such and gain their scientific status only secondarily through the testing of derived hypotheses. He pointed out that what one is able to formulate or (experimentally) observe regarding the assumptions about the interconnections is predetermined by the categories, and that the basic concepts are not arrived at through testing the assumptions.

With regard to the dimensions of reality grasped by a theory, the systematic assumptions formulated in the theoretical concepts, their assumed optimal operationalization in empirical variables, and the findings that can then accordingly be produced, all exist in a circular relation to one another. The only thing that is not circular is the degree of verifiability of hypotheses within the framework of the dimensions grasped by the theory. In other words, empirical testing in the conventional sense does not provide a sufficient criterion for the scientific value of theories, which may therefore pertain to entirely trivial or artificial effects. Since, on the other hand, the procedures for the derivation of hypotheses offer no standards for a scientifically proved formulation of "relevant" concepts, the precarious situation of indeterminacy, as we have described it, is the result.

Under the premises of the materialist theory of knowledge as reflection theory, "theoretical relevance" means that "essential" basic dimensions of objective reality are expressed in concepts, that is, such dimensions as underlie the lawful relationship of others and their determination of the variability of empirical phenomena. To the extent that the concepts of theories adequately reflect relevant dimensions, theories can be said to have real knowledge value, that is, integrative and explanatory power, relative to others.

It follows that elevating the relevance of psychological theory formation means basically guaranteeing its scientific status through the methodical and unequivocally testable constitution of a system of concepts, which distinguishes the object of psychology from other objects of knowledge and reveals its inner articulation. The knowledge value of other pertinent theory systems is then differentially assessed by comparing their object dimensions with this structure. The problem is one of an empirical decision, although not in the sense of current research practice. What, in effect, is demanded here is that validation procedures be extended to a process that, in traditional philosophy of science, has been left to the scientifically unbinding, unconstrained creative imagination of individual researchers.

In fact, Critical Psychology's most important contribution to the elevation of the scientific status of psychology is its historical-empirical approach to the constitution of categories. If this should seem strange, think of the decisive scientific progress that was achieved, for example, in biological taxonomy when organisms were no longer classified according to an external (morphological) point of view, but (as in Haeckel's systematization of the different forms of animals) according to conceptual orderings that reflected the phylogenetic degrees of relationship. What is this but an empirical-historical procedure for the development and critique of concepts?[4]

Before moving on to a presentation of our procedure for the analysis of psychological categories, I will have to describe how we arrived at it.

6

I have said that the materialistic account of the limited rationality of "bourgeois psychology" points to a need for more than a mere critique of ideology and urges a concrete revision of the conceptual contents of theory. This presupposes a standpoint that opens up an extended and more profound perspective on empirical subjectivity, thus allowing further scientific development of psychology. The implied transition from the mere critique of psychology to a Critical Psychology has been carried out programmatically since 1971/2.

The trail was blazed by the works of Soviet psychologists like Rubinstein's *Sein und Bewusstsein* [Being and consciousness] (1961) and especially Leontyev's "Historical Approach to the Study of the Human Psyche" (1971), which stressed the internal unity of natural, societal, and individual history and demonstrated the possibility of a nonsubjectivistic understanding of the subjective.

The epistemological background was provided by the positive reception of the dialectics of nature, which stimulated renewed discussions about the relationship between human historicity and nature in the sense of the insight of early Marxian developmental theory that "History itself is a real part of natural history, of nature becoming human" (1844/1981: 544). This was linked to a new understanding of the logical-historical method as represented in Marx's analysis of the development of societal modes of production in *Capital*. It was taken as a model for a dialectical materialist investigation of historical-empirical problems, a model, that is, to be realized as a method for understanding a broad range of other scientific objects.

In this connection, there emerged three important differences between Critical Psychology and various other psychology-critical or critical psychological positions tantamount to opposition. First, by understanding Marxism as limited to the critique of ideology, some of the latter positions came to doubt the possibility of radicalizing the critique of science into a "positive science." Second, these positions often reduced Marxism to a theory of society and declared it therefore to be incompetent on the issue of subjectivity and hence in need of a supplementary subject psychology sui generis. Third (under the hidden premise of the same reduction), statements about individuality were thought to be possible on the basis alone of a concretization of politicoeconomic analyses. Altogether, the latter positions disputed or severely circumscribed the competence of Marxism to deal directly with psychological and other special scientific problems. Critical Psychology became distinguished by its assertion of Marxism's full competence in such matters.

On this orientational basis (cf. Holzkamp and Schurig's introduction to the 1973 West German edition of Leontyev, 1971) Ute Holzkamp-Osterkamp sketched the fundamentals of our concept of motivation in 1972 and Holzkamp published *Sinnliche Erkenntnis* in 1973, the first monograph that was "critical psychological" in the strict sense of the word. In it the primacy of "object-related historical analyses" was laid out in detail as the methodical guide for critical psychological work. (See the further argumentation in Maiers, 1979, in which objections to this conception are refuted.) Since that time, the results of the method have filled numerous monographs.

7

In this section I will describe how the historical materialist view has been translated into a method for the development of concepts. Based on what I have said up to now, the elementary requirement can be formulated that human subjects should not be conceived in such a way that their societally mediated existence, though difficult to deny, appears in basic psychological concepts as impossible. This implies that the historical investigation of psychical processes and phenomena cannot be directly fixated on the empirical givens of the individual life, let alone their abstract treatment as isolated, desubjectified psychic functions. Rather, it must be recognized that the ontogenesis of behavior and experience is part of an historical process of another order of magnitude, that is, societal-historical development, which determines the psychical dimensions and functional aspects of individual development. The nonpsychical reality that transcends individual existence must therefore be brought into the psychological field of vision.

Now it would be a fundamental error to take the mere statement that human beings are determined by their objective historical relations as the essence of

Marxist argumentation. To do so would reflect not dialectical materialism, but that variant of metaphysical materialism that Marx criticized in the first thesis on Feuerbach as the "chief defect of all hitherto existing materialism" because "the thing, reality, sensuousness, is conceived only in the form of the object or of contemplation, but not as sensuous activity, practice, not subjectively" (Marx, 1845/1969a). On the one hand, because of the material necessity of maintaining existence, people's activity and consciousness are determined by the objective conditions of their lives, that is, by the "nature" reproduced in collective labor and the societal relations in which it occurs. On the other hand, humans are, by their practice, the source of active creation and conscious control of their lives' circumstances and thus subjects of their societal life process.[5] Reduction of this two-sided relation to a one-sided determination of the subject by societal circumstances misses not only people's sensuous reality, but also the very possibility of the societal reproduction process sustained by them. Objective determinedness – living under conditions – and subjective determining – the possibility of their alteration – are necessary, interconnected fundamentals of human societal activity that must be understood in their psychological aspects.

If we want to avoid ahistorically presupposing societal relations as external conditions for psychical development, we must find a natural explanation for the "triviality" that only human beings are capable of developing into concrete historical, societal relationships and, in that process, participate in the creation of their life circumstances. The historical materialist analysis of the societal foundation of psychical ontogenesis leads, when correctly understood, beyond the history of society. In this deepening of the historical perspective, it makes possible a scientific conceptualization of "human nature" that overcomes the traditional mystification of an opposition between the natural and societal characters of the individual.[6]

It has been sufficiently demonstrated in the largely fruitless and unresolved instinct-versus-learning controversy that the categorial determinations of this relationship cannot be obtained in the unmediated approach to psychoontogenesis since natural potentials here always manifest themselves in socialized forms. The key to the "riddle of psychogenesis" (W. Stern) lies not (as Stern guessed) in ontogenesis. Nor are the determinations found by abstract comparisons with the most highly developed subhuman species. For one thing, they represent their own evolutionary path, with species characteristics that have evolved to different levels. For another, the species-specific characteristics of human beings must not be taken without further distinction as determining the development of their specificity as humans. How can we distinguish between that which is specifically determining and that which is specific but secondary or that which is a nonspecific character of human nature? How can we oppose bourgeois psychological biologism or the theoretical "vacuum" of sociologism with substantial statements about the natural aspect of human existence?

Our answer to this is that we must examine how in the process of anthropogenesis the beginnings of an evolutionarily advantageous "economic" mode of reproduction developed, with its characteristic progression from the organismic adaptation to the species environment to the adaptation of the latter to the vital necessities of humans through the objectifying alteration of nature. That is, we need to discover developments that had such an effect upon the genomic information of hominids that their psychical capacities were altered so as to support participation in a new form of living, with a generalized cooperative-social provision for needs. This development, which is the key to solving the seeming paradox of a "societal nature," must be pursued to the point of transition from phylogenetic evolution to the dominance of a unique kind of historical process characterized by societal modes of production. On the other hand, in order to determine the initial conditions of anthropogenesis, a reconstruction of the entire natural history that led up to it is required. This must explain parsimoniously the origin and differentiation of the psychical as an evolutionary, organismic adaptation to – or "functional reflection" of – radical changes in the species-specific environment, such as is necessary and sufficient for the maintenance of the biological systemic balance. The conventional absence or lack of application of such a "functional-historical" principle to explain teleonomic changes appears to us to be the reason that the usual *Homo psychologicus* appears in many respects as not only incapable of taking part in society, but as a homunculus incapable even of biological life.

In summary, it is precisely when one is interested in a sensible empirical study of actual psychical processes and their ontogenetic development that the question about the psychical constitution of societally existing beings must be clarified beforehand. The categorial determination of the human societal specificity of consciousness for its part raises the more general problem of explaining the natural historical origin of the psychical.

The initial material of our historical-empirical analyses are the existing concepts of scientific (or everyday) psychology; it is their indeterminacy that must be overcome. By using relevant materials of biology and human science we try to reconstruct the historical origin and development of the objective properties that can be extracted from the handed-down concepts. The aim is to obtain a system of conceptual qualifications, the differentiations and relations of which correspond to the "real logic" of the development of the psychical as a special "subjective-active" reflection of objective reality through to the "end product" of consciousness as a reflective relationship to the world and the self on the part of the practically engaged human subject. It is expected that the most elementary forms would yield the most general concepts, phylogenetic differentiations would appear as conceptual distinctions, and "qualitative leaps" in phylogenesis would manifest themselves as various distinct qualities in the psychological conceptual system. With such an historical-empirical unraveling of the genetic relationships of the psychical as they are currently preserved, we shall be able to determine the extent to which the existing basic concepts are categorially undifferentiated and distorted, confuse differing levels of specificity, and so forth. We should also be able to judge the extent to which they might be retained.

The crucial feature of the "functional-historical analysis of the origin, differentiation, and qualification" of the psychic is its reconstruction of the constellations of contradictions in the organism–environment relationship, out of which it becomes understandable that, and how, in view of the altered conditions of the internal and external systems, the dynamic balance between the organisms and the environment could be maintained only by a qualitative restructuring of the morphological-physiological or psychological constitution. The methodic guideline for this basic procedure determining the categories of a particular scientific discipline can be summarized in the following five steps (Holzkamp, 1983: 78):

1. Identify the real historical dimensions within the preceding developmental stage of the organisms at which the qualitative transformation in question took place; that is, determine the "position" that is dialectically "negated" by the qualitative transformation and thereby bring the specificity of the new developmental stage into relief.

2. Identify in the external conditions the objective alterations that constitute the "environmental pole" of the inner developmental contradiction that causes the new quality to emerge. Such alterations involve a "moderate discrepancy" that, on the one hand, demands "compensations" from the organismic system, yet is supportable within its capacity. If it is not, the overall organism–environment system collapses, the inner contradiction is turned into an external opposition, and its antipodes will no longer be mediated as "poles" in further development.

3. Identify the change in function of the relevant dimension demonstrated in step 1 as the "organism pole" of the developmental contradiction and with it the origin of the first qualitative leap, that is, the development of the specificity of the new function under the altered conditions. This dialectical negation of a previously prevalent function does not determine the overall process but, in a sense, still serves to maintain the system at the earlier stage.

4. Identify the change of dominance between the earlier function characteristic of the system's maintenance and the new function, which then determines the specifics of the system. (This change presents itself as a discontinuous reversal of the relationship between two continuously changing dimensions.)

5. Identify the ways in which the overall development of the system is restructured and assumes new direction (that is, analyze the "specific-secondary alterations," and so on) after the qualitatively more specific function has become determining for the system's maintenance. With this identification of the qualitatively new dimensional structure, in which further qualitative

transformations will occur, follows a return to the first step of the analysis but at a higher level.

8

Using this procedure, which utilized natural historical materials available from other pertinent scientific disciplines (biology, paleontology, anthropology, and so forth) we have been able (in our opinion, more adequately in a dialectical sense that was achieved by Leontyev's historical investigation) to identify the following qualitative transitions in the development of psychical functioning:

1. The transition from prepsychic life process to the genesis of psychic reflection. Based on Leontyev's paradigmatic hypothesis regarding the origin of sensitivity (Leontyev, 1971: 5ff; see also Holzkamp & Schurig, 1973, Messmann & Rückriem, 1978), the category "psychical" represents the original form of a life activity that, in contradistinction to the more elementary processes of direct response to stimulation (irritability), is mediated by receptivity to metabolically neutral signals for vitally relevant factors. This definition of "sensibility" as signal mediatedness simultaneously provides, hypothetically, the abstract, general characterization of all succeeding, more specialized psychical vital phenomena, up to their final conscious form. Through pertinent evidence from the further course of analysis comes the objectification of the hypothetical basic form and thus the verification of the initial category "psychical" (cf. the "ascent from the abstract to the concrete" in Marx, 1857–8/1974: 631ff).

2. The genetic differentiation (and integration) of the special functions/dimensions within this elementary stage of psychical development was then understood. These functions and their related structures were orientation/meaning structures; emotionality/need structures; communication/social structures. In this context a new quality in the organism's relationship to its environment emerged with the origin of the capacity for learning and individual development, that is, the adaptive modifiability of previously differentiated basic psychical functions through individual experience.

3. The species-specific evolution of this capacity for learning and individual development was followed through anthropogenesis. As the last qualitative leap in psychophylogenesis linked with the "human phase of hominization," recent human nature could be worked out. This was defined as the psychophysical basis for the possibility of individual socialization [Vergesellschaftung] through the ontogenetic realization of societal-historically produced possibilities of development in the activity of knowing, emotional, and motivational processes, and social modes of communication (cf. Maiers, 1985, on the relevance of the concept of "human nature" to a science of the subject).

I cannot go into the details of hominization that are relevant for the qualitatively new human capacity for learning and development, which bring about the functional change from animals' ad hoc use of means to the production and retention of tools (end–means reversal), with all its implications for the way in which humans divide up their activity related to collectively providing for themselves a process that is generalized as the development of societal labor (see Chapter 3, below; Holzkamp, 1973; Holzkamp-Osterkamp, 1975, 1976; Schurig, 1976; Seidel, 1976; these works are integrated by Holzkamp, 1983). When the common form of vital maintenance requires that individuals take conscious control of individually relevant societal conditions in common with others, the psychical functions are necessarily restructured from their prehuman level.

We can say this much: Not only can the peculiarly human cognitive processes of orientation be adequately understood only as the individual realization of societal-historically developed modes of perceiving, speaking, and thinking, in which the mediational connections are apparent, but the emotional-motivational aspect of the psychical, too, is centered on the subjective necessity for controlling the conditions that are important in securing the quality of the individual life. As an anticipation by an individual of future possibilities of greater satisfaction with its corresponding organization of activity and motivation, generally speaking, it represents a special form of emotionality that appears relatively late in the course of the evolution of the subhuman capacity for learning and development. On a human level it assumes the quality of a supraindividual anticipation. More precisely, it is the anticipation of an individual goal of action as a partial aspect of an overarching constellation of goals in collective action, the results of which are understood to be in the existential interests of the individual (for example, coordination of hunter and beater). Isolation of an individual from existing possibilities of collective control over the circumstances of life and subjection to the fortuity of existing conditions result in subjective suffering, which we have identified as a specifically human anxiety – a fear of impotence of action. The category "productive needs" refers to the necessity felt in subjective experience to prevent or overcome such restrictions. It designates therefore the emotional side of action potence. The satisfaction of the so-called sensuous-vital needs cannot be attained at the human level within the dynamics of immediate individual pleasure or simple tension reduction alone, but is linked to the experiential certainty regarding control over the societal sources of need satisfaction. It thus presupposes freedom from anxiety. "Sensuous-vital" and "productive" needs designate two sides of the single interconnection of personal action potence and subjective situation.

9

The historical-empirical unraveling of the connection between societal reproduction and individual maintenance of life has been assumed to be essential in all Critical Psychological analyses. But in order to be carried out fruitfully, certain corrections had to be made. Thus in Holzkamp's book *Sinnliche*

Erkenntnis [Sensuous cognition] (1973) a three-stage "logic of derivation" was adopted that sharply separated the analysis of the "natural-historical genesis of basic biological-organismic characteristics" from the analysis of the "societal-historical origin of the most general, specifically human characteristics" of the psychical. In a third stage, the latter were to be given a concrete analysis in terms of their "determination by bourgeois society." This misunderstanding was later corrected in favor of a consistent natural historical derivation of the human societal type of psychical individual development. The lawful character of the development of the subject was then to be inferred from its relation to the historically concrete societal conditions required for its realization.

In this improved understanding of the three historical steps (Holzkamp, 1979) there was a tendency to equate the most general societal determinants of the psychical with the functionally and historically reconstructed psychical aspects of human nature. This ignored the fact that, since the societal-historical process has become dominant, the natural potential for socialization [*Vergesellschaftung*] unfolds under the conditions of economic societal formations as independent maintenance systems marked by division of labor. In them, in contrast to the early and transitional forms of cooperative-social living, in which the objective reciprocality of individual contributions and societal reproduction were both immediate and immediately intelligible, the "burden" of the necessity to participate is to a certain extent removed from individuals. Such structural characteristics of an "overall societal mediation of individual existence" remain to be considered categorially with regard to general, historical "human" features of psychoontogenesis. If the abstract-general characteristics of overall societal relations as such remain unexplained, then particular societal relationships and their psychical implications cannot be fully understood in all their specificity. Moreover, in the concepts of the necessary interconnection between societal and individual reproduction it is suggested that it is the phenomenal standpoint of the individual that is being dealt with; objective and subjective necessities are conceptually contaminated with matching normative consequences.

This set of problems is not found throughout the Critical Psychological works before Holzkamp's *Grundlegung der Psychologie* [Foundation of psychology] (1983). In Holzkamp-Osterkamp's "reinterpretation" of Freudian psychoanalysis (1976) there appeared subject-scientific concretizations of our categorial determinations with regard to empirical subjectivity in bourgeois society. These were, however, not fully covered by the explicitly elaborated general definitions and procedural prescriptions (cf. Holzkamp's critical review of former work, 1984), and this contradiction demanded a systematic solution. It could, of course, not be sought ad hoc in an immediate empirical orientation to the subject, but only in a precise historical reconstruction of the psychical side of human history. The individual-scientific analysis of the categories of the psychical can accordingly only be carried out functional-historically, where it aims at aspects that can be understood as results of a genetically based, continuous, and progressive process of evolution. Further categorial qualifications of the societal possibilities for development of the psychical are obtained by switching the analysis to the societal-theoretical level, and objectively characterizing the concrete, historical life situations as determined by social formation, class, or position in society. These are then considered in terms of their reflection in the psychical subjective situation: "The individual-scientific categories that we want to elaborate for the purpose of revealing the human, societal specificity of the psychical must therefore not only grasp the new quality of the previously differentiated functional aspects of the psychical in the transformation to the stage of societal development, they must at the same time represent mediational categories in which the mediation between the objective (that is, material, economic, and so on) and the psychical determinants of the societal person–world relationship is conceptually portrayed in an adequate fashion" (Holzkamp, 1983: 188ff, 192; Holzkamp, 1984, on the methodological marking of the boundaries of functional-historical analysis and on the guidelines for individual-scientific category analysis that goes beyond it).

How then are the dimensions and aspects of the psychical to be qualified by its relationship to the societal-historical process as a whole? It is critical to see that the objective meaning structures indicate actions that must be carried out by members of society if the societal mechanism of reproduction is to be maintained. From the standpoint of the individual they only represent generalized societal possibilities for action. In principle, there is always the alternative to reject them instead of doing them. The decision is in no way arbitrary. How I relate myself subjectively to meanings depends upon the extent to which I can or must expect my action to result in an increase or decrease in my control over the conditions and satisfactions of life. Included here is a new specificity of subjectivity as intersubjectivity: In that I experience myself as the source of intentions and actions, I am aware that others, too, act for reasons of extending their own control and that, in principle, this is understandable for me.

The objective societal possibility and the essential quality of human subjectivity that depends on it, viz. of being able to relate oneself consciously to the world and oneself, imply that human action cannot be understood simply as "conditional"; it must be understood as "grounded." Vital conditions do not directly determine the actions of individuals, but work as objective meanings in the sense of premises in the context of subjective grounds. Traditionally, conditionality is absolutized (as I have already indicated), and by the same token, subjectivity is understood as nonobjectifiable. Alternatively (as in symbolic interactionism), the meaningfulness and groundedness of human action are stressed at the expense of any understanding of how the grounds for action are mediated in objective conditions. In one case as in the other, the specificity of the human person–world relationship gets lost.

From our conception of the action–meaning interconnection it follows that there is no opposition between subjectivity and societality. The subjective, active characteristic of action – that is, the fact that the way of realizing generalized societal possibilities for action that objectively determine the dimensions and scope of individual action has subjective grounds – represents a necessary aspect of overall societal system maintenance.

10

All of this should, of course, be made concrete with respect to specific life circumstances – in our case, those of bourgeois society, with its antagonism between societal production and private appropriation. This contradiction between the rich material possibilities for individual development and satisfaction of needs and their lack of realization owing to a massive exclusion from self-determining control over individually relevant vital societal conditions pervades a very wide variety of everyday life situations – and is, at the same time, mystified there. Individuals never confront societal relations in their entirety but live their lives in immediate reference to their everyday practical life world. This forms an objectively determined part of the overall societal structure, without, however, its being evident in the context of meanings and grounds (for action) at the subject's standpoint in his or her life world. The interconnection is both contained and hidden here in a contradictory way that is determined historically by the bourgeois relations of production.

We have taken up the contradictory relationship between "immediacy" and "mediatedness" by differentiating the double possibility given in every existentially relevant situation. Individuals are confronted by the "restrictive" and "generalized" alternatives, either to seek action potence within the limits of given or allowed conditions or to develop it through the expansion of the existing framework. The latter implies the risk of failure, especially where the attempt comes up against externally set barriers.

The category pair "generalized versus restrictive" action potence helps to make understandable the extent to which individuals can resist societal pressures to sacrifice the extension of their possibilities for action and the quality of their lives, and whether and to what extent the societally suggested adaptations seem reasonable to them. For the latter case, which is typical of our circumstances, it needs to be understood how, under the premise that no one consciously becomes his or her own enemy, it is subjectively reasonable to submit oneself to conditions that are limiting and cause suffering and therefore also contribute to the consolidation of the restrictive framework. That is, it is necessary to work out what, in the face of actual or presumed threat of sanctions by which even the present level of action potence is placed into question, are the short-term advantages of relief from conflict and immediate fulfillment of needs. Such advantages are usually gained only at the expense of others, instead of getting together with them to strive for control over the conditions of existence, and so forth. Here a person must always fear or really experience that he or she is diminishing the basis of his or her own life and the chances for overcoming, in common with others, individual suffering because, on the basis of the same calculation of interests by others, one is threatened with identical, reciprocal treatment.

We should not imagine only contradictory relations in the political sphere: The power structures, competition, and conflicts of interests of bourgeois society cannot be escaped by retreat into a presumed privacy. One might think here of the situation of a child who, in breaking close ties with a mother who would prefer to maintain the childish dependency, risks losing maternal care and existing possibilities for action. The alternative to keep these by acting "childishly" may be hard to resist, even if it stands in the way of development in the long run.

In general, the concepts of "generalized" and "restrictive" action potence do not refer to any specific situation, but rather to the universal conflict involved in the pursuit of one's own interests, having to do with the decision whether to reconcile oneself to what is given or to make a move toward extending one's own control.

The contradictory relationship between generalized and restrictive action potence has been substantiated with respect to various aspects of psychical functioning. I can mention the categorial distinction between "comprehensive thinking" [*Begreifen*] and "interpretative thinking" [*Deuten*]. These are not just cognitive psychological opposite numbers; they actually form a principal aspect of the concept of action potence insofar as the latter depends on the kind of cognitive understanding of the nonevident overall societal context of determinants in the immediate life world. "Interpretation" is the way of thinking in which a pragmatic order is brought to superficial conditions, relations are simplified and personalized, and threats to action potence and the quality of life are interpreted as arising where they are experienced and as being changeable there as well, namely in the life world. "Interpretation" is, so to speak, a mode of thinking that is short-sighted with respect to the double possibility of action. "Comprehension," by contrast, means a cognitive transcendence of this immediacy, insight into the implications of a determination by the subject of his or her life chances through active attempts to influence societal conditions. To this corresponds an emotional readiness for action that, as "generalized emotional engagement," we contrast with "inwardness," an emotional state that involves a fictitious separation of "feelings" from thought and action. It has been further shown that motivation is not a psychical matter that can be generated in just any way at all. "Motivated" action is essentially dependent upon the objective and cognized real possibility linked to individual goals of extending control over reality and increasing the subjective quality of life. In contrast to this is "inner compulsion" as a quasi-motivational internalization of determination by alien others, in the course of which the inner connection to the external compulsion that determines action is no longer seen. Action under inner compulsion indicates therefore the subjective mystification of suppression by the dominant forces in life. (Osterkamp studied the contradictions of "restrictive action potence," "inner compulsion," and so forth, as aspects of "hostility to self" and was led by this to a reinterpretation of the psychoanalytic conceptions of superego, unconscious, and the defense processes.)

With this pair of categories, "generalized" and "restrictive" action potence, together with their functional aspects, we are dealing with general determinations of the direction of the subject's development in bourgeois society, not with immediate empirical descriptions. How the alternatives for action contained in such possibilities are actually experienced and translated into practice is a question for empirical research.

What, however, can be achieved at the level of the analysis of categories on the basis of the conceptual distinctions I have described is a "re-ductive" reconstruction of necessary and possible ontogenetic forms of development from the "helplessness" of the infant to the "personal action potence" of the adult individual? Holzkamp (1983: 417ff) explained the transition from the quasi-natural world of the child to the earliest possibilities for realizing societal meanings (as possibilities for action) in the child's practice as a "developmental-logical" sequence from "social signal learning," through "social intentionality," to the "generalization of meanings." One developmental sequence that builds on this is the transition from immediate, cooperative forms of coping in the framework of the home to the "transcendence of immediacy" in external centers of control. This results in an extension of the child's action potence. Both possible lines of development were substantiated through identification of early forms of the "restrictive" and "generalized" alternatives for action potence. On this basis a relationship to one's own childhood that is either constrained or conscious was elaborated as a biographical dimension of adult action potence.

11

The clarification of fundamental methodological principles and the derivation of relevant categories have been central tasks of Critical Psychology. Substantial progress on both tasks has permitted us to translate the historical-empirically grounded categorial definition of our subject matter into empirical studies in the narrower sense and theoretical accounts of particular processes.

What we have said about groundedness and comprehensibility from the "standpoint of the subject" as specific features of the psychical at the societal level could possibly lead the reader to misunderstand our empirical approach as tending toward the "hermeneutic." We reject this inference. It is an expression of the traditional dichotomy of positivist-factual and hermeneutic-interpretive science. The rehabilitation of one's uniquely own experience that we intend should not be confused with the assumption that the individual is embedded within a framework of merely interpretable subjective meanings. The "immediate experience" forms an inescapable point of departure for psychological analysis because it is the subject's means of access, from the standpoint of the life world, to the objective societal conditions of life insofar as these, as meanings, become the premises of individual plans for action. Granting this experiential point of departure, a scientific character requires the guarantee that the inclusion of individual subjectivity adhere to scientific criteria for the generality and objectivity of knowledge. Therefore we are concerned with understanding the levels of psychical mediation between the subjective situation and objective circumstances on the basis of our categories. This means that the subjective situation of an individual can be comprehended as a special phenomenal form of the societally typical, basic psychical situation of individuals. This has nothing to do with typological classification; rather, it is concerned with analyzing, with the person involved, existentially concrete ways of coping with existing action space and (where possible, in common with others) of extending them. The point is to oppose tendencies to reinterpret objective constraints into subjective constraints, and to encourage steps toward subjective extension of control.

Following Lewin's (1931/1981) critique of frequency thinking and his conception of generalization from a "single case" to "such a case" qua "type of event," Holzkamp (1983) elaborated a Critical Psychological understanding of concrete generalization as "generalization of possibilities" or of "structures." This is not the place for a more detailed description of our conceptions of generalization, law, the singular, and the typical or of our ideas on the unity of practice and production of knowledge in empirical research and our intersubjective treatment of research subjects as coresearchers. Many of our definitions are still provisional in nature; the strategic status of traditional empirical method, especially, is still an open question.

There can be no doubt, however, that our analysis has methodological consequences for the experimental-statistical verifiability of psychological theories insofar as these are formulated or intended as statements about the context of grounding for human action. As Holzkamp (1986) was able to show, this intention strikes at the heart of nomothetic social psychology (at least implicitly): Most theories, insofar as they are not strictly behaviorist, imply grounds for action. Within the verification scheme of variable psychology such grounds are hidden behind terms of a merely conditional nature. This camouflage necessitates an interpretation of empirical results that might be described as a speculative clarification of the premises of individual action. It is not related in any appropriate representational way to operationalized if–then hypotheses; these therefore do not test what they claim to test. This is a radicalization of the earlier Critical Psychological finding of "scientific indeterminacy."

If this is so, then the need for a (new) "paradigmatic" foundation of psychology is not just the whim of Marxist scientific do-gooders in response to a "crisis in psychology" that they themselves have invented. This foundational task must be faced squarely by non-Marxist scientists, too, insofar as they make any claims at all to methodological rigor and empirically verifiable, meaningful findings.

Notes

1 When we speak of Critical Psychology in connection with the developments in West Berlin, it should not be understood to refer to a merely local phenomenon. There were "international congresses" in Marburg in 1977, 1979, and 1984, "vacation schools" in Graz, Austria, in 1983, in Fulda in 1984, in Innsbruck, Austria, in 1985, and again in Fulda in 1987. The existence of numerous research and study groups and professional practitioners, both in West Germany and in foreign countries, as well as the supraregional distribution of authors contributing to the series "Texte zur Kritischen Psychologie" (Frankfurt/M.: Campus) or to the journal *Forum Kritische Psychologie* (West Berlin: Argument), both testify to its nonlocal nature. The occasionally encountered labels "Holzkamp School" or "Berlin School of Critical Psychology," not to mention the misleading term "school," are merely personalized cryptograms that misapply the term "school." They are acceptable only considering the fact that with the university reforms of 1969, and especially after the winter term of 1970/1971, when the conservative faction of professors and assistants formed their own "Institute for Psychology" in the Faculty of Educational Sciences, the reorganization of academic training in psychology that was pursued at the "Psychological Institute" of the former Philosophical Faculty, then Faculty 11, Philosophy and Social Sciences, was unique to all institutions of higher learning of Berlin and the FRG. The progressive alternative that resulted (massively obstructed in its development by losses of positions and other politically motivated administrative attacks) was very much the work of those who participated in the development of Critical Psychology. It was, however, thoroughly shaped by the struggles within the institute, extending into the mid-

1970s, around the program for materialist research, professional training, and democratic practice oriented to the interests of working people in bourgeois society. This struggle took a generalized political form in the opposition between its protagonists, the Aktionsgemeinschaften von Demokraten und Sozialisten [Action Alliances of Democrats and Socialists] and the student organization of the Maoist Communist Party of Germany. In short, Critical Psychology (in the narrower sense) saw in this context its first and relatively most developed articulation in research and teaching and still finds its personal focus in the West Berlin working group around Klaus Holzkamp, notwithstanding the multiplication since then of regional centers of Critical Psychology.

2 Benno Ohnesorg was a student who, on 2 June 1967, was shot and killed by the West Berlin police in front of the Deutsche Oper at a demonstration against the visit of the Shah of Iran.

3 These contributions were mostly published in the *Zeitschrift für Sozialpsychologie* after having been circulated as first drafts for discussion in the student bodies of the psychological institutes.

4 There are further fundamental orientations that correspond to this in contemporary theories of science, including non-Marxist ones, that speak of the failure of mere (verificationist or falsificationist) logic of theory evaluation and – insofar as the methodological anarchism of Feyerabend is not favored as a way out – demand working toward a rationale of the genesis of concepts and theories.

5 Marx and Engels's conception of history as a subject-related process cannot be gone into in detail here. Because of its power as a programmatic statement, however, I mention the explanation of the "real premises" of all human history "from which abstraction can be made only in the imagination" in *Die deutsche Ideologie* (Marx & Engels, 1846/1969: 20). I would like further to draw attention to Marx's summary of "profane history" contained in his letter of December 1846 to Annenkov (Marx, 1846/1965: 451) and directed against Proudhon's Hegelianizing phantasms. The rubbish to the effect that "for Marx history is completely automatic without people taking part, as if these people were played upon like pure chess pieces by the economic relations, themselves the work of humans," was already in his time ridiculed by Engels as an "eccentric assertion" of the "metaphysician Dühring" (Engels, 1890/1970: 83).

6 This mystification is encountered in the common idea of an instinctual fate of compulsory socialization, which is regarded as lamentable or as civilizing, depending upon theoretical taste (see Maiers, 1985).

3 Societal and Individual Life Processes

Klaus Holzkamp

1

In its persistent effort to expose the limited knowledge content of bourgeois theories and their resulting subservience to the capitalistic class perspective, militant materialism often finds itself on the receiving end of a similar treatment. The Marxist approach is said, for example, to be an essentially *economic* analysis that is therefore necessarily limited where the concern goes beyond the bare *conditions* of human life to *the human being as such,* that is, to psychophysical dispositions, biological endowments, vital needs, in short to *human nature.* Such conclusions come not only from those who hold views of psychology, scientific or otherwise, in which the conditions of individual human life are thought not even to require an economic analysis, but are understood merely as "stimuli," as natural "environment," or the like. Similar opinions are found even among those with materialistic pretensions, representing positions that actually claim to understand human "relations" from a Marxist perspective, but for the purpose of apprehending human "nature" fall back upon non-Marxist, especially subject-scientific approaches like psychoanalysis. Indeed, in their practice many Marxists plainly declare themselves incapable of dealing with "psychological" questions, which they simply abandon to "the psychologists."

Can "militant materialists" afford to give up their militancy when it comes to "human nature" and its scientific understanding? The answer surely is "no," and not only from the perspective of a Marxism committed to raising the whole of human knowledge and practice to an historically higher level through its liberation from the constraints of bourgeois ideology, a level at which, in principle, questions of "appropriateness" do not arise. Even short of such fundamental considerations, it would be a curious "modesty" for Marxists to claim that, although human beings stand at the center of concern, it is unnecessary or impossible to say anything specific about them in their full sensuous reality.

50

Thus if dialectical materialism is to remain potentially "militant" with regard to questions about the psyche, or about the "nature" of human beings, it must be presumed that the possibilities of answering such questions exist in Marxist theory or can be developed from it. Moreover, since Marxism is unquestionably a theory in which the analysis of economic relations and movements assumes a central and absolute position, it will be necessary to comprehend economic analysis, and to define the concept "economy" in such a way that propositions about "human nature" can be understood and substantiated as results (in the broadest sense) of such an "economic" analysis. But how can this be done?

As many futile attempts have shown, progress in this direction cannot be made by starting with the Marxist "anatomy of bourgeois society" and expecting somehow to arrive at a conception of the individual from the dissection and specification of the mode of production in particular capitalist societies. No matter how precise and detailed such an analysis may be, the "individual as such" remains somehow out of reach. The choice remaining appears to be either to "economize" the individual, such that social relations are substituted for it, and wrongly understanding the Sixth Thesis on Feuerbach, the "individual" is looked upon as the "ensemble of social relations," or covertly to borrow the needed concepts from bourgeois positions, especially from psychoanalysis. This problematic situation is not fundamentally altered if, like Lucien Sève, one distinguishes "concrete individuals" from the ensemble of social relations as "human essence," but still understands the concrete individual only in terms of the Marxist "anatomy of bourgeois society." Here, too, the individual actually remains "out of reach," and Sève's readiness to compromise with respect to psychology and psychoanalysis, granting independent significance to them "within limits," is then the logical consequence.

This dilemma of the economic analysis of human individuality resolves itself in a single stroke if, following Marx and Engels, "we recognize only a single science, the science of history," or if we take seriously Lenin's view of the materialist dialectic as the most comprehensive and substantial "doctrine of development." This means, in our connection, that the economic analysis must be opened to its historical dimension. Insofar as it is clear that "economic" life relations are not simply "there," but rather have evolved as specifically human forms of life production from other, prehuman forms of life production, the appearance of the unmediated opposition between economic relations and the inner nature of individuals becomes transparent as mere appearance. It can then be understood that with the historical formation of the societal-economic form of life production, the "nature" of living beings must necessarily have developed such that they became capable of participating in the new economic process by which subsistence and other conditions of life are socially produced. This crucial circumstance becomes clearer when one considers the trivial fact that no nonhuman living being, no matter how highly it has developed or how much attention has been given it, is in the position individually to realize a societal-economic process of life production. The curious undertaking of the Kelloggs, in which they raised their own baby with a young chimpanzee under equal developmental and educational conditions, is well known. They came, not surprisingly, to the conclusion that the chimpanzee (following an advantageous beginning) could not keep up with the child in the socialization process, but rather remained behind within the confines of its species-specific, biological potential. In the similarly motivated more recent experimental attempts to teach chimpanzees to "speak," although some amount of sign language was acquired after months of systematic training, the results have not been interpreted even by the greatest optimists to mean that the chimpanzees had learned to speak in a truly human sense. It is too obvious that it was human beings who, with their training activities, brought "Sarah" or "Washoe" to behave in a limited, externally humanlike way and that the chimpanzees would never have been capable of such a learning process by themselves. In short, human beings obviously have at their disposal a "nature," according to which they are, alone among living creatures, capable individually of participating in the societal process by virtue of their "natural" developmental potential.

By introducing the concept of "societal nature," the opposition of "nature" and "sociality" is overcome by affirming that the "sociality" of humans is found already in their "nature." But, on the other hand, this concept flies in the face of traditional conceptions and of the established division of scientific disciplines. Nature, it might be objected, is investigated by the natural sciences, according to which biology or a natural-scientifically understood psychology is responsible for the "inner nature" of human beings, whereas societal relations are investigated by the social sciences, such as sociology and economics. Talk of "societal nature" would negate this established division of labor and what does not belong together, what is in fact in opposition, would be connected by a mere play on words. Paradoxical talk about a societal nature of human beings does nothing to reveal the actual mediation between inner nature and society, much less say anything about how the substance of this "societal nature" should be characterized.

This possible objection must, of course, be taken seriously. When we say that humans, in contrast to all other living beings, *must,* by virtue of their inner nature, be capable of socialization because they would otherwise be unable to develop into the societal life production process, and, accordingly, that with the historical emergence of the societal-economic life production form "societal nature" *must* have developed as the *subjective side of the economy,* this is only a postulate, albeit a reasonable one. It remains an open question *how* such an historic process, in which the "inner nature" of the individual becomes socialized simultaneously with the development of the societal-economic life production form, would be constituted, *how* it can be demonstrated by scientific means that such a thing can be possible at all and what kind of a "nature" is thereby produced.

2

It is clear that in the process of hominization and the attainment of the societal-economic level one may, in the first instance, assume only the effect of the laws of biological evolution, in particular the laws of development by mutation and selection. But this implies that the laws of evolution, by means of their own effectiveness, must have produced a phylogenetic developmental stage in which mutation and selection were replaced as determinants by the "economic" production of the means and conditions of life on the basis of the *"societal" nature* of human beings. This would mean, moreover, that with the emergence of the societal nature of the human being, the biological laws of evolution must have been abrogated as determining, developmental factors. Such would be the evolutionary-theoretical understanding of the above-mentioned *seeming paradox of the so-called societal nature* of the human being. But "paradoxes" of this kind do not signal an abandonment of the scientific process of explication. On the contrary, it can be shown that the assumption of such an anthropogenetic process of the evolutionary socialization of human nature is not only a *possible* interpretation of the human evolutionary process, but is at the moment the *most adequate* one from a scientific point of view. In order to demonstrate this, I shall turn now to some pertinent research findings of Critical Psychology (see Holzkamp, 1983).

It is necessary to work out in a dialectical materialist way the transition from the merely evolutionary-phylogenetic to societal-historical development as a great transformation of quantity into quality. In order to manage this, the qualitative transformation must be analytically decomposed into separate empirically demonstrable steps. In so doing, two developmental processes become conspicuous as conditions for the qualitative transformation. One of these is the development of learned social relations extending to supraindividual, collective coordination of life production, in which single individuals assume partial functions subordinated to a general goal (the classic example: Leontyev's "hunter–beater" coordination, in which the beater frightens the game that the hunter kills, and the prey is later shared between both). The other is the development of the use and production of tools, such as sticks for hitting, for reaching a wanted object, for fishing termites out of their holes, and so forth. On the basis of these two developments, a *first qualitative leap* toward hominization is brought about in which, in the production and use of mediating instruments, *ends and means are, so to speak, "reversed."* Whereas the instrument was earlier brought into play in the presence of a concrete, needed object, such as a stick that serves to reach a banana and is then discarded, a *functional change* in the instrument gradually comes about in which it is produced not just in immediate connection with actual activity, but for generalized purposes, such as obtaining fruit, and is therefore retained, improved, and so forth. The central significance of this functional change lies in the fact that it represents an instance of *planned generalized provision* finding its way into the life production process. Instruments, early forms of tools, are produced for the occasion that they will be needed, that is, that in the future a situation of need or deficiency will arise for which their use will be required. This new generalized form of tool production and use arose from the very beginning in connection with the above-mentioned supraindividual coordination of activities, in which, by means of the emergence of the capability for planned production of tools for future generalized purposes, the social coordination, in its turn, achieved a new quality: This new kind of tool was now available for collective use. In this new function-sharing coordination, it was possible to produce tools for others and to use those made by others, as well as to employ various tools collectively and cooperatively. This instance of generalized provision brought about by the functional change of instruments into tools within the social life production process thus became the earliest form of generalized societal provision *as the central determinant of the societal life production process.*

What is important for the purpose of our argument is that, in accordance with the fundamental characteristic of the evolution process, the new societal life production form did not become dominant with a single stroke, but only very gradually over long periods of time in which the biological form of life production in a natural world dominated. The new form of life production was therefore already specific to the life process, but not yet dominant. This means, however, that the laws of mutation and selection, despite the new societal life production form, were still in effect. The changes must therefore have come about on the basis of biological evolutionary processes. This was possible – and this is crucial – because the possibility of generalized provision by means of social tool production in this life production form represented an immense "selective advantage." We have thus broken down the development of so-called human societal nature evolutionary-theoretical manner: Societal nature developed in a phase of hominization in which the societal life production form reacted through its selective advantages upon the genomic information and thus upon the biological nature of the human being. A dialectical materialist, natural scientific analysis thus reveals the mediation process by which the biological developmental requirements became altered in the direction of a potential for participation in the societal life production form, whereby the inner nature of the living being became societal. The apparent paradox is thus easily resolved.

The development of the societal life production form and the development of human societal nature must have reciprocally reinforced one another in the hominization phase following the "first qualitative leap" toward humanity, since humans became, on the basis of their so-called societal nature, more and more competent with respect to the societal life production form and the "selective advantage" created by it, reacting upon the "nature" of the individual, must have become ever greater. By virtue of this reciprocal action and some further conditions, it came, gradually, as we have shown elsewhere, to an expanding importance of the societal, as opposed to the still present biological life production form. The actual *reversal of dominance* from solely phylogenetic-evolutionary to societal-historical development as the *second and final qualitative leap* toward humanity was accomplished in the following way: At a certain point in development, through ever more extensive tool production and use, dominance shifted from adaptation of the organism to the environment to the active adaptation of the environment to individuals by means of their objectifying alteration of nature in a process of generalized societal provision. In this way the life production form of social labor developed as a process of socially planned appropriation and objectification of nature. The objective world formed by human beings, together with the social relations that were simultaneously established, became an independent carrier of development. To the extent that the natural *ecology* became a social *economy*, the phylogenetic process was superimposed upon by the societal-historical process, in which the process of reciprocal adaptation of human being and world takes place through an active, collective alteration of nature, characterized by a new order of magnitude of effectiveness and rate of progress (phylogenetic development is measured in hundreds of thousands of years; societal-historical development, in centuries or decades, and it is increasingly cumulative and accelerating). At the same time the evolutionary laws lose their power as determining factors in development by virtue of their own previous effectiveness in the transition phase: Natural selection is no longer dominant in the "economic" societal life production form. On the contrary, there comes to prevail a strategy that reduces and transcends natural selection by means of the collective, generalized provision for the maintenance of social units and thus also of each individual. In addition, the now dominant societal-historical process brings with it such a rapid development of living conditions that selection-conditioned processes of evolutionary change, owing to their comparatively infinite slowness, come to approach zero in their developmental relevance. Instead, specific societal-historical developmental laws become effective, through which (according to the classical doctrine of social formations), out of the original society, slaveholder society, feudalism, capitalism, and socialism developed as stages of the societal process.

Now if the societal-historical process became dominant in this manner, this would mean that the development of the societal nature of humans through selection-conditioned reaction of the societal life production form on genomic information came to an end. Natural selection, which brought about the societal developmental process, is now, for all practical purposes, excluded by it. On the other hand, natural selection could only be replaced by societal processes because the individual capability for participation in the societal process had so augmented itself in the transition phase that individuals, on the basis of their natural developmental potentials, now become able *individually* to realize and to share in the societal developmental process. The specifically human learning and developmental capacity therefore does not find its absolute limits in the respective personal lifespan, but is, beyond that, the capacity for appropriation and objectification of ever-newer achievements and needs, in connection with ever-newer demands and possibilities for satisfaction that arise in the *historical process*. The "societal nature" of the human being consists therefore not of some sort of anthropological constants, but rather of *developmental potential* of an historic order of magnitude that makes it possible for individuals at each societal-historical stage of development, with its expanded social appropriation of nature (as Marx expressed it), also to change their own nature. Societal nature as natural developmental potential is at the same time, therefore, the condition for the possibility of concrete socialization of the individual nature according to formation-, class-, and position-specific life relations.

3

When the question is now asked, "What are the special features acquired by the inner nature of humans in the transition from phylogenetically dominated to societal-historically dominated development?" it is clear that the living being does not enter into this process of human evolution as a tabula rasa. On the contrary, humans already have behind them a long period of phylogenetic development of their natural life possibilities, which culminates in a particular concrete stage of development. Obviously we must be acquainted with this stage if we are to determine which of the characteristics arising with this qualitatively new level constitutes the *human* nature of the individual, that is, what precisely in the inner nature of the living being is becoming socialized through the specifically human learning and developmental potential that has come with the transition to the economic life production form.

In order to bring this problem to a solution, the historical dimension of the analysis must be extended further. It will not suffice to investigate only the transition from the merely phylogenetic to the societal-historically dominated life production form with regard to the implications for the "inner nature" of living beings. Rather, *the entire natural historical process* within which those new potentials of the "nature" of living beings came about must be reconstructed. Only in this way can we work out the differentiations in content, the various functional levels and aspects of individual developmental capacity.

In Critical Psychology we have carried out this reconstruction on the basis of Leontyev's objective definition of the psyche. I cannot describe the contents of our reconstruction here, but will only mention certain procedural steps. We began by focusing on the qualitative transformation of the prepsychic life process to the psychic stage in order to arrive at a definition and specification of *psychogenesis* within the overall phylogenetic process. Thus, "psyche" was introduced to designate the genetically most basic form, and thus also the most general basic category of the science of the individual. In addition, the earlier differentiation of the psyche was given an historical understanding in which, from an analysis of *genetic* origins and differentiations, we were able to arrive at *conceptual* differentiations of the psyche, such as the orientational, emotional, and social aspects of psychic life activity. In this way these traditional concepts acquired a new materialistic content, and on this basis we were able critically to reject the corresponding bourgeois psychological definitions. Building upon this, a new general qualitative level was reconstructed, this time *within* psychogenesis, a level marked by the emergence of *individual learning and developmental capacity.* The intention was to show what novel quality was acquired at the new level by the various cognitive, emotional, and social dimensions of the psyche that had been identified by genetic differentiation analysis. Following this, we continued our study of psychogenesis at this new stage up to the point at which *hominization* might be said to begin. Working in this way, we arrived at empirically differentiated, methodologically grounded ideas of the structure, that is, the various levels and aspects, of the nature of the living beings who entered into the process of development of the new societal-economic stage, and thus how the inner nature came to be socialized. The new quality of societal nature could then be identified with respect to the various functional aspects and levels of the psyche that had been revealed by the foregoing analyses of origin and differentiation as the societal *developmental potential* of individuals for orientation activity, emotional and motivational processes, needs, and social communication forms as they had previously been derived and defined. This genetic analysis also revealed the *inner connection* among these various functional aspects, with which, by means of their materialist definition, it became possible to overcome the traditional fragmentation of the psychological object into various independent approaches and disciplines dealing with thinking, perception, emotionality, action, and so forth.

Because in psychogenesis, as in historical development altogether, not all aspects develop evenly, but rather some are determining of others, whereas others are secondary or even remain fixated at earlier levels of development, we found a definite genetic differentiation with respect to the developmental potentials of the human psyche. It was possible to distinguish the psychical aspects that are specific and determining for the development of the human societal-economic form of life production from ones that are brought along secondarily by the determining factors and then, further, from those that indeed belong to humans but are more or less unspecific for the human mode of life production. Thus our conception of the inner nature of humans acquired a special *genetic structure,* according to which it was possible to distinguish among *specific and determining, specific but secondary,* and *nonspecific* characteristics. These various constituents could then be analyzed with regard to their relationship to each other, and so on.

4

How, then, are the dimensions and aspects of the societal developmental capacity of individuals to be understood as psychical potentials of their societal nature? As our extensive investigations have shown, the specific and determining moment of this individual learning and developmental capacity is *the individual participation in consciously provisioning determination of the societal conditions of life.* Generally speaking, this is due to the fact that humans cannot, like animals, maintain their life in a bare individual, natural environment; rather, the maintenance of individual existence is always an aspect of the maintenance of societal life. The individual life conditions of humans are consequently always in some manner and degree *individually relevant societal life conditions.* The securing and developing of individual existence therefore tends to be identical with individual participation in the control over the societal process, that is, over those of its aspects that are relevant to the individual.

Thus, generally speaking, the development of human subjectivity, as the possibility of conscious control over one's own life conditions, always and necessarily requires *moving beyond individuality* toward participation in the *collective determination* of the societal process: If the individual life conditions are the individually relevant societal life conditions, then the individual, taken as a solitary being, does not have the power consciously to determine them, but rather remains necessarily at the mercy of the circumstances of existence and can only react to present contingencies instead of providing for his or her own existence in a human manner. To the extent that the individual life circumstances are in fact relevant and that their societal interconnectedness and determinedness increase, the single individual can determine his or her own life circumstances and thus become an *individual subject,* but only in union with others as a moment of a social subject. This transcendence of individuality in union with others with the general aim of consciously provisioning control over societal–individual life conditions, we have called *personal action potence.*

From the point of view of action potence, it becomes possible to characterize more precisely the various functional aspects of the psyche in its specific determining, specific secondary, and nonspecific constituents, in that the fate of these functional aspects can be followed in the course of the transition to the individual-historical type of development, a transition that can be thought of in terms of developing into societal life production. With regard to the individual knowing process, for example, we were able in this way to determine that human thinking, in its specific and determining characteristics, must be understood not merely as the analysis/synthesis of individually posed problems, but rather as appropriation of societal modes of thinking with which the individual realizes socially developed forms of analysis/synthesis in his or her individual thinking and only in this way becomes able to contribute to the development of these thought forms.

With respect to the emotional aspect of the psyche, the fundamental concept of "productive needs" was genetically reconstructed as a specific and determining constituent of human, as opposed to animal, emotionality. In this reconstruction it became clear that with the *objective necessity* of having to participate in the social provisioning process in order to control individual life conditions, a *subjective necessity* also developed. The significance of this is that for the human being to be at the mercy of immediate contingencies and not able to participate in the possibilities of collective control over life conditions means subjective suffering, or what we have called human anxiety, that is, *action impotence* as a consequence of isolation from socially provided possibilities of control. The productive needs are thus categorial devices for the analysis of the immediate experience with respect to the subjective necessity to overcome isolation and helplessness, and thus also anxiety, by participating in the common provision of one's own life conditions. The productive needs are, so to speak, the emotional side of action potence. Their subjectively necessary character, that is, their "need quality," is such that the satisfaction of the elementary sensuous-vital needs at the human level attains a special quality: Humans are not satisfied when they merely reduce particular momentary need tensions, such as hunger or sexuality; rather, they achieve a fulfilled, satisfied state only when they can anticipate the possibility of satisfaction of their needs within the prospect of a provisioned and secure individual existence, that is, when they can develop their action potence in the process of participation in control over societal life conditions. We have shown in detail that the "human" quality of satisfaction of sensuous-vital needs is so formed that it can only be achieved in the context of generalized provision and, more broadly, that the development of sensuousness means at the same time freedom from anxiety; that is, it means the development of action potence.

Naturally, with such a sketchy account I have not been able to describe the contents of our findings regarding the character of human learning and developmental capacity; I only intended to indicate that these findings exist and are available elsewhere. For present purposes, however, the following points are necessary. The concept of personal action potence, together with its various functional aspects, is intended to emphasize the most general characteristics of the human type of individual development. This does not mean, however, that these characteristics are fully realized in, or adequately characterize, the development of each individual. We are speaking rather of the general *directional determinants* that, on the one hand, distinguish human from prehuman individual development but, on the other hand, may express themselves under particular historical conditions only in limited and contradictory ways. In this regard, the general determinants of individual development are to be understood in exactly the same way as those of superordinate societal-historical development, of which they are a part and an aspect. Although overall societal-historical development contrasts with animal life production forms in that it is life production by mean of cooperative, consciously provisioning labor, it is always the case that cooperation can express itself only in a reduced and partial way in antagonistic class society in which the mass of members is excluded from conscious control over affairs that affect them. Only in socialism is a stage reached at which a qualitatively new kind of social cooperation becomes generally determining and characteristic of the entire life production form. Only in socialism is a stage achieved in which the general determination of societal cooperation becomes characteristic for the whole life production process in a qualitatively new form.

The attributes of "action potence" and its functional aspects thus do not occur directly as analytic determinants in the observable course of individual development, but are always partial and mystified in bourgeois society by concrete class-specific obstacles to development. What we have here, then, is an *analytic category* that can help us to understand how the general directional determination of a tendency toward extended control over one's own life conditions through participation in societal provisioning manifests itself – however reduced, perverted, or mystified – under concrete social developmental conditions and obstacles. The surface appearances of individual courses of development that are ordinarily encountered can thus be analyzed in terms of the relationship they express between the generalized action potence and the developmental restrictions through which they are canalized and deformed. Thus it is necessary to understand not only social developmental obstacles by which action potence is concretely restricted, but also the subjective levels of mediation, modes of assimilation, and mechanisms of defense by which the subjective necessity to control conditions appears in possibly unrecognizable, perverted ways. It is out of this isolation from control over relevant life conditions, and of subjection to life's contingencies, when consciously understood and emotionally felt, that *individual suffering* arises. And it is in the attempts to overcome this suffering, attempts in which people, in the conscious conduct of their lives, strive for control over the circumstances of their existence under the restrictive and contradictory conditions of the moment, that one sees the malformations and perversions of action potence that we speak of as restrictive action potence. By taking the restrictive societal conditions for development and their subjective modes of assimilation into consideration, the modes of thought that are reduced and distorted for all of us in bourgeois society, as well as the emotions that are crippled, isolated, and diminished as "private" inner life, the social relations that appear as mere individual private relations can still be understood as special expressions of our tendency toward conscious control over our life conditions, that is, toward action potence.

With an analysis of this kind, in each particular instance it becomes scientifically ascertainable in what direction we must collectively change our societal life conditions such that action potence is increasingly freed from its limited and mystified forms, and how we can come to a satisfying, anxiety-free, and fulfilled existence by developing the possibilities for the cooperative self-determination of our affairs. The analysis of the limits and perversions of individual life possibilities and subjective situations, and the practical critique of social relations that produce them, are thus only two sides of the same subject-scientific investigational process (see Holzkamp, 1983: ch. 7, 8, 9).

With this we arrive at a *new level of the critique* of bourgeois psychology; it can be shown, namely, that conceptions in which the inner nature of humans is isolated from societal relations and in which the psyche is reduced to a bare "inwardness," in which humans are understood as having only to maintain their lives in a naturally given environment, and so forth, are not simply false, but are in fact the theoretical reproduction of the diminution and distortion of the tendency toward collective self-determination under bourgeois conditions of life.

I shall now give two concrete examples of this general approach to the critique of bourgeois psychology. In working through modern cognitive theories of emotion, Ute Holzkamp-Osterkamp has demonstrated that, for individuals who are excluded by bourgeois social relations from conscious cooperative control over the social process and therefore also over their own relevant life conditions, only the internalization and privatization of emotions, and thus their detachment from action, remains available as an alternative to the collective struggle. For the isolated individual this is a form of shutting out reality, in which the risk of altercation with the authorities, which is unbearable for isolated individuals, is, by denying the necessity and possibility of action, not even admitted to consciousness. As Holzkamp-Osterkamp showed, however, it is precisely this internalized and privatized emotionality that is portrayed by bourgeois theories as universal human emotionality in general, and in this portrayal forms of consciousness associated with adaptation and resignation to bourgeois class relations are blindly reproduced and reinforced (see Holzkamp-Osterkamp, 1978). As a further example, the analysis by Morus Markard of the social-psychological "attitude" concept can be cited [see Chapter 9 of the present volume]. Among other things, it was found that the attitude measures or scales currently in use necessarily eliminate the object-relatedness of the attitude as well as the possibility of the subject's acting consciously with respect to attitudes or to their objects. What is left is "attitude" as a bare, individual, inner psychical state of affairs that has nothing at all to do with the social reality outside the individual. This is, on its part, the theoretical duplication of a particular aspect of bourgeois ideology. It is the concept of pluralism, according to which anyone who holds to the possibility of real knowledge about societal relations, as opposed to mere diversity of opinion, is categorized as dogmatic. Under this concept, the dissemination of object-detached opinions and their manipulation in the sense of personal political opinions (read "class interests") appear as the central themes of democratic politics.

These and many other pertinent investigations not only yield new insights into the manifold appearance forms of restricted action potence and its related means of shutting out reality for the purpose of denying or avoiding conflict with those who hold power but also give the affected individuals the possibility of knowing what they need to do in order to overcome the restrictions of action and consciousness and move toward participation in the collective widening of control over societal life circumstances in the interest of enlarging personal action potence and improving the quality of life.

If, as we have said, bourgeois psychological theories do not in fact go beyond the scientifically styled reproduction of the surface features of bourgeois society, then a Marxist-based subject-science is more than merely well suited for the critique of both theories with scientific pretensions and the "everyday'' psychologies they duplicate; it becomes an important *instrument in the ideological struggle*. More than that, it allows Marxists to conduct the ideological struggle offensively, even where, from the bourgeois ideological side, questions of subjectivity – in whatever manner – are raised. Wherever conceptions, mainly psychoanalytic, of social conflict or aggression as products of unresolved denials of drive in early childhood, and the like, are current (as in the peace movement), they can be opposed not only by a Marxist class analysis, but beyond that, by exposing the helpless renunciation of the subjective fulfillment of life as implied by the view of oneself as a mere victim of past repressions and by demonstrating how this view turns attention away from the common task of creating humane life conditions and directs it to one's own childhood as the presumed "personal" source of subjective suffering. At the same time, the propagation of such views must be understood and made understandable in terms of their "consoling function" for the supposed victims; it must be shown how such views, by referring class conflict to early childhood, serve as pseudo-justification for the individual's avoidance of conflict by standing aside from the class struggle, this being a manifestation of restricted action potence.

Likewise, we must no longer puritanically treat as problematic and suspicious the demands raised in the new social movements for full enjoyment of existence here and now. It would be better to give these people the theoretical means by which to understand their own experience and recognize that under bourgeois class relations the enjoyment of existence they seek will again and again necessarily be undermined by competition, guilt feelings, and latent isolation anxiety, and that immediate efforts in that direction will not only be futile in the end, but will confirm the individual's personal impotence with respect to those who rule. We may then come to the shared insight that we are always best off here and now when we struggle to overcome those societal relations under which we must be at odds with ourselves, since in the struggle itself the very forms of relating and subjective situations pertaining to control over our life conditions are already partially anticipated. Further, we must no longer cling abstractly to the virtues of the collective when we are reproached about massing and leveling by communist collectivism: Rather, we are able to recognize the wish to be alone, to live one's own life, as fully legitimate for ourselves and others, providing we make clear at the same time that separation as a dominant way of living, under existing social relations, is synonymous with surrender and anxiety, and that social relations, based on a common responsibility for the whole, under which, one can be "separate in society" (Marx) and "at home with oneself" confidently and without anxiety, need yet to be struggled for in the development of collective power.

From these examples it should be clear that a Marxist-based subject-science is not only a technical affair for psychologists, but also an important means for achieving scientifically grounded ideological clarity in the debates of "militant materialists" around the question of what obstructs and what promotes the development of human subjectivity and the quality of human life.

4   Experience of Self and Scientific Objectivity

Klaus Holzkamp

1

Prior to 1968 our institute regularly observed the beginning of the new semester by holding a tea party. In an atmosphere of candlelight and biscuits, first-semester students were introduced to the faculty members and encouraged to feel at home with the study of psychology. On these occasions the director of the institute at the time made a humorous little speech, the quintessence of which was the following. Beginning students should forget everything they had previously heard or believed about psychology; from now on everything would be different. Especially they should abandon any hope that the study of psychology would have anything to do with them, their personal experiences and problems, or be able to help them in overcoming individual difficulties or anxieties. Such expectations were prescientific and would prove, more likely than not, an obstruction to the acquisition of an acceptable motivation for study. Rather it was important to understand that psychology is a science like all others and, as such, concerned with *objective* knowledge, and that whoever wants to learn and practice this science must accordingly put aside *subjective opinions,* that is, what one thought one knew from one's own experience, in favor of what was now designated as the scientific aspiration for knowledge . . . and so on and on in this vein.

Words like these by our former director still describe the methodological self-understanding of mainstream scientific psychology. But a great many students and an increasing number of psychologists can no longer reconcile themselves with the demand to deny the subjective as a necessary presupposition for scientific psychology. Indeed, whole branches of psychological research and practice must be put into doubt by such a conception of method, especially clinical psychology, which can less and less make do without drawing and reflecting upon self-experience, including that of the therapist. To pronounce such practices unscientific provides scientific-theoretical consecration to the de facto split between basic and specialized study and to the underlying

65

division between scientific and applied psychology. What's more, it asserts the split as necessary and immutable. So it is no wonder that in recent times distinct alternative conceptions of psychology that introduce subjectivity, everyday life, and spontaneity as objects of psychological investigation have emerged and become widespread.

What remains unclear, however, is how the inclusion of subjectivity in psychology as advocated by these conceptions squares with the demand for scientific objectivity. Does the assumption remain that subjectivity and objectivity are exclusive of one another, and is one thereby forced to reject or limit psychology's claim that it is scientific for the sake of subjectivity (as implied by the well-known dictum of humanistic psychology that American psychology exaggerates its scientific nature)? Or is it possible in psychology to develop a concept of scientific objectivity that does not require the elimination of subjective self-experience? We might even ask whether traditional psychology has actually achieved its aspiration to scientific status at the expense of subjectivity.

Questions like these are seldom precisely put, let alone adequately answered. It is therefore still necessary to consider subjectivity as a problem of psychological method. I hope that the following preliminary observations will help to achieve some clarity on this issue.

2

First, the scientific postulate that objective knowledge in psychology requires the exclusion or control of subjectivity demands closer examination. How is this postulate justified in current experimental-statistical psychology? What conceptions of subjectivity are assumed? And to what extent is the claim actually warranted, that scientific rigor and certainty have been achieved in psychological research by the elimination of the subjective?

With the customary experimental-statistical method of investigation, there are supposed to be tests of theoretical assumptions about the connection between the conditions in which individuals are placed and particular forms of individual behavior. The experimental conditions are operationalized as independent variables; the forms of behavior, as dependent variables. The procedural precaution of experimental control of variables is intended to ensure as far as possible that the data regarding the behavior of the subject are not influenced by factors other than those experimentally introduced, that is, are not influenced by "disturbing variables," since the findings are actually interpretable as an empirical test of the respective theoretically assumed connection only when such influence is minimized. According to current understanding, adequate control requires the use of frequency distributions, usually obtained by investigating several individuals under identical arrangements. Since control cannot eliminate extraneous factors completely, the experimental behavioral data (dependent variable) normally come out as a "scatter" distribution about a average value, such that it is impossible to judge by mere visual inspection the extent to which they are related to the experimental arrangements (independent variables). At this point another statistic enters the picture: the so-called inferential statistic, which interprets the scatter distribution in terms of the chance variability of independent elements and on this basis applies certain constructs from probability theory in order to ascertain the probability with which a confirmation of the test assumptions may be taken from the experimental data (or according to the traditional "null hypothesis" logic, the probability with which the opposing hypothesis that the distribution of experimental behavior data vary only in a chance way with respect to the introduced experimental arrangements can be rejected).

We have called this experimental-statistical procedural scheme variable-psychology. What is meant by this is the logic of psychological research just sketched. Variable-psychology arose historically as a consequence of functionalism-behaviorism, and although it hardly describes the methodology of all psychology, it still forms the core of academic psychology's conception of what constitutes its scientific nature. Variable-psychology, either as explicit or implicit research logic, is thus not characterized by a unitary conception of theory. On the contrary, the theories that fall under this rubric have been quite various. What is crucial, however, is that although the theories may range widely *in content* beyond the limits of variable-psychology, they are reduced by the variable-scheme in their empirical reference when they come to experimental testing, such that the distinctive theoretical content necessarily becomes "surplus meaning," lacking empirical support. Thus in methodological discussions it has been proposed that this surplus meaning be omitted, and this, in turn, has been opposed by those who understood that the substantive significance of psychological research would thereby be sacrificed. It is not possible here to discuss all the complex effects of the variable-scheme on the character and history of theory in psychology.

From this rather brief description of variable-psychology's research logic, I should be able to formulate its methodic grounds for excluding subjectivity for the sake of scientific objectivity. Subjectivity, as it is understood here, is the main source of the extraneous variation that must be eliminated or neutralized if the experimental-statistical testing of theoretical assumptions is to be possible in the manner we have described.

With the improvement of variable-psychological procedures, it has become increasingly clear that even the subjectivity of the experimenter can in various ways become a source of extraneous variation. As a result, all sorts of precautions have been introduced with the aim of controlling the influence of the experimenter and his or her expectations by standardizing or reducing contact with experimental subjects. But the ideas of variable-psychology about the subjectivity of the research subject as a source of error variance have been much more important.

Quite independent of how far a theory may appear to have gone beyond behaviorism, if it is governed by the variable-psychological experimental-statistical schema, the fundamental methodological assumption of behaviorism will be found concealed within it. This is the assumption that only stimulus conditions and externally observable behaviors are intersubjectively accessible. Subjective experiences and consciousness are accordingly treated as if they were private affairs of the individual, given only to the individual and therefore neither intersubjectively accessible nor scientifically objectifiable or generalizable.

Within the variable-schema the following picture emerges: Between the objective, scientifically accessible instances of stimulus conditions and behavior, that is, between independent and dependent variables, understood as measurement values in space and time, resides the subjective experience of consciousness of the experimental subject, about which, it is asserted, nothing immediate can be known or said, and which accordingly is designated by the lovely term "black box."

The multifarious gaps and contradictions that have resulted from the discrepancy between theoretical proposals on subjective, experiential states such as anxiety, emotionality, motivation, and so forth, and the methodological denial of their immediate empirical comprehensibility (as a hypostatization of the black box), has led to extended and complex controversies around concepts like "hypothetical construct" and "intervening variable." I need not elaborate on this here. In the present connection we are interested only in how the subjectivity of the experimental subject, thus understood, appears as an extraneous factor to be eliminated.

Subjective experience, consciousness, and so on, of the experimental subject generally do not appear within the conceptual world of variable-psychology as an error factor. They may even be accepted as an actual theme for theoretical development, *as long as* it is possible to assume that they are governed by the introduced independent variables. Indeed, one cannot peer immediately into the black box, but one can draw conclusions or guesses from what goes into the black box and how it comes out about what must have happened inside and then compose one's theoretical verse from that. The matter becomes problematic only when one does not close one's eyes to the fact that in psychological questions, except perhaps those concerned with automatic physiological responses, the conditions introduced by the experimenter do not have their effect directly upon the subject, but rather only to the degree that, or in the manner determined by how, they are apprehended by the subject and then converted into activity. Consciousness includes the fact that subjects can consciously relate to the experiment and the experimental conditions. But if this is so, then the presumed objective stimulus conditions must, in a certain sense, *pass into the black box.* One does not know whether the subjects are really following instructions and reacting to the stimulus conditions or, instead of pressing the key when the left of the two "presented" lines appears longer, are orienting with their key pressing on some internally conjured state of affairs. One therefore also does not know whether the objectively observed behavioral data actually count as a test of the assumed connection operationalized by the experimenter or of a quite different, unrecognized hypothesis residing in the subject's head. It is clear that subjectivity or consciousness, in the sense of individuals possibly relating spontaneously to the experimental arrangements, must be an error factor of the first magnitude for variable psychology. As such, subjectivity could be said to become *really* subjective, or the black box becomes *really* black.

So it is no wonder that an entire branch of research activity has emerged dedicated to solving the problem of how such an "extraneous" subjectivity can be eliminated or controlled. Within this branch of endeavor, known as the "social psychology of experiments," some researchers investigate experimentally the conditions under which experimental subjects develop their own hypotheses, which deviate from those intended by the experimenter. Others correctly conclude that this procedure is circular since the subjects can also formulate their own hypotheses in these new experiments. Some researchers appear to hope that they can get a grip on extraneous subjectivity gradually by means of increasingly refined manipulations and deception strategies and thus perpetuate the variable-psychological research logic. Others conclude correctly that what is involved here is a problem that, in principle, cannot be resolved by any immanent improvement in experimental technique. The contradictory nature of this dispute can be summarized as follows. On the one hand, penetrating analyses of the experimental situation bring us repeatedly to a questioning of the soundness of the variable-schema itself. On the other hand, one hesitates drawing the necessary conclusions owing to the absence of a visible alternative to the understanding of science contained in variable-psychology, and – against better judgment – the search for internal solutions continues. I will not pursue this further here.

Another aspect of the methodological necessity to eliminate subjectivity for the sake of scientific objectivity as required by variable-psychology emerges from the application of inferential statistics. Claims about the empirical verification of assumed connections are only possible according to this research logic when the random distributions conform to the minimal assumptions required for statistical test procedures. Psychological hypotheses therefore concern not each individual's subjectivity, but rather the statistics (means, variances, and so forth) in which distributions are reductively described. Ordinarily such values characterize distributions of data that several experimental subjects have produced under identical arrangements. But even where the very same subject has produced data in the so-called single-subject design and these are presented in a distribution, it is not "I" as I experience myself and my world here and now that is represented; rather, values are calculated from my life situations and translated into distributional characteristics in order to make them amenable to statistical evaluation. From all this it is evident what was meant by our former institute director in his speech to the students: I myself, in my concrete subjective life situation, in fact do not appear in the hypotheses of variable-psychology. Data about my person, my subjective experiences, my present situation, and so on, assume only the form of isolated particulars that appear as *elements* in the distribution and disappear hopelessly and irretrievably as *experimental data* in the distributional statistics with which the hypotheses to be tested are concerned. A further aspect of the understanding of subjectivity that places it into opposition to scientific objectivity is the idea that subjectivity is the merely particular, the individual, which must be sacrificed for scientific generalization, conceived as statistical or frequency generalization.

In such conceptions, contradictions between the variable psychological view of scientific objectification and generalization, and the theory and practice of clinical therapeutic treatment, which obviously has to do not with statistical values, but with particular clients and their concrete life situations, become especially clear. It becomes understandable why, for example, the old idea that behavior therapy is simply an application of experimental learning research had to fail. On the whole, controversies of the sort represented by the catchphrase "clinical versus statistical" are simply a new variant of the contradictory constellation we have described. In fact, it is clear that the variable-psychological approach as a method cannot begin to grasp clinical practice. In spite of this, the presumed equation of variable-psychology with science has inspired all manner of direct and devious means to trim here, compromise there, and so on, all intended to legitimize therapy as a variable-psychological procedure.

3

As can be seen from the foregoing, variable-psychology, with its premise that objectivity can only be achieved by the exclusion of subjectivity, finds itself faced with multifarious problems and contradictions. To be sure, this alone would not speak against it if one could at least move in the direction of the desired goal. Its advocates might be seen as conducting a courageous struggle for more rigorous science on difficult terrain. But whoever takes an unprejudiced look at research as it is guided by variable-psychology must conclude that no such claim is justified. The attempt has indeed been made to exclude subjectivity, but in no way has objectivity, in the sense of an unambiguous empirical reference of tested hypotheses, thereby been achieved. Rather, the *interpretation* of respective research results has obviously been to a large extent arbitrary. There are enormous quantities of experimentally produced and statistically tested findings, but one cannot claim to know what they really mean. Moreover, while in variable-psychology there are criteria regarding how to plan and evaluate experiments, there are absolutely no unambiguous criteria regarding the admissibility and adequacy of *interpretations* of the findings. Consequently, when, as is ordinarily the case, statistically secured findings are taken as verification of the experimentally operationalized theoretical hypothesis, this is done only because, from the start, no consideration is given to equally likely alternative explanations. Such an alternative may, however, be considered by the next experimenter, who will then find equally empirical verification for his or her explanation, which will prove to be just as arbitrary, and so forth. Accordingly, when a hypothesis cannot be verified empirically, one need not be disappointed; nothing stands in the way of citing numerous reasons why the hypothesis should come to nothing in these particular circumstances, and, too, it is only a matter of intellectual agility and imagination to represent apparently negative results as actually a tendency toward verification of the hypothesis. So the usual articles reporting experimental research are a mixture of presumably "hard," statistically tested data and more or less "soft" talk about what the data mean theoretically. The fact that for lack of firm evaluation criteria one theoretical explanation appears to be just as good or bad as another is surely one of the most important characteristics of the present state of affairs in psychology, as even those in the variable-psychology camp have repeatedly recognized. This is the state in which there exist row upon row of incommensurable minitheories without decisive empirical backing for their validity; fashionable changes in theoretical trends take the place of demonstrable scientific advance.

Why is it not possible in variable-psychological research to interpret results in a sufficiently reliable and unambiguous way; that is, why has scientific objectivity not yet been achieved? Is it because eliminating or controlling with adequate effectiveness the extraneous subjective factors has not been possible? Has the missing theoretical certainty nothing to do with the objectifying attempts of experimental-statistical planning? Or does there perhaps exist a necessary connection between the means by which subjectivity is supposed to be eliminated and the extensive uninterpretability of research findings arrived at by these means? I believe this last suggestion to be the right one, and I shall now try to show why.

I assume it to be the case that in everyday life, too, people form hypotheses of some sort about other people's subjective situations, motives, and reasons. Such hypotheses are correct and empirically confirmed at least to the extent that we are able to conduct our lives in common. How can this be? In short, because our daily world consists of a generally accessible *social nexus of meanings* in the sense of *generalized action possibilities.* When other people realize such action possibilities, their actions and subjective situations also become meaningful for me, that is, understood as *grounded.* For example, if I see someone approaching with a hammer in hand, a nail between his teeth, and a picture under his arm, it is normally clear to me from our common experience in life that he wants to hang the picture. His inwardness is thus for the most part no problem for me, since what he at the moment feels, thinks, and wants, externalizes itself in its practically relevant aspects for me out of his meaningful action. If he does something unexpected (contrary to hypothesis) puts the hammer away, spits out the nail, leans the picture against the wall, and walks quickly away – then he is still not really puzzling or incomprehensible. I assume that I am unaware of the particular *premises* of his new action, which nevertheless remains in principle understandable for me. I therefore ask him, in case he has not already offered some pertinent explanation, "What are you doing?" He will probably reply, "The milk's boiling over," or something of that sort, and with that, things are again clear to me. But even if he does not answer, although he must have heard me, there normally remains in everyday practice an easily testable hypothesis stemming from our common context of life and meaning. Perhaps he is not talking to me; he is still angry about yesterday. Even the extreme case of an inwardness that is shut off from me does not signify incomprehensibility or meaninglessness, but may even possibly have an especially serious and momentous meaning within the context of our shared life.

I need not describe this conception of intersubjective context of meaning and reasons more precisely. It has been developed elsewhere in great detail (Holzkamp, 1983). It already follows from what has been said here that the inaccessibility of the inwardness of the other person, which is designated by the term *black box*, is in no way a general characteristic of interpersonal relations, but is rather a deficiency of intersubjective understanding artificially produced in the variable-psychological experiment. It is this deficiency that includes directly within it the impossibility of unequivocal theoretical interpretation. Since, in keeping with the variable-psychological understanding of scientific objectivity, the experimenter may consider the behavior of the subject only insofar as it is understood as conditioned by the manipulated stimulus situation (independent variable), the framework for understanding the intersubjective contexts of meanings and reasons that I have described will systematically and necessarily be overlooked. As the experimental reality, which in fact consists of meaningful generalized action possibilities for the subject, is only recorded in its numerically measurable characteristics, it is impossible for the experimenter to grasp the activities of the subject as grounded in such generalized (and thus, to the experimenter, accessible) meaning references. Given the experimenter's position, it is impossible for him or her to initiate a *process of intersubjective understanding* such as I have described, which would clarify and render unambiguous the subjective situation of the other as an aspect of the experimenter's particular way of realizing meaning through action. One consequence of this is that the black box is constituted as the embodiment of the subject's subjective experiences and situations, which *must* become an inaccessible, private inwardness in the variable-psychological order of things because they are cut off from their objective, intersubjective reference of meaning. A second consequence is the impossibility of unequivocal interpretations of findings. All the mediating processes to which I have referred and through which my situation becomes intersubjectively accessible as an aspect of my socially meaningful actions are here excluded. There thus remains between the measured stimulus conditions and externally measurable behaviors of the subject a great empty space that can only be bridged "free-floatingly" with more or less unsupportable speculations about what may have been going on inside. The black box as supplier of uninterpretable data is therefore the result of procedural requirements in which the possibility of finding out anything about the subject and his subjective situation is deliberately and systematically removed from the experimenter.

This dilemma can be illuminated from another side if we consider the obvious protest that it is erroneous to assert, as we have done, that the experimenter is cut off from the intersubjective understanding process. He or she is able during the experiment or afterward to ask about the respective situations. In fact, such postexperimental questioning is often used in variable-psychological research. But what exactly is gained thereby? There are two possibilities here. In the first, the questioning occurs, so to speak, outside the official program, that is, outside the variable-psychological experimental design. In this case the results of the questioning are not under the control of the stimulus conditions and have therefore nothing at all to do with the testing of the hypothesis about the connection between independent and dependent variables. At best they are suited to the illustrative garnishing of the – as ever – equivocal theoretical interpretations, or they fulfill merely an alibi function, by which it is concealed that in the actual experiment the subject *qua subject* had nothing to say. In the second possibility, the questioning is introduced as a part of the experimental design and test of the hypothesis. This has to do with verbal responses as a dependent variable that, again, can only be interpreted in light of the independent variables as quantifiable stimulus conditions. The dilemma is therefore not overcome, but is rather reproduced. Owing to the variable-psychological reduction of humans acting in the contexts of intersubjective societal meanings to "conditioned" subjects, the interpersonal processes of understanding within which the reciprocal clarification of the subjective situation of the other person in the context of action can be achieved are fundamentally suspended.

In summary, if an experimenter would just give a little thought to the fact that he or she is a person and thus affected by personal hypotheses, and if this experimenter would ask the variable-psychological question, "Do people do this or that under these and those conditions?" then he or she would have to see immediately that the question in this form is unanswerable. What one does is determined by one's real action possibilities within the concrete intersubjective life context and is accordingly, quantitatively and qualitatively, hopelessly underdetermined by what the hypothesis refers to as "stimulus conditions." If this is so, then the actions of other people must, insofar as they are understood merely as dependent variables related to stimulus conditions, necessarily be uninterpretable. (By the way, concepts such as Skinner's "operant conditioning" are not exempt from this judgment; in his case "operants" are indeed conceived of as spontaneous acts whose frequency of occurrence is, again, simply seen as conditioned by their experimentally arranged consequences – which I shall not discuss further here.)

The reasons for the scientific arbitrariness of theoretical interpretations of variable-psychological findings become evident on yet another level when the question of *statistical verification* is considered. It was alleged earlier that, in the interest of their testability and generalizability, theoretical hypotheses cannot refer to individuals or to concrete individual life situations, but only to values in statistical distributions. A statistical average, for instance, comes into existence when characteristics identifying various individuals or situations as similar elements in a distribution are taken from them and certain procedures are employed to calculate the central tendency of the quantitative expression of these characteristics. In this way, the respective particulars of the concrete historical life context are reduced to mere quantitative differences with respect to a homogeneous characteristic and are thus torn from the only context within which they are comprehensible as intersubjectively meaningful. What's more, the average thus calculated is nothing more than a statistical artifact, a *fictional value,* immediately corresponding to nothing in psychic reality. The characteristics of the real experience and subjective situation of a concrete subject represent, even in their quantitatively reduced form, only the distributional elements from which the statistic was calculated and which becomes the basis for the statistical judgment; they themselves have disappeared. Although the researchers may want to interpret the calculated statistical values (or their relation to one another) theoretically, they must nevertheless act and talk *as if* they were able to refer to the unity of subjective experience of the world and of self. Otherwise psychological interpretations would not be possible. It makes no sense, for example, to speak of anxiety without presupposing that a particular person in a particular situation *has* anxiety. Variable-psychology, then, creates an artificial nonperson by means of its measurement-bound statements, a statistical ghost as the location in which the assumed psychic processes are actually supposed to be found. This statistical ghost is, like all ghosts, a totally abstract being; we do not relate to it in any life context, we do not know its concrete circumstances of existence, and we can say nothing about it that reflects reality. This is true not only for the interpretation of averages, but for the theoretical signification of all statistical values, including complex ones like factor loadings. The adventurous caprice with which factors are named is so obvious that even some factor analyzers have begun to see it. And so it is clear what has come of the attempt to overcome the presumed mere particularity and contingency of individual subjectivity by means of statistical objectification and generalization: One went out to search for what was general and found – or better, invented – the variable-psychological homunculus.

I hope that these considerations have helped to make it clear that my earlier claim about the arbitrariness and unfoundedness of variable-psychological theorizing was in no way a merely personal impression or a mean-spirited exaggeration. From various aspects of the variable-psychological research logic we are brought to the conclusion that the elimination of individual subjectivity, thought to be necessary for methodological reasons, entails the uninterpretability, and thus a lack of scientific objectivity, of the data thereby obtained. It would be interesting now to pursue further how one might try to reduce the interpretational uncertainty by means of recourse to a vulgar everyday consensus, disregarding the concrete living conditions of the subject, or how one might make an effort to reduce the theoretical equivocality by means of secondary rules of interpretation pertaining to closed artificial languages invented for this purpose on the occasion of any and every theoretical minitrend. But the terminological certainty sought in this way turns out to be "lifted by its own bootstraps," because the superordinate interpretation rules themselves are not objectively grounded, but merely of traditional or conventional character, and so on and on.

I cannot, however, avoid the question about the consequences of my analysis. If it is correct that the variable-psychological street is a dead-end but one wishes nevertheless to maintain a claim to the scientific nature of psychological practice (if only to prove the responsibility of one's practice to the subject), then it must be possible to establish a foundation for scientific objectivity and generalizability without the variable-psychological elimination of subjectivity. But what would such a foundation look like?

4

This much should be clear: Nothing is accomplished by simply excluding the experiment and statistical analysis from psychology. Our critique has been directed only at the ways in which the experiment and statistics are used in variable-psychology, namely as methodological expression of the dogma of "people as conditioned." If the arbitrariness and unfoundedness of psychological theorizing are to be overcome, then the action of people in the intersubjective societal nexus of meaning, and with it the subject's experience of self and world, with individual consciousness as its location, may not be reduced in any respect for reasons of method. If psychological results are to be scientifically interpretable, the subjective self-experience as we have understood it must rather be presupposed as the absolute foundation of all methodic arrangements for achieving a scientific status for psychology. Since self-experience or consciousness are always "my" experience or "my" consciousness and thus are, so to speak, first-person in their givenness, an alternative to variable-psychology as psychology from an external standpoint would be a psychology from the standpoint of the generalized "me." This, naturally, is not to speak of anything like solipsism, but rather of what is expressed in each and every "me," to emphasize that social relations at the human level are intersubjective relations, that is, relations in which different subjective "centers of intentionality" are related to one another. Thus at any given moment, in that I perceive the other person from my standpoint, I perceive at the same time that he or she perceives me from his or her standpoint as someone who is perceiving him or her, and in this sense our perspectives cross over into each other.

Thus if one understands psychology as an intersubjective science, or (since subjectivity always implies intersubjectivity) more briefly as subject-science, this means that, as a researcher, one does not relate one's theories and procedures merely to others, keeping oneself out of it, but rather sees oneself as a subject fully involved in them. Since intersubjectivity is the specifically human level of relating, in a psychology that does not want to miss this level, not only the subjectivity of the other, but also the overlapping subjectivity of the researcher, will belong to the empirical that it is psychology's job to research. This also means that subject-scientific theories and procedures are not "about people, but rather "for" people. They serve (in favorable cases) each "me" in clarifying and altering "my" own experience and life practice.

Out of the subject-scientific position comes what in this connection can alone be called *scientific objectivity and generalizability.* "Objectivity" and "subjectivity" are to be understood in their relation to one another, such that objectivity is not attained at the cost of subjectivity, but rather means "objectification of the subjective." And "generalizability" is to be understood in relation to me as a single individual and to my immediate experience, such that the "generalization" does not lead to the disappearance of the individual, but rather means the "generalization of the individual."

Surely many will be at a loss to imagine how a subject-scientific program that sublates the opposition between objective and subjective, between the individual and the general, can be realized. In order to overcome this helplessness, it is necessary, first, to take leave of the idea of a necessary solipsism, inaccessibility, and impenetrability of subjective self-experience and individual consciousness as it is expressed in variable-psychology by the black box. One should then examine more closely the earlier discussion in which I tried to show that human actions and the subjective situations in which they are grounded are realizations of general societal action possibilities that, insofar as they are meaningful for me, have in principle meaning for others as well, and that this intersubjective context of meanings and reasons cannot be seen in variable-psychology because it has been methodologically eliminated. When one thinks this through further, it becomes clear how under the presupposition of such intersubjective meaning contexts the problem of objectification and generalization should be approached. My subjective self-experience is indeed at the moment given only to "me," but it is nevertheless not exhausted by that, but rather, as an aspect of the subjective aspect of my action, only an individual variant of experience, which in its general characteristics is related to objective societal action possibilities and the concrete-historical obstacles and contradictions connected with them. Therefore, in most personal experiences I am, through the societal relations by which the possibilities and necessities of my action are determined, connected to other people who see themselves facing the same possibilities and necessities in their actions. Consequently, insofar as the manner and means of my personal assimilation and transformation of concrete social action possibilities and limitations are understood, my experiences are objectifiable and generalizable *as* subjective experiences within this context of intersubjective experience.

When we speak thus of generalization, it is certainly not to be understood as frequency generalization from samples to populations. *Generalization* here means recognizing and accounting for those mediational levels and aspects by which each particular case of subjective–intersubjective experience or situations is understandable as a special manifestation of a general case. This kind of generalization, which we distinguish from the statistical form (frequency generalization) by calling it *structural generalization,* is nothing exceptional in sciences other than psychology. For instance, a physicist who tests the law of falling bodies and obtains a measurement that deviates from the general formula $v = (g/2)t^2$ can nevertheless understand it without much ado as a particular instance of a strictly valid general law by accounting for mediational factors like friction or atmospheric resistance. It would never occur to the physicist to let the object fall a hundred times just to be sure, to form a distribution of the obtained measurements, calculate an average and variance, and proceed further in this manner to test statistically the law of falling bodies. The universalization of that kind of procedure as the scientific procedure par excellence was reserved for variable-psychologists.

Now if we are to develop structural generalization as a subject-scientific procedure, we must proceed from the fact that it is not immediately apparent that, and at what levels, my everyday subjective situations are mediated by various levels of generalized, societally determined possibilities and limitations of action. Only because of this is a scientific analysis at this point necessary and possible. (According to Marx, science would be neither necessary nor possible if essence and appearance were identical.) In the everyday practice of life the generality that lies within my experience asserts itself there and in my thinking only sporadically and piecemeal. Thus I also recognize my connectedness in experience with other people in societal situations like my own and with resulting interests like mine only as a partial and occasional penetration into the seeming privateness of my subjective situation. The causes for this deficient clarity of the general societal connections of my subjective situation lie in the particular characteristics of individual life practice, especially in its "private existence" in bourgeois social relations.

The general aim of subject-scientific research is therefore to work out in a general way the *mediating levels* by which the experiences of subjects under particular contradictory social relations can be understood as special individual instances of certain objective possibilities and limitations of action. This is equivalent to working out the common action possibilities and necessities within respectively analyzed social constellations. The interest in *knowing* for subject science thus proves to be a generalized form of the individual interest in expanding control over conditions of existence, thereby improving the subjective quality of life.

In order to realize the subject-scientific program, it is above all necessary to have carried out the historical-empirical derivation and grounding of *categories* with which subjects can adequately grasp the levels and aspects of the mediation of their experiences with general social relations. (Similarly atmospheric resistance and friction as mediational levels between particular instances and the general law of falling bodies are not self-evident, but the outcome of a long scientific process.) The well-grounded elaboration of such a subject-scientific system of mediational categories has been the chief occupation of Critical Psychology for a long time. Centered around the fundamental categories of "societal meaning" and "subjective action potence" and working from the point of view of mediation between social and individual existence, new definitions of psychic functions life cognition, emotionality, and motivation have been developed as aspects of subjective–intersubjective action potence, and new foundations have been laid for understanding personal conflict, defense mechanisms, and the unconscious.

Recently the implications of the results of categorial analysis for an appropriate *system of subject-scientific research methods* have become increasingly clear to us. We have come to recognize, for instance, the important role that a scientific approach to practice plays in the testing and objectification of subject-scientific theories. For its part this has meant the possibility of overcoming the separation of basic scientific psychology and psychological practice, since research and practice prove to be only different emphases within a unitary scientific process. What we understand of this has been presented in the ninth chapter of my book *Grundlegung der Psychologie*. Newer aspects are being presented and discussed elsewhere (Holzkamp, 1983).

5

If we stand back to ascertain more precisely Critical Psychology's historical position, a position outside variable-psychology but within psychology, a number of interesting connections become evident. For example, one notes with interest that Wundt had specified immediate experience as the subject matter of psychology; are approaches to an understanding of consciousness as a medium of interpersonal world experience already to be found there and then buried by variable psychology's privatization of consciousness? Likewise, in regard to Lewin's old critique of thinking in terms of frequencies and averages and his idea of rising from the single case to the "pure case," could it be that possibilities of avoiding the variable-psychological dead-end might be found there, although Lewin, in emigration, had lost sight of them under the pressure of behaviorist ideology in the United States? One notes further that Piaget discovered obviously significant principles of lawful cognitive development without the least statistical finery simply by interacting with his own children. Does it perhaps have to do here with experimental arrangements that did not succumb to the variable-psychological reduction, but in the hands of the subjects were able to yield important contributions to subject-scientific knowledge? One might even be tempted to look again more closely at the so-called *verstehende* or *geisteswissenschaftliche* psychology: Was it perhaps swept prematurely from the stage of scientific debate by a psychology that wanted to act as if it were a form of "natural science"?

Together with a review of this sort, one ought to analyze closely the contemporary parallel attempts to develop an alternative to variable-psychology, such as action research, ethnomethodology, phenomenological psychology, qualitative social research, biographical research, and critical hermeneutic: To what extent are these approaches making compromises with variable-psychology on purely eclectic grounds? To what extent are they moving in the same direction as our approach, such that a reciprocal promotion of scientific developmental work might be possible? And are there perhaps totally different yet well reasoned and promising alternatives to the variable-psychological dead-end that should be taken into account? We would be interested in getting clear answers to questions like these.

5 Psychoanalysis and Marxist Psychology

Klaus Holzkamp

1

The suggestion that psychoanalysis has significance for Marxist psychology may give rise to doubts in some readers about the author's standpoint: Haven't Marxists (and Marxist–Leninists) always been sharply critical of psychoanalysis, and hasn't it been shown that every integration of psychoanalysis and Marxism, every "Freudo-Marxism," whatever its particular form, is necessarily untenable because psychoanalysis, owing to its inextricable connection to bourgeois ideology, is genuinely irreconcilable with Marxism? So it must be said very clearly at the beginning of my remarks that I am basically in agreement with the Marxist–Leninist assessment that psychoanalysis essentially biologizes and individualizes its subject matter, that it psychologizes social conflicts, postulates a universal opposition between the repressing society and the unsocial drive-determined individual, abets irrationalism, and so forth. Accordingly, I share the opinion that any attempt to round out Marxism with psychoanalytic concepts in Freudo-Marxist fashion in the intention of making it capable of grasping the subjective motives of individuals or the masses will be accomplished only at the expense of the scientific and ideological foundations of Marxism.

In order to underscore my position on this issue, I can point to the fact that at this very moment, Critical Psychology is in sharp and sustained conflict with psychoanalytic views, especially with those with leftist or anticapitalist pretenses, including positions that are explicitly Freudo-Marxist, such as the "Critical Theory of the Subject" (Horn, Lorenzer, Brückner, Leithäuser, and so on), and those less obvious and programmatic attempts to modernize Marxism psychoanalytically, such as in the Althusserian and similar traditions. The debate has become especially intense in the controversy around the *Projekt Ideologietheorie* [ideology-theory project] (Elfferding, W. F. Haug, Holzkamp-Osterkamp, Wilhelm, all 1983). We have repeatedly and explicitly opposed the assumption that newer versions of psychoanalysis such as those of Horney,

81

Fromm, Lacan, Lorenzer, and so forth, are less vulnerable than the original Freudian version. Rather, we maintain that the deviations from Freud's positions carried out by these newer versions are regressive through and through (as I shall explain in a moment). Our critique of modern Freudo-Marxism is summarized in the book by K. -H. Braun, *Kritik des Freudo-Marxismus* (1979).

Even in our day-to-day ideological-political debates psychoanalytic positions are our chief opponents. We have taken issue, for example, with the views of Alice Miller, whose books are bestsellers at present and have been well received by many members of the democratic movement. Gabi Minz (1983) has analyzed the ways in which psychoanalytic ideas about the genuine powerlessness of individuals against societal forces are expressed and disguised, and how class-determined repression is psychologized in Miller's treatment of the suffering of children and adults in bourgeois society. Our continuing debates with Horst Eberhard Richter have been especially delicate. He is actively engaged in the struggle for peace but, at the same time, offers interpretations of the international conflict and the causes of the nuclear threat in his books *Alle redeten vom Frieden* [They all spoke of peace] (1981a) and *Zur Psychologie des Friedens* [On the psychology of peace] (1982) that, because of their psychoanalytic alignment, are bound to have seriously disorienting effects in the peace movement. Richter analyzes the antagonisms between West and East not as instances or escalations of crises in the international class struggle, but, in the tedious psychoanalytic manner, as collective neuroses that have their "deepest" causes in the unresolved conflicts of early childhood. Thus, according to Richter, "actually, the secret destructive tendencies [reside] within us. . . . " (1981b: 42), and it is therefore "our own raging sadism that we actually see in the mirror image of the diabolical enemy" (1982: 56). Accordingly he understands the present struggle for peace as a struggle "to heal the mental illness known as peacelessness" (1982: 28) and urges us to seek the underlying "experiential prototype" in "our childhood" (1982: 46). At the First Peace Congress of the Psycho-Social Professions in Dortmund, in June 1983, I took issue with the psychoanalytic psychologizing – or psychiatrizing – of societal relations as they are applied by Richter to the problem of peace and the threat of nuclear war and met with agreement among many of the hundreds of participants, but there was also bitter resistance.

2

So, if it is understood that in speaking of the "significance of psychoanalysis of Marxist psychology" I am not proposing any kind of Freudo-Marxist integration, what is it that I intend? It is certainly not a return to the popular view that Freud's system, though it is on the whole scientifically and ideologically untenable, may contain valuable insights into such matters as mental dynamics, the origin of neuroses, or the therapist–patient relationship. How should correct consequences be derived from false premises? Just as certainly I do not hold the view that Freud asked correct and important questions but, because of his mistaken overall conceptions, came to the wrong answers. How could it have been possible for him, if his assumptions were mistaken, to arrive at the correct questions? I wish neither to insinuate that Freud was an eclectic nor to use eclecticism to facilitate my own arguments. When I speak of Freud's significance for Marxist psychology, I mean this in an entirely principled way. An adequate reception and consideration of psychoanalysis, in my view, has decisive consequences for the correct conceptual and methodological foundation of Marxist psychology. But doesn't this put me into an irreconcilable contradiction with the fundamental Marxist critique of psychoanalysis and Freudo-Marxism which I have just claimed to accept? I want to approach clarification of this problem in several steps, the first of which will be to put my foregoing critical exposition of psychoanalysis into a different light by interpreting it, so to speak, "against the grain."

When I sketched our current debates with psychoanalytic positions in order to demonstrate our agreement with the Marxist critique, it was clear that our arguments are, in principle, very much the same as those advanced in the early 1920s by Jurinetz, Thalheimer, Voloshinov, Sapir, and, in the meantime, by many other Marxists. One might ask, then, why, historically speaking, the Marxist critique has been so unsuccessful if it has in fact been so right and so convincing? Why has psychoanalysis not long ago been superseded and laid to rest as alchemy was? Why, despite its recurrent refutation, is it today enjoying the greatest vitality, especially right now in the ideological offensive?

One might think of defusing all this by appealing to the arsenal of the Marxist critique of psychoanalysis, in particular by suggesting that psychoanalysis is a particular expression of bourgeois ideology, not least of the petit bourgeois consciousness of the intellectual opinion makers. This would allow us to understand why psychoanalytic positions are constantly employed as weapons against the progressive forces in the ideological class struggle and why, owing to bourgeois ideological prejudice, they find a corresponding popular resonance. This Marxist argument is, like all the others, surely correct. But does it give us an understanding of the influence of psychoanalysis?

I doubt that the history of the effectiveness of psychoanalysis can be adequately understood from an exclusively ideological-critical point of view when I see that the acceptance or rejection of psychoanalytic views simply never coincides with the fronts in the class struggle. It is never the case that psychoanalysis finds resonance only with conservative circles or members of the petit bourgeois "left." Rather, its influence reaches far into the ranks of the democrats, socialists, and communists. Thus constantly new variations on psychoanalytic ideas, such as those found in the books by Miller and Richter or in works like *Having and Being* by Fromm, are welcomed as important and progressive contributions to the elucidation of subjectivity in bourgeois society even by many of our own political friends (who do not always clearly identify their psychoanalytic foundations). And then, each time we try warningly to reveal what in fact lies behind these proposals, the task becomes truly Sisyphean: No sooner is one book criticized, than the next appears on the scene, and our successes remain doubtful and fragile at best.

Doubts about the sufficiency of an ideological-critical analysis become stronger when I consider the case of bourgeois academic psychology. For example, although behaviorism is the most influential point of view within psychology, it has no popular resonance or political-ideological influence that comes anywhere near that of psychoanalysis. Is traditional academic psychology any less in the grips of bourgeois ideology than psychoanalysis? What explains the fact that behavioristic ideas find no massive popular resonance among democrats, socialists, and communists outside the limits of the psychological discipline? Why is it that only specialists ever see reasons to debate behavioristic issues and that no essential clarification of the problem of subjectivity is expected to result? If we play this line of thinking out a bit further, it becomes evident that an explanation is desperately needed for the fact that there is a *Freudo*-Marxism, but no Hullo-Marxism, Lewino-Marxism, or Skinnero-Marxism. (Neurath's attempt in the 1920s to adopt Marxism as a behavioristic-physicalistic sociology for neopositivism can be considered a mere curiosity, the importance of which is peripheral at best.) When Marxists find their existing concepts of individual subjectivity inadequate or problematic, why do they repeatedly turn to *psychoanalytic* foundations, despite all evident difficulties and reservations and although many other psychological theories and findings are available that appear to be scientifically better grounded and less hotly disputed by Marxists?

The problem takes on yet another wrinkle when we turn our attention from popular influence to interdisciplinary influence in the social, cultural, and historical sciences. Practically everywhere (in literary studies, art, linguistics, religious studies, ethnology, and especially in sociology), when there is need for an explanation of a specialized psychological question, it is almost taken for granted in bourgeois society that one must turn to psychoanalysis. In this connection, in fact, psychology is frequently equated with psychoanalysis. Attempts to apply other kinds of psychological principles in the interdisciplinary setting remain comparatively rare and have only limited influence. Why, given bourgeois psychological alternatives, is it psychoanalysis that is seen by other disciplines to be exciting, useful, illuminating, heuristic, and so on, whereas, despite all its scientific efforts and trimmings, academic psychology is left alone in its scientific ghetto?

These various problematic aspects of the current Marxist critique of psychoanalysis fall into place for me *at the vanishing point of my own experience with the works of Freud.* Each time I read him I find his ideas annoying and provocative. Nevertheless I gain new and surprising insights and important stimulation to thought. Despite all my serious reservations, I can't but see Freud as a *great researcher fully dedicated to the advancement of knowledge,* whose standard is not approached by academic psychology with all its formal scientific appearance, nor is it done justice to by Marxist critique, no matter how correct the latter might be.

From these considerations it appears that if the significance of psychoanalysis for Marxist psychology is to be adequately clarified, it will not do simply to keep repeating or adapting the old critical arguments. Although they are accurate, they are obviously not adequately suited to grasp the character and historical magnitude of psychoanalysis. We must rather strive to achieve a new approach. We shall have to mobilize more of what Marx called the "power of abstraction" in order to identify those *fundamental knowledge qualities of psychoanalysis that remain when its obvious weaknesses are disregarded.* The relationship between psychoanalysis and academic psychology must also be seen in a new way such that the question becomes whether or why academic psychology, despite or because of the methodological assumptions by which it intends to arrive at more certain scientific propositions than psychoanalysis, does *not* achieve the level of knowledge of the latter. In the context of this problem we shall also want to examine the view held by many Marxist psychologists that they must ignore psychoanalysis because of its subjection to bourgeois ideology, whereas they feel they can move more freely among the conceptual and methodological assumptions of traditional academic psychology because it is supposedly less "bourgeois."

3

In order to get an adequate account of the scientific status of psychoanalysis vis-à-vis that of academic psychology, it will be useful, first, to give some attention to the historical fact that these psychologies have come to form two separate branches of science. It is not at all self-evident why an integration of psychology and psychoanalysis has not yet taken place and does not appear imminent. Even today psychoanalysis has its own journals, training facilities, and institutional roots independent of those of academic psychology, and when a psychoanalyst gets a teaching position (a rare occurrence), it is hardly ever in a psychology department, but in sociology or medicine. This separation is often attributed to a tendency in psychoanalysis itself for the building of schools or sects. But this opinion is surely more than just a little shallow. It can hardly be overlooked, for example, that various attempts to integrate psychoanalytic concepts into academic psychology indeed exist. Not only is the "dynamic" aspect in the psychoanalytic sense recognized by most personality theories, but psychoanalytic concepts like "repression," "regression," "projection," and "anxiety" have been incorporated in psychological theories, operationalized, and experimentally tested. It is obvious as well that psychoanalytic concepts have not remained unaltered by their association with academic psychological concepts and methods; their function and meaning have in fact been changed extensively. This only increased the necessity to retain the respective concepts in their original psychoanalytic context. There are therefore obviously substantive reasons for the failure of psychoanalysis to become integrated with academic psychology, and it is my intention here to bring these reasons into clearer focus.

Preliminary to further considerations, it will be useful briefly to reconstruct the historical origins and development of academic psychology and psychoanalysis in relation each other.

In the early classical period of psychology as a separate science, before both the emergence of psychoanalysis and the development of academic psychology in its modern form, Wilhelm Wundt, as we know, emphasized "immediate experience" as subject matter (cf., for example, 1896/1913: 1ff). This "immediate experience" was not a special "inner" state of affairs detached from external reality, but was rather the human experience of the world taken from a particular point of view. For each experience the "objects" were supposed to be differentiated from the "experiencing subject." Whereas natural science was understood to be concerned with "mediate experience," that is, experience independent of the experiencing subject, psychology was supposed to investigate the "entire content of experience in its relationship to the subject." From the psychological standpoint this "abstraction" from the experiencing subject "and all the consequences that arise from it" were thought to be overcome (1896/1913: 3). In the Wundtian view, individual subjectivity thus achieved intersubjective accessibility in that it represented the subjective aspect of the experience of the *one, objective reality* as it is given to us all. The task of psychology could be understood here to be the determination of the *generally valid laws* according to which *the real world is constituted as subjective experience*. The attempt to reach the ultimate abstract elements of immediate experience and to explain the constitution of this experience in terms of associative connections of these elements was Wundt's way of arriving at such general laws.

This understanding of the object of psychological investigation was retained in several historical lines of development even after the Wundtian era. For example, it is obvious that as the Würzburg School pursued its concern with "imageless thought" it was still looking for the elements and constitutive principles of immediate experience. Perhaps it is not so obvious that Gestalt psychology also belongs unequivocally to this tradition of understanding the object of psychological investigation. In their radical critique of Wundtian elemental psychology they did not direct their attack against the fact that Wundt was investigating the laws of the constitution of immediate experience, but rather only against his understanding of how the assumed laws should be formed. They maintained that immediate experience could not be adequately explained as the synthetic sum of elements and required the analytic identification of immanent relational and organizational principles. Thus for Gestalt psychology, as for element psychology, the concern was not the description of a private inner world, but rather to grasp the general laws by which immediate experience, although subjective, is constituted as intersubjectively accessible and homogeneous experience of the one objective external world. It was assumed the Gestalt principles of nearness, similarity, continuation, prägnanz, and so forth, would, on presentation of identical objective stimulus patterns, lead with lawful necessity to identical subjective organization of the experiential field. In this understanding of the object of psychological investigation as we have outlined it here, can be found the methodological foundation of this "classical" form of psychology, experimental arrangements served here essentially to produce the conditions under which the elements and principles of either structure or organization, which are found in and govern subjective experience, can be understood most precisely and with the greatest generality.

I have laid out the Wundtian view in some detail in order to make as visible as possible the radical historical break and the related reductionistic distortion that came at the beginning of this century with psychology's turn to functionalism-behaviorism, that is, the original phase of mainstream modern academic psychology. Whereas "classical" psychology, despite all its empiristic and sensationistic errors, took account of consciousness as the specifically human level of subjective–intersubjective experience of the world, the new functionalistic-behavioristic understanding of the psychological object radically reduced human activity to an *unspecific, organismic* level, or even further to *physicalistic* conceptions of the determination of human activity. In this process of reduction several steps or aspects can be discerned.

In the earliest functionalistic phase of the "new psychology," under the influence of the pragmatic philosophies of James and Dewey, a social-Darwinist conception of the psychological object emerged in terms of the adaptation of humans, understood principally as "organisms," to their environment. "Consciousness" was thereby not immediately excluded from psychology by early functionalists like Angell, McGeoch, Woodworth, but rather, following James, it was conceptualized as an especially complex "organ" of adaptation found in each individual person. This "biologization" of consciousness, however, laid the foundation for its elimination from psychology by the behavioristic radicalization of functionalism. Whereas classical psychology considered consciousness to be the specific focus of subjective-intersubjective experience, that is, as a characteristic of the subject–object relationship, functionalism's individualization of consciousness as an organismic organ of adaptation led to an understanding of immediate experience as, so to speak, stuffed into each single individual and as narrowed to a private "inner world" and isolated from the external world. This accomplished the separation that Wundt had so decidedly rejected.

With the behavioristic radicalization of functionalism, the narrowed concept of "consciousness" was taken over and, at the same time, attributed to classical psychology. Obscurities of classical psychology, such as its unfortunate term *introspection*, which, owing to its own privatized conception of consciousness, the "new psychology" understood literally, encouraged such historical errors. It followed that behaviorism, seemingly at variance with the conception of consciousness that classical psychology and functionalism had in common, excluded consciousness from the scientific vocabulary of psychology on the grounds that it was intersubjectively inaccessible because it was a "private matter" of each individual. Only data on "stimuli" and "responses" were allowed as scientifically objective. Thus the behavioristic *stimulus–response scheme*, by which psychology was to be placed on an objective footing, was itself based upon a subjectivistic assumption, that is, an abstract negation of a subjectivistically narrowed conception of consciousness. Biologism/physicalism, on the one hand, and subjectivism, on the other, were in fact but two sides of the same coin.

In the further history of academic psychology the crude stimulus–response formula has been manifestly modified and softened at the theoretical level, but methodological expressions of this formula still form the basis of the mainstream of modern bourgeois psychology. The biologistic concept of function has been reduced to a mathematical-physical concept of function in which the "response" as "dependent variable" is seen as a "function" of the "stimulus" as "independent variable." The "organism", as connecting point between "stimulus" and "response," became thereby the locus of "intervening variables" that themselves could not be researched empirically but had to be theoretically assumed in order to make predictions regarding the manner of connection between the "independent" stimulus variables and the "dependent" response variables. This methodological "*variable scheme*" underlies the entire experimental-statistical method of the new psychology. For this reason we call mainstream psychology *"variable psychology."*

Now it is necessary to show how and in what forms the reductionistic-subjectivistic basis of the S–R formula manifests itself in modern bourgeois psychology by means of its methodological expression in the variable scheme. Although this cannot be done here in any detail, in the interest of moving my considerations forward it will be necessary to clarify at least in rough terms the principal transformation that took place on the historical path from classical psychology to modern variable psychology with respect to the general scientific understanding of psychological *theory construction and generalization.*

When the understanding of consciousness as the medium of the intersubjective relation to the world was narrowed to that of the mere "inner world" of individuals, the *exclusively external view of "other organisms"* replaced the analysis of human experience of self and world. With that, individual subjectivity "evaporated" in the variable psychological understanding of methods in two ways. First, each person's own subjectivity, and with it the subject–object connection of scientific knowledge, was excluded from theoretical reflection. Second, the "subjectivity of the other" disappeared into the empirically inaccessible "black box" between stimulus and response variables. Thus whereas, as we have said, classical theory construction was directed at the understanding of the structural or organizational laws of subjective–intersubjective human experience, variable psychological theories formulated "predictions" about which connections exist between certain conditions in which other organisms/individuals are found and the reactions or behaviors of those individuals as they are determined by those conditions. The *hypothetical* or *constructive* part of variable psychological theory therefore is concerned with precisely that which classical psychology took to be the *direct empirical reference* of theory construction, that is, immediate experience. Since, therefore, according to variable psychology, subjective experience functions only as a hypothetical "connecting point" between stimulus and response variables, reference to it, for its part, can be omitted. In fact it is left out of those theories that seek to understand the process of translating stimuli into responses, not in psychological terms, but in physiological or pseudophysiological terms. On the other hand, the evaporation of the individual subjectivity is not altered by the periodic attempts of academic psychologists to moderate the behavioristic constraints by reintroducing "mentalistic," cognitive, and similar terminology. Since, owing to the methodic structure of the variable scheme, experience and consciousness cannot be grasped except as "intervening variables," they disappear hopelessly into the black box of scientific inaccessibility. Because of this internalization of consciousness, relaxation of the constraints of procedural principles seems to be inevitable; fidelity to life and experience would seem to be attainable only by reducing scientific exactitude. This "rolling back" of the explicit behaviorist position, which behaviorists rightly denounce as unscientific, occurs with such regularity that the mainstream of bourgeois psychology takes on the appearance of an alternation between "hard" and "soft" waves, an alternation based upon a common subjectivism.

This fundamental scientific difference between the classical and variable psychological understanding of theory implies as well a fundamental difference in methodological concepts of *scientific generalization.* In the classical concept of generalization as analysis and investigation of immediate experience that reveal its immanent laws of mediation with objective reality, the transcendence of subjectivity toward its inherent intersubjective structure must remain totally invisible and truly incomprehensible for variable psychology because it has put the subjective into an irreconcilable, abstract opposition to the objective, thus excluding subjectivity from any possibility of conceptualization. After variable psychology has eliminated subjective experience, and with it the shared connection of individuals to the world, on the basis of which experience can be generalized, what remain is a multitude of organisms/individuals isolated from one another. It is here that generalizations are to be sought. The way is thus prepared for the psychological adoption of the concept of *statistical frequency generalization,* which had been developed in botany. It now follows almost naturally that – after ignoring their subjective relation to reality – the isolated individuals who remain should be defined by means of the abstraction of certain measurable differences as homogeneous, independent elements of a statistical distribution in the same manner as a population of peas. Thus all the assumptions required to estimate populations from samples are met. Generalization here no longer means the *scientific analysis of appearance in terms of its essential determinants;* it now means absolutely nothing more than *the drawing of conclusions from a distribution of a smaller number of elements about a larger, or an infinite, distribution of like elements.* Let us not deceive ourselves: Since estimations are always made from statistics to parameters or their combinational equivalents, even the most complicated statistical procedures, including the multivariate kind, are based on this uninspired reductionistic concept of generalization, according to which one only moves back and forth between various large piles of surface data, and which in psychology is often held to be the *non plus ultra* of scientific methodology.

4

This broadly historical reconstruction of the relationship between the classical psychology of consciousness and "modern" variable psychology should now make it possible to elucidate the scientific status of psychoanalysis by locating its position in the relationship. I believe the decisive key to an adequate understanding of the character of basic psychoanalytic concepts and methods of procedure is to show that psychoanalysis did not follow the functionalist-behaviorist direction, and therefore did not go along with the variable psychological elimination of human consciousness which resulted from its being misunderstood as mere private inwardness and from all of the reductionistic-subjectivistic consequences that followed from that. If we want to do justice to psychoanalysis, then, we must place it directly in the developmental line of classical psychology. Despite all their otherwise serious differences, classical psychology and psychoanalysis shared the same fundamental understanding of the object and task of psychology. Whatever obscurities and misunderstandings it may harbor, psychoanalysis, too, sees immediate experience as the object of its investigation and understands its task to be the objective clarification and investigation of this experience as subjective–intersubjective relation to self and the world. Psychoanalysis does not understand this to mean, as it does for classical psychology, the analysis of experience in terms of the general structural and organizational principles by which it is mediated with objective reality. It is less concerned with such epistemological questions than it is with investigating the immediate experience in which lies concealed the socially repressive relations as they are felt in people's concrete life circumstances.

In order to support this thesis (which may at first appear bizarre) and to work out its consequences, I turn first to the fundamental fact that the basic theoretical concepts of psychoanalysis have a radically different categorial structure and function from those in variable psychology. Concepts like defense and repression, regression and projection, id, ego, and superego are not part of a theoretical context in which "predictions" about connections between independent and dependent variables are supposed to be made and empirically tested. Such concepts are not applied "from outside" onto "others," but are put into the hands of the persons concerned as a means of clarification and understanding of their own immediate experience. They have the virtual function of "means" by which, "in dealing with oneself," the appearance of one's subjective situation [*Befindlichkeit*] can be analyzed to reveal its inherent dependencies, conflicts, denials, compulsions, and circumscriptions, thus allowing the person to achieve a more conscious, reflective, and responsible life practice. If one puts basic psychoanalytic concepts into the context of variable psychology, in order to make them scientific, and judges them from that point of view, then one is simply subjecting them to precisely the categorial criteria for which they are not suited. This would be about as intelligent as attempting to study meteorological phenomena in terms of psychological motivational concepts in order to find out why clouds drop rain. Concepts like ego, id, and superego were intended as a means of dramatizing the contradictory tendencies and impulses in immediate experience in order to deal with them more consciously, that is, to bring them under control. Whoever wants to reject such concepts with the argument that they are neither operationalizable nor experimentally testable and are therefore speculative is missing the point, since psychoanalytic concepts are, of course, meaningless in the variable psychological context, as are motivational concepts in the meteorological context. From this point of view it becomes understandable that, as we mentioned earlier, psychoanalytic concepts have resisted all attempts at integration into modern psychology. A concept like regression is meaningful in the psychoanalytic context in that infantile impulses in experience, which make it impossible for a person to gain an adequate level of control over present conflicts, are made comprehensible and potentially surmountable. Now if "regression" is operationalized by variable psychology as the movement, under stress, from a later learned behavior pattern to one that had been learned earlier, it may become possible to test it empirically, even in experiments on rats, but this takes the regression concept out of the subjective–intersubjective experiential context and puts it into the context of external, successive activities and thus totally robs it of its meaning and function. Such a distorting trivialization and leveling can be demonstrated for all psychoanalytic concepts that have been subjected to variable psychological procedures in the name of scientific precision.

The function of psychoanalytic concepts as means toward a clarification of surface experience in the context of subjective understanding of self and the world can also be demonstrated for those concepts that were introduced in "natural scientific" dress. These were introduced, I believe, out of lack of clarity on the part of psychoanalysis about the status of its own conceptual base. Thus the concept of libido was accounted for in terms of physical energy, and Bernfeld and Feitelberg even made suggestions on how it might be objectively measured. On a closer look, it is clear that Freud's intended quantitative understanding of the libido concept was immediately connected to its function in the analysis of the subjective situation. Only on the assumption that at any given moment a limited amount of libido is available does it make any sense to inquire about its "place of residence," about its fixation in objects, about its narcissistic disposition, and about its regressive fixation on infantile object choices or stages of instinctual development as they are applied in psychoanalysis. Also the concept of sublimation, by which psychoanalysis recommends that instinctual sexual wishes be tamed through transformation of the libido into socially acceptable needs, is not thinkable without the "libido quantum theorem" and the "libido economy" based upon it. These kinds of physicalized concepts do not have any value in themselves in psychoanalysis and do not make it into a "natural science" (as some of its representatives claim), but are rather merely analogies in the service of the psychoanalytic work of interpretation.

From the fact that psychoanalysis belongs to the tradition of the classical understanding of the psychological object as immediate experience, it is understandable that psychoanalysis, like classical psychology, has been accused of a lack of scientific objectivity owing to its concern with mere subjective experience, of being limited to intersubjectively undemonstrable introspection, and the like. Allegations like these rest, in my opinion, on the same subjectivistic reduction of consciousness to mere private inwardness, in which, as we have shown, the particular means by which classical psychology proposed to achieve scientific objectivity and generality was overlooked.

If we examine more closely the character and function of basic psychoanalytic concepts, it becomes clear that the analysis of immediate experience is in no way limited to providing the individual with plausible but otherwise coincidental and nonbinding interpretations. Rather it has to do with an understanding of experience that aims at working out the hidden lawful connections with objective relations that extend beyond mere individual circumstances and points of view. Classical psychology attempted, on the basis of the epistemological premises of "neutral monism," to understand the structural and organizational principles by which, through its mediation with the external objective world, subjective experience could be made accessible and compelling. Freud, by contrast, was asking in a down-to-earth, psychological way about the lawful mediational levels through which the themes and contradictions of what appeared to be *mere individual* experience could be understood as individual expressions of *general human-social* themes of existence and constellations of conflict.

This can be seen clearly from that basic constellation and its scientific function that Freud regarded as the touchstone for affiliation with psychoanalysis: the Oedipus complex. The concept of the Oedipus complex has often been misunderstood as simply a theoretical statement about the occurrence of a particular familial constellation, and in this form it has been subjected to repeated empirical refutation. But for Freud the Oedipus complex is a *fundamental human constellation of conflict* that exists not simply at the empirical level, but must be arrived at through the analytic investigation of appearance in order to grasp the momentary, seemingly merely individual conflicts as *their* special expression; it is the mode of appearance of the inexorable and irrevocable suppression of the possibilities for satisfaction and fulfillment by an overpowering and punitive authority. From this function of the essential definition of the suppression of individual life possibilities as a special case of repressive human relations, it is understandable that Freud did not confine his substantiation of the Oedipus complex to statements about concrete familial triangular relationships, but rather sought a *phylogenetic derivation of the Oedipus complex*. No matter how dubious the details of this derivation were, being based on Lamarckian ideas, what is significant for our argument is that, in doing this, Freud was attempting a *categorical foundation* for his theory that would make possible the *scientifically objectifying investigation of immediate human experience*. It becomes clearer what kind of objective relations are intended when one considers Freud's conception of the *necessary suppression of the Oedipus complex resulting in the establishment of the superego within the subject*. With the aid of the category, superego, the individual was supposed to be given the means with which to elucidate his tendencies to self-inhibition and self-punishment as "internalizations" of objective social compulsions and threats and thus to understand the true, that is, objective, cause of his subjective impairments so as to deal with them without self-destructive anxiety and guilt feelings. The superego concept thus had the function of making it possible to penetrate the subjectively given appearance of conscience, with its related guilt feelings, and to see the social repressive relations that are hidden in it. In this way the individual is supposed to become able to quit holding himself accountable for the existence and consequences of general human repression, to give up his infantile aspirations, and, instead, as a "mature personality," to reconcile himself to the limited and diluted possibilities for fulfillment that exist under the conditions of irrevocable social repression.

It would not be difficult to demonstrate that other basic categories of Freudian psychoanalysis also serve the function of mediating between subjective experience and objective social relations. I will only discuss here, however, the concept of *scientific generalization* found in the psychoanalytic construction of categories. Here, too, it is clearly the case that Freud did not adopt the variable-psychology trend, with its statistical approach to frequency generalization, but carried on with the classical approach to generalization. In the classical view a theoretical conception of the structural and organizational principles of the psyche is general if, by demonstrating the immanent objective structure of immediate experience, it makes that experience comprehensible as intersubjectively homogeneous and accessible. The theoretical concepts of psychoanalysis are generalizable to the extent that what appears at the moment as merely individual experience is decipherable as an "instance" of general human conflict. Despite its similarity to the classical concept of generalization, there is an important advancement here: According to the classical formulation of generalization, *individual deviations* from the principles of experiential structure or organization are set aside as due to "accidental extraneous factors." In the psychoanalytic approach to generality, by contrast, the *mediation process*, the particular expressions of conflict, adjustment, and related defenses by which the general social constellations express themselves, are taken into account. Generalizing, therefore, does not require abstraction from the individual case since *the differences in personal experience are not eliminated through recourse to extraneous factors* but rather are *elucidated by the mediational processes and levels* that are part and parcel of the theory. Through the exploration of one's experience one is able to find oneself again in the general constellations of conflict thus discovered, or more correctly, *one finds these constellations in oneself.* On the other hand, on the basis of one's insight into the mediational processes through which the general takes its particular appearance, it is possible for one to accept the uniqueness and distinctiveness of one's subjective situation. This avoids the formation of an opposition between the singular and the general, and one no longer needs to be abstracted from one's individual situation and circumstances in order to achieve scientific generality.

Freud once summarized his scientific convictions by saying that it is the aim of scientific thinking "to arrive at agreement with reality, that is, with that which exists outside and independent of us and which, as experience has taught us, is determining in the fulfillment or thwarting of our wishes. This agreement with the real external world we call truth" (Freud, 1933/1967: 194). This statement has often been understood as mere lip service that contrasts with the actual unscientific and speculative nature of psychoanalytic research practice. In my view Freud has captured here the very heart of his scientific endeavor. The "fulfillment or thwarting of our wishes" as the object of psychoanalytic investigation is elucidated for Freud when it is recognized in its mediation with that objective reality that is "definitive" – that is, the fulfilling or thwarting social authorities. This is the special psychoanalytic procedure for the production of "agreement with the real external world," that is, the psychoanalytic effort to establish the "truth."

5

With this historical reconstruction of the scientific status of the basic categories of psychoanalysis, we are closer to understanding the reasons for the widespread popularity and scientific influence of psychoanalysis despite its obvious mistakes and errors. Variable psychology, in breaking from the classical understanding of psychology and under its program of excluding or reducing subjectivity for the sake of a more restricted understanding of science, became degenerate as a science of the control of human behavior. Psychoanalysis embraced the classical understanding and initiated a psychological science of the subject in which the subjective situation, the world- and self-views of the person, personal suffering, conflicts and anxieties, guilt feelings, feelings of being torn and vulnerable were not transferred from the subject to the object and thereby reified and distorted in their essence, but were rather taken in their full subjective reality as the foundation of scientific analysis and generalization.

Viewed from this subject-scientific vantage point, the achievements of psychoanalysis as the first historically concrete development of subject-science can be distinguished from its errors and weaknesses. What's more, it becomes clear that even Freud's errors, in the context of a subject-science, possess a significance and dignity that is not matched by the limited correctness of the variable-psychological science of control. These errors, however, include scientific and political consequences of such a magnitude that they cannot be ignored, but compel us constantly to take issue with psychoanalysis scientifically and ideologically.

It is in the recognition of its new subject-scientific status that the problems and contradictions of psychoanalytic categories became clear. On the one hand, only on this basis does it become understandable why Freud's premise about the irreconcilability of personal aspirations and social demands is not merely a false universalization of bourgeois capitalist relations, but rather describes certain aspects of the subjective situation of persons under these relations in a generalized way that is both so rich and uncompromising that everyone can find himself in it and can grasp his or her individual situation as an instance of general repression. It is precisely in the often faulted biologistic anthropologization of antagonisms between instinctual demands and society that the entire significance of Freud as a great, incorruptible, bourgeois scientist is manifested, whereas all attempts by later psychoanalysts to "sociologize" Freud's ideas, closely viewed, have been apologetic in covering up and denying the harsh and relentless nature of bourgeois class contradictions.

On the other hand, Freud's conception of the fatal unchangeability of the societal repression of subjective aspirations, which reflected his universalization of bourgeois relations, revealed the problematic nature of such an assumption precisely because of its subject-scientific character. When the various subjective manifestations of failure and denial of reality, and also of managing and coping in the face of unavoidable suppression, become comprehensible "for each person" in a generalized way through elucidation of the conflict constellations *hypostasized as generally human*, it is affirmed that *the appearance forms change, but the suppression remains.* The individual in bourgeois society thus always rediscovers him or herself in psychoanalytic interpretations as a *"victim of relations."* To the extent that the subject comes to recognize and deal with his or her personal or immediate social conflicts, he or she is relieved of the burden of the great, all-embracing conflict, that is, the conflict with the ruling powers and their representatives. The decision, whether to struggle or not, is thereby removed from the individual, in that the various categorial elaborations of psychoanalysis do not at all account for or admit to a struggle against the *conditions* under which one suffers, for example, when the supposed conflicts are ultimately referred to one's early childhood and thus designated as lapsed, or when disputes with present authorities are defused and underestimated by suggesting that they are not the ones actually intended, that it is in fact the authority of the father against which one is rebelling. It is precisely the subject-scientific dignity of psychoanalytic categories that makes possible real insights into the subjective consequences of societal repression but, when universalized, offers individuals "solutions" in which the *actual conditions of their misery are obscured.* When one constantly seeks new ways of coping under existing conditions, always necessarily in vain, one permanently violates one's own interests in that the common struggle to overcome the restricting life circumstances is ignored as a possibility. The psychoanalytic conception of overcoming repressions is founded upon the all-embracing repression of the connection between the improvement of the subjective situation and the struggle for social conditions, that is, for conditions under which a restricted mode of living that for the sake of short-term avoidance of conflict sacrifices long-term interests is no longer subjectively "functional."

It would surely be shortsighted to assert that the Freudian analysis "psychologizes" all societal relations and neglects every kind of societally conditioned subjective conflict. But societal contradictions are, according to the specifically "genetic" model of psychoanalysis, only taken into consideration as conditions of fundamental conflicts in *early childhood,* and the working through of conflicts appears as necessarily only a task of *each particular individual,* who in the interest of his or her present coping with life must work through the consequences of his or her early childhood conflicts. This excludes repressive societal relations as conditions of each and every person's *present* suffering and the common struggle for changing these relations as a means of overcoming suffering. Also coming from this is something that is (despite all its pessimistic and resignative characteristics) peculiarly consoling in the psychoanalytic point of view: Although everyone *must* individually work through the consequences of his or her own early childhood repression in order to arrive at a relatively tolerable adult existence, it *is possible* to do so. At the same time one is relieved of participation in the collective struggle against the dominant relations, together with all the danger and risks associated with that; one can work out one's problems by oneself at home. Who is then to wonder that the way for the individual solution of societal contradictions suggested here finds such a great response precisely from bourgeois intellectuals? With regard to this suspension of real political struggle, the situation of the individual is not at all changed when, as in Freudo-Marxism, the social relations that are blamed for the early childhood repression are understood, with the aid of Marxist categories, to be "as such" historically determined and changeable. The particular individual is, in the psychoanalytic view, cut off from any influence upon a societal process thus understood. Participation in the transforming of bourgeois class reality into living conditions more fit for human beings in the interest of the development of one's subjective life-chances appears neither possible nor necessary. The individual person is, as before, a mere victim of circumstances and is directed back to work upon him or herself as the actual location of the difficulties.

From the psychoanalytic point of view, it is understood that every kind of individual participation in the political struggle appears suspect. Isn't it simply a projection of personal conflicts and thus a diversion from the actual problems within? In somewhat disguised form this view is found in the cheap bit of advice to "start with yourself," in which this "beginning," in accordance with the structure of the psychoanalytic conflict model, is already the "end." In this connection it also becomes clear that psychoanalysis can, on the basis of its specific categorial presuppositions, do nothing but psychologize societal class antagonisms as an expression of collective neuroticism – and it has always done this wherever it has dealt with such problems, beginning with Freud's idea that in the October Revolution the "instinctual restrictions necessitated by society" and the aggressive tendencies arising from them were redirected outward as hostility of the poor against the rich, of the formerly powerless against the earlier holders of power (Freud, 1933/1967: 195), and ending with the above-mentioned psychiatrization of the current nuclear threat as an expression of a collective persecution complex by H. E. Richter. At this point the scientific and ideological untenability of every "Freudo-Marxist" attempt at an integration of the psychoanalytic form of subject-scientific categories with Marxism becomes especially plain.

6

On the basis of the preceding considerations it should be clear in principle how the question with which this essay began about the *significance of psychoanalysis for Marxist psychology* should be answered: The significance lies in the new subject-scientific level of psychoanalytic categories and procedures. In elaborating its own position within the historical development of basic psychological approaches, Marxist psychology must reject the psychoanalytic categories in their concrete, historically limited expression but, at the same time, preserve the subject-scientific level that psychoanalysis has achieved by the way in which it formulated psychological questions and carried out their investigation. This also means that the classical tradition in the understanding of the psychological object, which was suppressed by the functionalist-behaviorist trend, must also be reactualized and developed further. This will include a critical reevaluation of the various forms of modern psychology, especially all of those peripheral conceptions and procedures that have not been completely under the influence of variable-psychology, and that therefore ought to have their relevant implications reconstructed.

It is thus not at all consonant with a psychology based on Marxist principles to embrace either the subjectivist internalization of human consciousness inaugurated by the functionalist-behaviorist movement or the resulting pseudo-objectivity of variable psychological concepts and methods. On the contrary, only on the basis of Marxism does it become possible to liberate the classical psychological conception of consciousness as a medium of intersubjective relations between people and the world from its idealistic shortcomings. Only from this standpoint can consciousness, as specific to the human experience of self and the world, be understood as coming from the necessities of material production and a reproduction of societal–individual life and thus also be understood in its historical determination by particular modes of production (as Leontyev has carried this out in his famous chapter "On the Historical Development of Consciousness," 1971: 177–215). In this way, the equating of consciousness with the black box of private inwardness becomes comprehensible as an historically determined limitation and distortion of consciousness in the form of isolated private persons in their practical-ideological subjugation to bourgeois conditions of reproduction. Thus the variable psychological conception of science can be understood as having been arrested in the interests of capitalist exploitation. In this way, too, the subject-scientific conception of the basic structure of immediate experience can be freed from its psychoanalytic distortion, and it is made obvious that the difference between the *appearance and essence* of subjective experience of self and the world as explicated by Freud (a difference without which, according to Marx, science would be neither possible nor necessary) cannot be allowed again to get lost in Marxist psychology. It is also clear that individual consciousness is not a static condition, but a contradictory process in which the conscious conduct of life must, in face of the exceeding complexity of objective societal relations, be wrested again and again away from the subjective tendencies toward a simplifying and harmonizing obfuscation of societal possibilities and necessities. The Freudian conception of the unconscious will thus have to be rejected in its metaphysical, irrationalist form. At the same time, however, it must be understood that, owing to the ineradicable contradiction between immediate experience and the societally mediated nature of individual existence, unconscious aspects of subjective experience of self and the world play a necessary role in the struggle for a conscious mode of living. Hence, the means and forms of the subjective exclusion of reality and elimination of contradictions must form a central theme of a Marxist psychology. In this connection the question arises: What particular expressions must these tendencies toward denial of reality assume, and how strongly, if the contradiction between immediate experience and societal relations is not a surmountable, developmental contradiction, but rather, owing to the exclusion of the affected person from the common control over societal processes under capitalist relations, is an antagonistic contradiction that cannot be overcome? In this connection it must also be asked whether the Freudian conception of the independence, isolation, and inaccessibility of a substantial unconscious – though it must indeed be rejected as a universal concept – can be taken as offering an adequate description of certain forms of reality loss in the subjective self-accommodation to the ruling capitalist relations by means of giving in to dependence (Holzkamp-Osterkamp, 1976).

It should now have become clear that the Marxist psychological concept of scientific generalization cannot in any case submit to the universality claim of the variable-psychological model of statistical frequency generalization. There is absolutely no sensible reason for accepting the alternative, "either" immediate subjective experience "or" scientific generalization, thereby reductively abstracting away the specifics of human life activity in the name of science. After all, on the basis of his classical understanding of object Lewin already demonstrated that structural generalization that mediates between individual appearance and general law was the characteristic of the modern "Galileian" mode of thought, as opposed to what he called Aristotelian frequency thinking. It was on this basis that he developed his scientific-theoretical conception of rising from the singular to the "pure "case. These Lewinian conceptions, so far as I can see, have never been refuted in modern psychology, but rather (and sadly later by Lewin himself) have simply been ignored (Lewin, 1981).

That Marxist psychology must begin its methodological developmental efforts here, and not with the variable-psychological frequency thinking, becomes clear from Marx's conception of "rising from the abstract to the concrete." As reconstructed by Marx, the path from the concrete image, by way of the abstractive elaboration of its most general determinants, to the concrete thought, in which the levels of the most general determinants are comprehended, thus revealing the particular as the specific appearance form of the general, implies the concept of "structural generalization." This conception of Marx's pertains not only to *Capital*, but represents a profoundly comprehensive clarification of how scientific knowledge is acquired altogether. Rubinstein has demonstrated this forcefully and convincingly in his chapter on "thinking as cognition" (1961: 98ff.), particularly with respect to natural scientific knowledge. By critically reformulating and further developing the subject-scientific ideas of structural generalization as the elucidation of the individual experience and situation as mediated by the objective societal form, Marxist psychology can, on the one hand, like psychoanalysis, leave unreduced the subjective–intersubjective reality of the experience of self and of the human world, and thus also of suffering and inescapable conflict, and, on the other hand, make it possible for individuals to understand the societal possibilities and contradictions that appear in individualized form. And it can do this for the affected person without the scientific and ideological disadvantages found in the psychoanalytic understanding. In this way Marxist psychology can become, in the subject-scientific perspective, an effective means for clarification of each person's own life conduct through subjective reconstruction of the internal connection between genuine individual life interests and societal responsibility for action.

How the categorial foundations of the subject-scientific development of knowledge should be advanced is easy to see from the research results that have so far been produced by Marxist psychology. *On the side of the individual,* all psychoanalytic ideas of an unchangeable unsocial "drive structure" have to be shown to be scientifically untenable by demonstrating the cognitive, emotional, and motivational dimensions through which individuals are able and ready to become involved in the societal life process and, by way of contributing to societal reproduction, to take part in the creation of conditions for the reproduction of each person's subjective existence. *On the side of societal relations,* the psychoanalytic idea that these are solely limiting and repressing is overcome by elaborating the connection between the development of subjective quality of the life and the individual's participation in societal control over the conditions of life, that is, by the integration of the individual into the collective subjectivity.

The present emphasis on the subject-scientific perspective of Marxist psychology, however, is intended less as a demonstration of how a problem can be clarified than as an indication of precisely what requires future clarification. Especially in working out the procedural consequences of the subject-scientific conception of structural generalization, the largest share of the work lies before us. Naturally, too, the traditional psychological conceptions of method, including the variable-psychological concept of frequency generalization, should not be abstractly negated but are rather to be rejected solely with regard to their claim to universality as a guarantee of psychology's scientific status. Assuming the primacy of structural generalization, questions can be asked about the conditions of applicability and status of such method concepts within the framework of subject-scientific research. The essential intent of this chapter has been to provide a more precise foundation for the consensus and thus also to affirm that the essential future tasks of the collective work of Marxist psychologists lie on the level of the subject-scientific problem described and that in this there is no way around psychoanalysis.

6 Emotion, Cognition, and Action Potence

Ute Holzkamp-Osterkamp

In order to analyze the relationship of cognitive and emotional processes to action preparedness or action potence, we must pay attention to the subject's capacity to alter or not to alter relevant living conditions. This is important because it is precisely the active altering and cooperative influencing of relevant life relations that is specific to "human" life activity. That is what fundamentally distinguishes the human from the merely organismic mode of life. It is also important because it tends to be ignored by traditional psychology.

I will develop some aspects of this problem here and indicate some general conclusions. Some basic types of theories about the cognitive–emotional relationship will be examined for the ways in which they deal with the alterability or nonalterability of relevant living conditions by the individual. My analysis will be based on the functional and historical categories worked out earlier in Critical Psychological research on the relationship between cognitive and emotional processes (Holzkamp-Osterkamp, 1975, 1976; Holzkamp and Holzkamp-Osterkamp, 1977).

The procedure for critically working through traditional theories is one application of the general Critical Psychological methods for analyzing bourgeois theories (Holzkamp, 1977): The "one-sidedness" of particular theoretical conceptions is exposed by applying more comprehensive Critical Psychological categories; that is, their claims to universality are refuted, and it is shown how they are only relatively valid under particular historically determined conditions. Their relative knowledge value is then subsumed into the more comprehensive conceptions of Critical Psychology, which then gain for themselves a higher level of organization, differentiation, and empirical concreteness. These improved conceptions then form the basis for further positive Critical Psychological research.

One problem encountered by the Critical Psychological reinterpretation of bourgeois theories is that in granting bourgeois psychological approaches a validity within their own bailiwicks, it must be assumed that the findings of bourgeois psychology are sound in terms of their own methods. This, however,

102

cannot be taken for granted. As the methodological analyses of Critical Psychology have demonstrated, this assumption is *extremely problematic* (cf. Jäger, 1977; Keiler, 1977; Leiser, 1977; Maschewsky, 1977; Jäger et al., 1978). This means that we must first determine whether the results we are concerned with are empirically founded and thus warrant critical preservation of their relative knowledge content. We are only just beginning to elaborate the criteria for this kind of methodological assessment. But it is not too early, in my opinion, for the reappraisal of bourgeois theories with an eye to furthering the elaboration and development of our Critical Psychological conceptions. We have to proceed with both the theoretical reappraisal and methodological critique of bourgeois psychology so that insights gained in each area become available for the critique and improvement of the other. This is the only way in which stagnation of research can be avoided and a progressive optimization of the state of research be maintained. It must be granted, however, that at the current stage of methodological development we cannot use bourgeois psychological findings in their own frames of reference as evidence for or against Critical Psychological claims. At best they provide illustrations and empirical "enlargements" of the Critical Psychological assumptions.

Our main purpose here will be to examine the essential determinants and distortions of emotion found in bourgeois psychology and to offer a Critical Psychological reappraisal of emotion's relation to cognition and its implications for work and education. We will be further interested in implications for a Critical Psychological theory of psychic disorders and their treatment and for the relationship between the client's interests and those of the therapist in psychotherapy.

The Relation Between Emotion, Cognition, and Action from the Point of View of Critical Psychology

To assist the reader's understanding of the theoretical basis of our analysis and reinterpretation of existing theories of emotion, the main points of the Critical Psychological conception of emotionality will be sketched out. Of course, this can be done only globally and roughly here. Some finer detail will be presented in the discussions of particular theories. As our functional-historical analysis of the emergence and differentiation of emotionality in the general life process has revealed (cf. Holzkamp-Osterkamp, 1975, 1976), emotion functions as an evaluation of the environmental conditions as they are apprehended cognitively. The standard of evaluation is the subjective meaning of the cognized environmental conditions and the individual possibilities for action they present. Emotions are thus an essential determinant of actions related to cognized circumstances and events. These emotional evaluations of environmental conditions underlie every life activity; at the organismic level of specificity they are not conscious, but result from the immediate coordination of individual behavior with concrete environmental conditions or, in the general regulation of behavior, direct the organismic adaptation toward pertinent aspects of the environment. They develop as aspects of the development and differentiation of species-specific and individual relations to the environment. The evaluative feedback of the adaptiveness of individual behavior is thus reflected in the individual organism not for each separate level of the relationship to the environment, but rather as a "complex quality," that is, as an overall emotional tone, that condenses all particular evaluations automatically into a unitary execution of action, on the basis of which alone goal-directed action is possible. Such emotional evaluations generally occur only with the "interference" of habitualized and automatic action sequences and with dangers to action potence stemming from current threats or situations demanding a "new," heightened "attention." It is therefore characteristic of phases of "reorientation" within the environmental relations of organisms.

Societal existence is the uniting of the powers of individuals in the common task of maintaining and expanding the conditions in which life takes place. It is therefore an essential precondition for the possibilities that an individual has for living and experiencing and presupposes a fundamental alteration in the individual's relationship to his or her own needs and thus to emotionality. People no longer become active out of the immediate pressure of needs, but rather in the cognizance of their general state of need, that is, independently of current need tensions. Thus the individual interest in societal relations, that is, in the long-term securing and conscious determination of individual existence, presumes a reciprocal liberation from the immediate need state that acts on the isolated, struggling individual for whom the "goals" of action are dictated by accidentally given conditions. At the specifically human level, therefore, the agreement of action with needs is no longer a natural given, but a problem to be solved. Goals no longer come from spontaneous impulses to action, but are determined by the necessities of making a secure societal existence and are tested by individuals – as it were, after the fact – against the background of a range of concrete action alternatives and according to their value of subjective satisfaction.

So people are no longer channeled into a predetermined action by whatever need is momentarily dominant, but know at all times more or less clearly about all of their needs and are to a large extent responsible for the way in which they satisfy them. This necessarily implies that they must take into account the effects of current satisfactions on long-term interests and goals, must respond consciously to their needs and plan for their satisfaction. In short, they determine their living conditions, instead of being determined by them through their need states.

Checking societal goals for their satisfaction value, that is, not acting automatically but by conscious direction, always presupposes the analysis of emotionality, that is, breaking down its unitary complexity and tracing its particular qualities to their objective sources so as to be able to influence the subjective situation by changing objective reality. A "positive" change of the subjective situation at the human level of development is not a short-term, hedonistic striving for immediate individual well-being. Because they reflect societal existence, human emotions transcend the momentary individual situation. Knowing about the general state of need requires not just the satisfaction of the current need, but also the subjective assurance that the need will be satisfied in the future, that is, in principle. And since at the specifically human level of development the competence of action is no longer determined only by individual capabilities but by the extent and quality of societal relations, others' emotional evaluation of the objective situation becomes especially significant for individual existence and its enrichment. At the same time, evaluative consensus on objective circumstances reflects the emotional connectedness to others as a subjective evaluation of the possibilities for action through community with them.

Under the conditions of general insecurity of individual existence, that is, of deficient social integration, the striving for consensus with others can become detached from the evaluation of objective environmental circumstances. It can appear as an independent action tendency, in which the emotional connectedness with others does not result in the promotion of mutual development through the common improvement of life conditions, but in fact limits the individual possibilities for development because the individual no longer risks doing what is frowned upon by this short-circuited emotional consensus.

According to our theory, the emotional evaluation of environmental conditions is the basis and first step of every cognitive process, that is, of the thinking and acting that seeks information about existing conditions. The cognition of the new is always dependent upon earlier experience or evaluation, but in the emotional reaction, owing to its all-embracing character, information is mediated and accentuated that remains subliminal and left out of account in the conscious coordination of action. The emotional reaction, generally a more or less diffuse feeling of "ease" or "unease" evoked by the complex situation, serves to inform and correct the conscious goal- or task-oriented exchange with the environment.

The elucidation of individual emotionality, that is, the transformation of spontaneous impulses into directed action, depends upon finding subjective security in the support of other persons, on being accepted in the social environment and not existentially threatened by contradiction and conflict with it. The emotions, as expression of these spontaneous impulses to action, are stronger when an unhindered realization in action can be anticipated and are more inhibited when the consequences of action are threatening.

The clarity, strength, and vigor of the emotions are thus determined by the clarity of demands and goals to which the individual feels him- or herself obliged and by the explicitness and distinctness of the social relations and the potential for development that they offer. This, in turn, is determined by the openness with which the interests of individuals are taken into consideration by the living and working community. Emotions are clear when the individual knows about them and feels secure with them, when his or her relations to the environment are unequivocal and he or she can take appropriate action based on his or her experience without concern about possible conflicts. Emotions are unclear when the environmental relations are contradictory, when certain developmental possibilities are simultaneously offered and obstructed, when the support of others is ambivalent, when one is dependent upon others and restricted and exploited by them as well and hindered in articulating and confronting these contradictions, when one can neither openly express the emotional impulses to action nor shield oneself from them. When one tries to avoid conflicts, the emotions become characterized qualitatively and quantitatively by weakness, the immediate expression of one's own impotence and helplessness. Or, in order to avoid the impetus to societally unwanted and thus risky action, emotions generally become withdrawn, thin, and bloodless. The fear of the emotions or the tendency to avoid strong emotions, that is, the fear of the consequences of one's impulses, channels thinking into safe, relatively neutral directions, and by creating a distance from things, impairs the capacity for thinking and makes it impossible for a person really to understand problems and to engage effectively in action.

The Cognition-Guiding Function of Emotionality in the Theories of Volkelt, Bruschlinski and Tichomirow, and Simonow

The first type of theory that we shall deal with is concerned with the *significance of experience that is still emotional and not yet conceptualized and that forms a first step toward conscious knowledge.* Some of these theories stem from the early "introspective" phase of scientific psychology (for example, Lipps, 1902; Szymanski, 1929; Maier, 1965). Especially important is the analysis of Johannes Volkelt in his *Die Gefühlsgewissheit* (The Certainty of Feeling) of 1922, which is concerned with the *relationship of emotional and rational thinking and the cognition-guiding function of emotions.* I shall cite some characteristic passages.

According to Volkelt, "the certainty of feeling must be related at its roots in deliberation, thinking, and logic." "It is not a feeling for particular facts, but *feeling for the connection of facts.''* Since grasping connections is a primeval category of thought according to Volkelt, "the logical occurs in two forms: first, in the form of conceptual thinking that is active in deliberation, discussion, justification, and proof; and second, in a kind of condensed, obscured, abbreviated, nonconceptual form, the form of a *logical feeling, a logical tact''* (p. 24). The obscure, unitary "certainty of feeling," characterized by "the color of the undivided, the individual, the melted-together," is, according to Volkelt, to be seen as "feeling of a logical kind," as "the sensing of connections . . . virtually as a *first step toward thinking,''* as "thinking, translated back into the conditions of nonexplicitness" (p. 25). Volkelt discusses the possibility "that logical tact intervenes in a preparatory, procuring, directing way in the course of knowing, but then makes room for justification, implication, in short, for strictly scientific procedures" (p. 37).

In more recent times, the problem of the cognition-guiding function of emotions has only been treated, so far as I can see, by Soviet psychologists, not by employing introspective-descriptive methods, but by controlled, experimental observations. Bruschlinski and Tichomirow (1975) proceed, for example, like Volkelt, from the assumption that emotional and thought processes should not be opposed to each another. They demonstrate that emotion is necessary in discovering the basic principle of a problem solution. They speak of an interim "emotional solution," a conviction that a particular solution is correct even before it is objectively identified.

According to their findings, the discovery of the solution comes about in two phases. First, an approximate area is marked off in which the solution principle can be found; then the principle itself is discovered. Emotional activation is associated with the first phase and determines the subjective value of a particular line of search. It serves to indicate when to start and when to stop and where to search for what is not yet found. To illustrate, the authors point to the children's game in which finding the hidden object is guided and facilitated by the shouts of "cold" and "hot." The work of Bruschlinski and Tichomirow showed, too, that where there was insufficient emotional engagement or interest – as indicated by statements by the experimental subjects or from physiological activation – complicated problems whose principles of solution were not yet known could not be solved.

The significance of emotional arousal for creative accomplishment is also emphasized by Simonow (1975), although his observations are limited to its quantitative aspects. One interesting result was that for creative thinking certain reorganizational processes evoked by emotional arousal were essential, and these – since they are repressed in consciousness by rational selection – carry on unconsciously or by "switching off" consciousness.

Emotion is viewed by Simonow as "one of the most effective means of 'struggling' against the 'probability prognosis' with its detrimental tendency to persistence and bias of previous experiences." At the same time, however, he speaks of "mutagenesis" and of knowledge gained through production of relatively improbably connections among neural traces of past events. According to Simonow, mutagenesis has to do with a "directed accidentalness," with "searching in a direction in which the probability of discovery . . . is greater relative to the other directions" (p. 87). The mechanisms of mutagenesis also work, Simonow explains, in a waking state, "but lie outside of consciousness and are repressed by incoming information and rational selection and are most effective in sleep" (p. 91). For this reason, "periodic sleep is not only necessary for the restoration of metabolism and the fitness of the nerve cells," but is even more important for "the processing and ordering of information gathered during the waking state" (p. 90). The prevention of such ordering activities apparently leads to strong emotional states of insecurity, anxiety, and irritability.

The Cognition-Guiding or "Disturbing" Function of Emotionality as a Consequence of Action in Concrete Life Situations

The studies we have cited yield important insights regarding the connection between cognitive and emotional processes. Their procedures, however, whether introspective or experimental, abstract from the concrete living conditions of individuals, and consequently overlook a more comprehensive and essential connection: the one among cognition, emotionality, and action. When this connection is considered and it is recalled that the possibilities of the single individual are measured at the human level of existence by his or her relations with the remaining members of society, then it is obvious how limited our conceptions will be if we treat individuals as if they gained their knowledge in a vacuum instead of in the concrete, societally determined situations and webs of interest into which their actions must be integrated and within which their existence must be established. This means that the positive cognition-guiding function of emotionality treated in the cited studies is not a *general* characteristic of the relation between cognition and emotional processes, but can only be effective where the need to act in order to alter relevant conditions of life in one's own interest does not meet with conflict.

The problem situation is different, however, when, the individual confronts a hostile complex of interests and power relations. In this case one's cognitions alone cannot serve to guide action; it must be recognized that the action demanded by those cognitions could cause the loss of social support and consequently also the security of existence.

Given such an ambivalent emotional subjective situation, the cognitive process cannot provide unambiguous direction; "certainty of feeling" and engagement are impaired. Moreover, in acute conflict emotion can disturb or even block the acquisition of knowledge itself. Fear of knowledge or of the consequences of action and conflict has an immediately disabling effect upon the capacity for thought. In such threatening situations emotionality turns from a *facilitator* into an *obstacle* to action that might otherwise improve the circumstances of living. The emotional tendencies to action that are produced when possibilities of improving living conditions are recognized become detached, through defense mechanisms, for cognition and action owing to the threat that their realization poses to existence; they come to express themselves in general, diffused unrest and lack of concentration; they finally turn into a kind of "disturbed inner life" and subjective burden for the individual.

This will especially be the case – because at the human level of development the possibilities of individuals are determined by their relationships to others – when current security of existence is sought, not as the self-evident prerequisite for action, but as an immediate solution to the problem, and striving to overcome social isolation and its consequent threat to existence overlaps with the actual problem. Reactions of others to problem solution, then, gain a greater weight than the problem solution itself; the assessment by the others, on the whole, is not of the concrete problem, but rather of the person. This is all the more the case when the problem is not distinguished by its meaning to the subject, but assumed out of some sort of direct compulsion. The striving for personal recognition can at least lend the task a secondary meaning.

To the extent, however, that the reactions of others are taken as the standard for self-assessment, the situation becomes a matter of existential preservation. The accompanying stress increases when the need for, that is, reliance on, the immediate benevolence of others is greater and the specific demands are less well known or are contradictory. Stress is also produced by perceived discrepancies between the positive expectations arising from a general readiness to adapt and one's capability.

Such social insecurity impairs concentration upon practical demands; the dominating effort for social approval represents an additional burden because it makes the existentially important problem solution all the more difficult to attain. The resulting state of overmotivation leads to failure both through its direct debilitating effect on the person and because the consternation it creates leads to assessment of partial successes as insufficient and leading to nothing. Thus Rubinstein (1968: 700–701) says that where immediate evaluation by others becomes the subject's actual goal and the concrete action is only a means for achieving that goal, the subject, by diverting attention to the effect upon others, frequently cuts him- or herself off from the success of concrete action and thereby also from the recognition by others.

An essential cause of the diversion of attention to the level of subjective approval, according to Rubinstein, is the feeling of insecurity that comes from a lack of preparation for concrete demands, leads to an outcome that is uncertain and accidental, and depends on the kind of relations one has with others: In a generally positive atmosphere individual potentials for constructive engagement that otherwise would be tied up by the concern for social approval would be set free.

In this connection we can mention the work of Mandler and Sarason (1952) on the effects on achievement of attending to evaluations by others. As is typical for bourgeois psychology, the authors interpret the effects not in terms of objective conditions, but rather as personality traits, for example, general anxiety that cannot be further analyzed. Mandler and Sarason distinguish task-relevant and task-irrelevant, that is, object- and person-oriented, reactions. As demands get more difficult, "anxious" persons show more task-irrelevant reactions, and these in turn affect actual task achievement negatively, which increases concern for one's effect upon others, thus making it all the more difficult to carry out the task successfully.

We can also cite many studies of the effects of various achievement demands on the behavior of "anxious" and "nonanxious" subjects (for example, Spielberger, 1966) and the great number of investigations by Lewin and his followers on demand and ego level, in which the diversion of attention to individual approval, typical of general insecurity, is absolutized as a general characteristic of human life.

What findings like this actually demonstrate is the dependence of the direction and intensity of individual thought and action upon the quality of social relations. Our understanding of emotional security and self-confidence as stemming from the clarification of environmental relations, that is, from the extent to which one's own needs and interests are given practical recognition by others, is confirmed – negatively – by the results of these studies, in which the possibilities of the individual are limited and the emotional and cognitive direction is left to the individual in uncertain social relations.

Societal existence as precondition for the diverse vital and experiential possibilities of human individuals always implies well the possibility of individual existential insecurity stemming from ambiguity or insecurity of vitally necessary social relations, which always implies a threat to the action potence of the individual.

The Absolutization of the "Disturbance Function" of the Emotions in the "Cognitive Emotion Theories" of Epstein, Lazarus, Mandler, Pribram, and Schachter

Whereas in older theories and in Soviet psychology only the *positive knowledge-guiding* function of emotionality is considered, in modern "cognitive" theories of emotion like those of Epstein, Lazarus, Mandler, Pribram, and Schachter, the "disturbance" function of emotions is widely absolutized. In these theories the functionalist preoccupation with the adaptation of the individual to existing environmental conditions or to psychological control stands at the center of interest. Although there are important differences among cognitive theories of emotion, they have the following essential points in common.

Emotional events are related essentially only to the adaptation to existing life circumstances. The active production of life circumstances by individuals as a precondition for a successful agreement of the subjective and objective moments is shoved to the periphery of discussion from the start. The result is that only those emotional processes that arise during *adaptational difficulties* in situations of *disorientation* are studied. The "disturbance" function of emotions thus becomes emphasized. According to the underlying concept of "adaptation," the problem of reducing the disturbance function of emotions is treated not as a problem of regaining self-control through extension of the active influence of the individual upon the relevant vital conditions, but rather as a problem simply of the psychic reduction of emotional excitement and the alteration of its focus on the environment.

Theories that emphasize the predictability of events as a prerequisite for the individual's adaptive capacity and use the concept of control in this connection still speak as if the subjection to existing power relations and alien interests were unavoidable. The word *control* is understood as the capacity for adaptation to vital conditions as determined by others. In order to avoid conflict and to maintain the psychic stability of the individual under existing conditions, a relative openness to various trends, detached from all contents, is recommended in order to attach oneself opportunistically and as quickly as possible to whatever assertive tendencies are prevailing, that is, to secure one's own advantage by joining the ruling forces.

"Cognitive" theories of emotion all refer more or less strictly to currently popular conceptions of orientation or habituation such as those developed by Sokolov (1960, 1963) and Groves and Thompson (1970). On this basis one assumes a general experiential framework, a "system of reference," from which the various events can be interpreted. This interpretation is at the same time treated as a subjective need.

As long as the new environmental givens are still not familiar, processed, or arranged, there is a special orientation to them accompanied by a relative rise in physiological arousal as an expression of general activation. Once the new givens are arranged within the existing reference system, they no longer arouse any special attention; habituation, that is, emotional blunting, to them occurs. The formerly new facts lose their arousing quality, become neutral, and are noticed only if there is some disturbance or interruption in our processing of the environment.

Below the level of attention and actual orientation there is thus a general orientation that is the generalized resultant of many actual orientations and that regulates the customary life activities and receives, registers, and processes information, and only in the case of disturbance, when accustomed modes of behaving no longer function freely, when established expectations are not confirmed, and a reorientation becomes necessary, does it come to an "objectivization" (Uznadze) and a particular form of arousal that beyond a certain level assumes a negative quality. The "biological sense" of such a negative-experiential quality of heightened arousal is, according to the interpretation of many authors (for example, Epstein, 1972; Lazarus and Averill, 1972), as an incentive to withdraw from the evoking situation to which the individual has not developed an appropriate response or to intensify the search for possibilities of directing the arousal into an adequate, existence-securing behavior.

If the organism is unable to develop an adequate behavioral strategy for dealing with novel environmental events, if the information exceeds an individual's processing capacity, then there occurs a greater-than-optimal arousal, which is an expression of the necessity for appropriate action. This, however, does not make finding a solution to the problem easier. Such a solution may in fact be obstructed and, given the general disorientation of the behavior, can lead to a generalized unease, leading, in turn, to further behavioral disorientation that is usually experienced by the individual as "anxiety."

According to the view of Lazarus and Averill (1972), Lazarus, Averill, and Opton (1973) and Lazarus (1977), some of the best-known representatives of the cognitive theory of emotion, the individual, owing to phylogenetic, cultural, and individual developmental conditions, is equipped with certain dispositions to judge environmental givens by means of a "cognitive filter" through which the environment is assessed for its subjective significance and manageability. According to this theory, emotions are a complex reaction syndrome consisting of physiological arousal, the assessment of the adaptive difficulties as expressed in arousal, and observable behavior – restlessness, flushing, and so forth. Emotions reflect the environmental relations of the individual, the manner of adjustment to the prevailing givens, and the action potence that they allow, whereby, as the theory basically emphasizes, the cognitive processes not only determine the quality and intensity of the emotional reactions, but indeed form the very basis of the coping processes, that is, of the ability of the individual to have effective influence.

Further discussion, then, deals with the negative emotions above all, mainly the feeling of anxiety and helplessness and its management by the individual under conditions of deficient predictability of events. In one of his most recent studies Lazarus (1977) even defines emotions generally as a disturbance of the relationship to the environment that is experienced as a threat, whereby, as already emphasized in earlier studies (for example, Lazarus and Averill, 1972: 250), the experience of threat is more significant for the psychological understanding of reality than is the objective threat itself.

According to Lazarus and his co-workers, emotions do not mediate between cognition and action, as deduced by our functional-historical analysis; cognition is defined as an instance of mediation between environmental circumstances and emotions. The emotions, thus understood, appear as ends in themselves. They are no longer discussed in terms of their action-guiding function, but rather are described – more or less sweepingly, often only in terms of physiological activation – only as the object of immediate influence or therapeutic treatment.

Emotions as an expression of the subjective situation is thus not dealt with in its function of assessing the individual's relation to the environment and as a guideline for the active influence upon the objective conditions of life. Instead, it is dealt with under the tacit assumption of the immutability of existing power relationships and the necessity of individual subordination to these as a universal source of threat that can only be overcome or at least subdued within the individual, thus avoiding concrete alteration of circumstances.

It is not the objective living conditions that are to be altered to correspond to the subjective situation; rather, the subjective situation must be adjusted to the existing living conditions or relations of authority, which are not to be questioned, but accepted or assessed as emotionally positive. Deviations from this expectation are blamed solely upon the individual as an aberration of feeling. The general disorientation of behavior is the essential foundation for manipulability by others since the individual in this situation becomes more or less "grateful" for every offered behavioral orientation as a way of achieving social recognition. It becomes a problem in these theories only when the functioning of such individual adaptive performance is endangered by "disturbing" emotionality as a consequence of repressed needs and the corresponding impulses to action.

Thus in dealing with ways in which emotional reactions are managed, the possibilities of active alteration of living conditions are given only sketchy consideration. According to the view of Lazarus and co-workers, there are two fundamental strategies for coping: direct action and cognitive assimilation. Attack and flight are mentioned as forms of direct action. These, according to the authors, are aimed at changing the organism–environment relationship such that the threat is reduced or eliminated, but little more is said of this strategy except that it can now and then lead to further difficulties that in turn can lead to further alteration of the emotional situation (Lazarus et al., 1973: 171). Cognitive assimilation, according to this theory, is invoked when there is no possibility for direct action. It amounts to giving a "new interpretation to existing environmental conditions. This is accomplished either by acquiring new information that leads to more "reality-appropriate" behavior or by a "cognitive tour de force" (Lazarus and Averill, 1972: 251), that is, by defense processes.

Aside from these strategies, Lazarus mention self-regulation as one more form of adaptation. This is the possibility of the individual, when overly pressed by environmental circumstances, to gain direct influence over emotional arousal through the reinterpretation of the situation or even by reducing arousal by physiological means, such as tranquilizers, drugs, and relaxation exercises; that is, the importance of the event is deflated in one way or another by "toning down" one's own reactions.

The tactic of directly influencing physiological arousal, is, as Lazarus says, often the only one available and is therefore very important because the generalized reduction of physiological arousal or anxiety is an essential precondition for adequate adaptive performance. Lazarus (1977) tells us little more about the conditions under which one or the other form of "coping" or "self-regulation" occur, nor does he tell us about the long-term efficacy of the adjustment processes.

Lazarus (1977) emphasizes that through "self-regulation," that is, immediate influence on emotional arousal, the person is capable of directing his or her emotional reactions at will instead of reacting passively or automatically to internal and external events. By his understanding this means a certain freedom. The freedom of individuals in relations over which they exert no influence thus consists in the "freedom" from engagement, the freedom to reduce one's capacity for experience, that is, generalized indifference and blunting of feelings. It does not appear to occur to Lazarus that the development of one individual might be arbitrarily limited by the interests of another or that individual development and undistorted emotionality might depend upon rebelling against repression and finding ways of enduring the conflicts aroused by rebellion. He also fails to recognize that it is precisely the task of psychological work to promote the process of self-determination and the individual's active influence on relevant living conditions, instead of supporting the denial of the subjective needs through a generalized avoidance of conflicts and thereby contributing essentially to an acceptance of emotionality as "disturbing" factor.

The separation of emotions and action becomes even clearer in the work of Mandler, Pribram, and Epstein. According to Mandler's theory (for example, Kessen & Mandler, 1961; Mandler & Watson, 1966; and Mandler, 1972) the interruption of organized behavior or of plans where no alternative action is possible causes a general physiological arousal that, at a certain level, expresses itself as anxiety. Generalized arousal results in further disorganization of behavior, yielding the typical picture of behavior disturbed by anxiety. This physiological arousal, Mandler argues, can be brought under control by substitute behaviors that frequently become resistent to change and become established as symptoms. According to Mandler's theory (1964), the establishment of such a behavior is all the stronger, the lower the "frustration tolerance" for physiological arousal and the stress connected with it, or the lower the tolerance of general disorientation, and the greater the inclination to accept the next-best possibility as a kind of bulwark against disorientation and the helplessness it entails.

According to this theory the general behavioral orientation is at least as important for the individual as the goal to which it is subordinated. But this means that under conditions of general disorientation and of social insecurity each offered orientation, independent of its concrete content, will be experienced and generally accepted by the individual as a relief. That is, in individual goallessness is given the absolute manipulability by others. The subjective compulsion, from which comes the willing assumption of every offered orientation, often expresses itself in the rigidity with which precisely these substantively unidentified goals are defended against all change. This rigidity of behavior can lead secondarily to further adaptive difficulties.

Since helplessness is a reaction to disorientation, as Mandler argues (1972), repeated experience of individual impotence and incapacity can develop into chronic hopelessness, characterized by general passivity, immobility, and intense feelings of inferiority and anxiety.

In his attempt to develop a neurophysiological theory of emotions, Pribram (1967a, b) speaks of neural plans and programs, the organization of genetic and acquired experiences, that govern the equilibrium or internal stability of the organism–environment system that is presupposed by all perception and action and to which all new information about the environment is related. Emotions occur, according to this theory, when the information to be processed cannot be brought into agreement with the reference system established on the basis of past experience. The existing plans and programs, that is, expectations, are thus disturbed, and discontinuity, e-motion, a state of being thrown out of motion, that is, a temporary state of action impotence, occurs.

According to Pribram's view, activation is an indication of the incongruence between the input structures and the already established neural structures. Regarding the processing of incongruent environmental information, Pribram believes that pertinent physiological data demonstrate two tendencies: a tendency that accentuates the disturbance created by input in the system and the corresponding orientational reactions and a tendency toward preservation and securing of the existing "habitualized" experiences and attenuation of the disturbance, that is, of the information that cannot be reconciled with the existing reference system. In this connection, Pribram speaks of "participatory" and "preparatory" processes or of "external" and "internal" control. According to Pribram, these two processes move between the poles of maximal information density and maximal information redundance.

The participatory processes are aimed at incorporating the input into the existing reference system and at producing agreement between old and new experiences through alteration of the neural model, restructuring the existing organization against which input is measured. The preparatory processes are aimed at the protection of the old system through the attenuation of, or resistance to, noncongruent experiences. Whereas the participatory processes are thus open to alteration of the environment and achieve flexibility through a more complex form of organization, that is, the external control over the development of new congruences and the extension of existing plans and programs, the preparatory processes produce the continuity and stability of the system through simplification, that is, the defensive exclusion of all aspects of reality that initiate the emotional conditions by the ignoring or repressing of incongruent experience. Pribram mentions sleep's function as a particular form of informational defense.

Pribram aims at a conceptual clarification of the relationship between motivation and emotion: "Emotions are . . . essentially neural dispositions which regulate input when action is temporarily interrupted, literally when an e-motion exists. Motivation, on the other hand, is concerned with the organism in action and the carrying out of plans. Emotion and motivation, passion and action, are the two poles of the plane" (1967a: 38). The organism reacts then, as indicated elsewhere (1967b), with motivation to the incongruent information when it tries to extend its behavioral repertoire through learning and to adjust to the new perceptual facts. By contrast, emotional reactions occur when for some reason the organism does not succeed in the extension and adjustment of its behavioral repertoire, so that the discrepancy between perceptual variety and behavioral repertoire must be bridged by internal mechanisms of self-regulation and self-control. This happens when new perceptual facts become reinterpreted by and included in the already available reference system. When this is successful, positive emotions result; if such a reinterpretation and inclusion is not successful, the organism seeks to secure its existence by withdrawing from the new perceptual facts, which signify a negative emotional situation. Under what conditions one or the other occurs is not explained by Pribram. He merely concludes generally that, with respect to the information flowing in from the environment, control is possible to the extent that it can be shut off, but the consequences of one's own action are unforeseeable: "One can only be sure that what will happen in the environment is a consequence of the action" (1967a: 38). Action always contains risks for which, according to Pribram, one cannot adapt or prepare oneself. They are encountered only in the immediate situation: "Risk is countered only by experience" (1967a: 38).

All concepts that describe emotions, in Pribram's interpretation, can also be used to characterize motives or motivation. "Love as an emotion has its counterpart in love as a motive. The emotion of fear has it mirror image in the motive of fear. Being moved by music can be apposed to being moved to make music. And so on" (1967a: 38). Passion and action, in Pribram's opinion, must, however, always stand in a balanced relation to one another; relative imbalance between the active and passive sides leads to maladjustment, which Pribram clarifies only regarding the emotions, that is, for the circumstance of present action impotence. On the one hand, overly strong emotions can have immediate negative effects on the behavioral organization and adaptive performance, but they can also lead to an extreme preference for one or another form of processing, and through this, again, to adjustment difficulties. If the source of threatening input is not removed, the defense of the existing reference system in opposition to new contradictory information can lead to a broader and broader shielding and thus to an increasing independence of the "inner plans" from external reality and finally to psychic collapse. When this happens, reality crashes in on the completely unprepared individual and, as Pribram says, "all hell breaks loose" (1967a: 37). Too great an openness to reality, a spontaneous, uncritical engagement with the environment, leads, according to Pribram, to the fragmentation of existing plans of action and finally to the instability of the reference system and the discontinuity of psychic processes. This is apparently associated with adjustment difficulties that Pribram does not describe. His prescription for the good life is to hold the middle ground between these two extremes.

Pribram makes it clear that in this kind of theory emotions are positive only if associated with reproducing a state of adaptedness to concrete environmental conditions, and negative when adaptation fails. The neglect of subjectivity, that is, the concrete meaning of objective environmental conditions for the individual, is expressed by the fact that it is not the goals and their subjective meaning that are taken to be at issue, but the plans alone. The means of responding to unquestioned demands and the interruption of plans are treated only as momentary disturbances in adjustment, not as frustrations of particular substantive ideas and needs. Along with the problem of goals, the objective causes of the obstacles to goal attainment are also neglected in the discussion. What is left is a contentless individual oriented to mere adjustment, who feels secure when adjustment is successful – and aspires to nothing more than this – and resorts to panic when it fails to achieve the lofty goal of adjustment to the given conditions of life.

Epstein (1972) goes one step further toward absolutizing emotions in opposition to cognition and action. Epstein, too, following the theories of orientation and habituation, assumes that the individual needs to formulate a consistent and predictable model out of the data of the external world, and that an increase in physiological arousal occurs when this system or its elements do not meet expectations or contradict one another. By this theory, anxiety then arises when this "arousal" cannot be redirected into appropriate actions.

General arousal, cognitive incongruence, and a lack of possibilities for action that can reduce arousal are, according to Epstein's interpretation, essential elements in anxiety that express themselves in subjective experience as feelings of being overwhelmed and overstimulated, of disorientation, disorganization, and helplessness. Epstein's remarks on this are contradictory. From the fact that physiological activation, in contrast to anxiety, can be evoked by all internal and external stimuli and not only by danger or the unexpected, he infers the higher significance of physiological arousal as opposed to the concrete, anxiety-eliciting threat (pp. 308–309).

The emotions are, then, viewed by him not as the assessment of environmental circumstances, which is accompanied by particular physiological arousal. Stimulus and emotional reaction are alike presented as causes of physiological arousal, and strong physiological arousal is described as the actual evil. The reduction of physiological arousal is therefore defined as the essential task of psychologists or therapists, and the question of the origin and functional significance of this arousal is totally ignored. Thus Epstein claims that too high an activation and its defense mechanisms are primarily responsible for behavioral disturbance, not anxiety and its defense mechanisms. The concrete threat from which the heightened activation or anxiety resulted gets lost in the analysis. In the discussion that follows, anxiety is reinterpreted as a defense mechanism against extreme physiological arousal, helping the organism avoid the conditions that produce the overly high activation, which, whatever the source, cannot be tolerated over an extended period of time. Since for Epstein the physiological arousal is the individual's obvious central problem, and since the solution to the problem, namely escape, arises from its aversiveness, it is not clear why he used the concept of anxiety at all.

Individual efforts to deal with physiological activation arising from the blocking of the original goal of activity, according to Epstein, fall into the following categories: (1) direct manifestations of increased activation, for example, restlessness and general tension; (2) behavioral and perceptual disturbances conditioned by the overarousal, for example, fixation, disorganization, regression; (3) channeling of arousal into unblocked actions, for example, aggression, escape, substitute activities; and (4) attempts to reduce arousal through avoidance, denial, and reinterpretation of the situation, for example, general apathy, regression, defense mechanisms.

According to Epstein, the intolerability of increased physiological activation also accounts for people's intense need to find explanations for threatening situations and to preserve possibilities of action for themselves, however unclear and ineffective these may be. This explains everyday phenomena like superstition, magical practices, religion, compulsive acts, and even individual gullibility.

Epstein thus comes summarily to the conclusion that the principle motivation for individuals to structure their world and find responses to it is anxiety. Small doses of anxiety have the constructive effect of extending perception and increasing "control over nature," while overly high levels of anxiety lead to defensive restrictions, including violent reinterpretations of events and compulsive rituals – as if "any explanation is better than none" or "any action is better than none" (p. 314).

As in the previously described "cognitive" theories, two points are conspicuous in Epstein's conception: First, the theory is obviously contradictory and unclear as a result of the exclusion of objective living conditions, in terms of which alone individual subjective action can be coherently explained, and, second, it results in a picture of the individual under conditions of disorientation stemming from a lack of clear goals and possibilities for effective action constantly searching for an orientation, a subjective hold on things. Individuals appear in these theories (and are experimentally "produced" by them) not in the conscious assertion of their own needs and interests as a basis for seizing possibilities for active influence over relevant conditions, but rather as adjusting to existing expectations, aligning their needs accordingly. And insofar as such adjustment represents the highest maxim, knowledge is not only useless, but can actually be dangerous since it may give rise to doubts about the correctness and durability of the received orientation. These, in turn, result in a general insecurity, which is just what it is presumed we need to escape from.

In the theory of Schachter and co-workers (for example Schachter & Singer, 1962; Nisbett and Schachter, 1966; Schachter, 1966) the state of physiological arousal and its belated interpretation with appropriate reference to the environment, as already discussed by others in connection with the state of disorientation, provides a universal model of human behavior. Schachter assumes that the emotional experience is always determined by both physiological reaction and cognition but understands this relationship in a special way: Mere physiological arousal is not experienced as emotion, but implies a strong need for substantiation and definition of the general arousal, and the most threatening environmental circumstances can be without effect if the physiological activation is reduced, as with a tranquilizer. According to Schachter's theory, an assessment of circumstances and mode of action are not indicated by the physiological arousal. Rather, the physiological arousal is by itself without content, though disquieting. The disquiet is abated only when the physiological arousal can be interpreted by the use of corresponding cognitive cues that may then lead to an appropriate adjustment to the situation.

To test this theory, Schachter and his co-workers carried out a series of very interesting investigations. For example, Schachter and Singer (1962) injected their subjects with epinephrine. The subjects then defined their increasing activation as anger or euphoria, depending upon the concrete environmental circumstances. Schachter (1966) took this as proof of the relative indeterminateness or contingent nature of emotions and "openness" of physiological arousal. In further experiments (Nisbett & Schachter, 1966) subjects were given a placebo, and half were told that as a side effect of the injection they should expect a general physiological arousal, trembling, sweaty hands, and so forth, whereas the other half were given no information at all. In the actual experimental situation both groups were given electric shocks. The subjects who could attribute the resulting increase in arousal to the injection generally felt the shock as less painful and were ready to tolerate stronger currents than the subjects who had no other explanation for their physiological arousal and thus attributed it directly to the shocks. The interpretation of the events therefore has, as Lazarus (for example, 1966), too, was able to show in earlier experiments that we have not described here, an immediate effect upon the intensity of the experience.

Schachter's theory of emotion goes beyond earlier cognitive approaches by eliminating the conflict between the actual directedness of concrete action and the assumption of universal nondirectedness of physiological arousal, thus avoiding the problems that stem from assuming, on the one hand, that the autonomy and lack of direction of emotional arousal are an expression of disorientation or misdirection of action, and then, however, ignoring the concrete, objective causes for this. In Schachter's theory the emotions lose all of their compelling character for the individual. They serve adjustment to whatever environmental conditions that happen to be present, become the mere rationalization of inner arousal and are readily channeled into by environmental information. Manipulability in situations of disorientation and general insecurity, already discussed in our criticism of earlier theories, here becomes absolutely limitless and treated as a species-specific human characteristic. These "exaggerations" of Schachter's theory led Lazarus and Averill (1972) to criticize it for not going far enough and failing to solve the central problem of how physiological activation arises in the first place. The confirmation of the theory in Schachter's results can be accounted for by the fact that activation was artificially induced, thus leaving the environmental conditions as the only possible basis for interpretation. Under normal conditions arousal is less likely to precede the emotional assessment than it is to be part, or a consequence, of it. It is sometimes possible that the conditions of arousal may be reinterpreted or attributed to relatively accidental or false causes, but that is not the usual course of emotion. Emotion is not just the indication of a reaction, but the reaction itself, formed by the subject's judgment of the significance of the environmental circumstances. The primary thing for Lazarus is the assessment of the environmental circumstances by the organism, which, again, may lead to physiological arousal. Under certain – personal or situational – conditions the original arousal can be reinterpreted and steered in other directions. Lazarus argues that Schachter's theory raises this exception to the general case. An approach, however, that emphasizes the description of the existing situation and fails to explain its coming into being necessarily bridles the horse from behind. Lazarus has identified essential weaknesses in Schachter's theory. He does not appear to have recognized, however, that these weaknesses are only an extreme expression of the theoretical isolation of emotionality from the action of individuals in concrete life situations, which is also characteristic of Lazarus's theory.

Similar reasoning is found in many other psychological theories that have to do with therapy, such as the work of Beech and Liddell (1974), in which a general disposition for conditions of pathological arousal coupled with a belated interpretation of such arousal is viewed as an essential cause of mental disturbances. It is assumed that the interpretation is dependent on coincidentally available information but usually attaches itself to the factors eliciting the reaction. The mental disturbance, according to such a theory, only becomes the object of "therapeutic" activity when it has developed and become so independent that it undermines the action potence of the individual even in the available frame of adjustment. Therapeutic interruption of this negative circle, then, will usually be assessed as successful by the affected individual who, for the sake of maintaining existence, must be interested in the recovery of his acceptability or usefulness. Therapeutic success here is the individual's return to an "average degree of mental disturbance," which, since no fundamental change of the individual–environmental relationship is brought about, can always go back to a "conspicuous" degree of disturbance.

In these theories the physiological arousal is understood not as a reaction of the individual to particular *environmental circumstances,* but rather as a cause of behavior, which in the final analysis means that certain behavioral patterns of the individual are in turn explained by other individual behavior patterns, that is, circularly. It is not seen that physiological processes – as reflections of particular individual – environment relationships – are the primary causes of behavioral disturbances, nor that they develop a relative autonomy only under very particular circumstances, leading to loss of control by and overtaxing of the individual.

How the analysis of physiological processes contributes to the clarification of specific behavior patterns is convincingly demonstrated by Holland's work (1974), following a suggestion made by Delius (1970), on the origin of the compulsion neurosis. Delius began with the well-known connection between physiological arousal and the occurrence of substitute actions (see, for example, Bindra, 1959) and the observation that substitute actions often involve behavior patterns that normally occur under conditions of inactivity or sleep, which itself can be a substitute action. He adopts the hypothesis of Chance (1962), that substitute actions have the function of reducing physiological overarousal. He refers to the findings of Dell, Bonvallet, and Hugelin (1961), according to which strong physiological arousal leads to activation of the sleep system, through which, as Delius (1970) notes, there results a general reduction in attention span and an increased prominence of the skin senses and olfactory system. With overloading of environmental information, that is, in situations of excessive physiological excitation, according to Delius, the sleep system can be activated, resulting in a sudden reversal into a general deactivation or sleepiness, or to activities closely associated with it.

Especially frequent are substitute activities, such as attending to the skin, that occur in reduced orientation to the environment and reflect a heightened sensitivity of the skin receptors. Skin-caring activities that are evoked by the activation of the sleep system (cf. Roitbak, 1960; Pompeiano, 1965) tend themselves to evoke sleep – probably by way of the relatively systematic, monotone stimulation of the skin senses. Using these considerations of Delius's, Holland tries to explain the compulsive washing behavior of the neurotic, which he attributes to the heightened sensitivity of the skin senses occurring in situations of overtaxation and which, lacking any better hypothesis, are usually interpreted as having to do with dirt or germs. Through association of conditions of filth with physiological arousal, these objects, situations, or events become signals of danger that for their part contribute to the overtaxation of the situation or evoke washing behavior directly.

A careful examination of physiological processes and their control by individuals is important, and the work of Delius and Holland is very informative, but they give no answers to questions about the conditions under which the information overload arises, to which the physiological arousal is a particular answer. And they do not tell us how informational defense and its consequences are initiated. Once again, Holland has nothing better to offer than the "lack of processing capacity," the causes of which are not further examined.

The Function of Traditional Psychological Concepts of Emotion in Strategies for Worker Satisfaction in the Workplace: N. R. F. Maier, Lewin, Maslow

Human emotionality is devalued by the fact that the only means toward individual mastery of life considered by cognitive emotion theories are the *attitudes* of the individual toward existing conditions, the *anticipation* of particular events, and so forth, but not the active *alteration* of the objective relations of existence.

Whereas an adequate theoretical reconstruction of the connection between cognition, emotions, and action requires that we take negative emotional subjective states seriously as expressions of the unsatisfactoriness of objective living conditions, and emotionality must therefore be seen as serving as a subjective guide for the improvement of environmental relations, the cognitive emotion theories that we have described analyze life activity as if the relevant circumstances were immutable, which amounts to an assumption of subordination to existing power structures. This means that emotionality, since it is not understood as the subjective reflection of the necessity to improve human circumstances, is effectively deprived of function, appearing only as a disturbing excess to be alleviated when possible.

But excluding the possibility of individuals to influence the conditions relevant to their lives *effectively negates their subjectivity*. Individuals become *objects of alien interests*. Only insofar as individuals have not completely given up their developmental entitlement to determination of relevant life conditions, only insofar as they have undertaken to resist the prevailing developmental limitations and not simply adjust their emotional impulses in accordance with them, insofar as they have revolted against those limitations in some kind of diffuse, emotional way in preparation for conscious action against a *disturbing environment*, only then do they become interesting for this kind of psychology, though only as *objects* of activities directed at alleviating the disturbance. Since the emotional "revolt" of individuals against a diffuse, negatively assessed life situation becomes stronger when possibilities for improvement are at least sensed, the ruling powers and their scientific helpers become more intensively interested in the emotionality of those affected by their actions as the danger increases that the revolt thus expressed threatens to erupt into actions. And the more far-reaching the consequences of such an eruption would be, the greater it would be in its expressive force and the less easily suppressed.

These implications of cognitive theories of emotion may appear to be exaggerated since they seem only to be concerned with basic scientific *theoretical* conceptions that therefore should be criticized only on a theoretical level. But justification for the emphasis on these implications can be found, in my opinion, in an analysis of the *societal application* of these theories, especially in the central realm of *production*. It is here that the one-sidedness that seems merely theoretical, that is, the exclusion of emotionality from the connection between cognition and action and the restriction of attention to the disturbance function of emotions, takes on the *normative dimension of a psychological strategy for the management of conflicts with workers in the interest of capital.* According to this strategy, which of course is not openly declared, the actions of management or of psychologists in the service of management must remove emotions from their function of mediating between cognitions and actions and limit themselves to the possibilities of processing emotional arousal within the realm of the psychic, so that the preparedness and action potence of the workers in pursuit of their own interests in opposition to capital can be undermined. In this way the supposed merely "theoretical" consequence of the depreciation of human emotionality and formation of the subject as an object of alien interests suddenly takes on the material force of a psychological assistance in assuring the subjection of workers to the conditions of work and life dictated by the power of capital. I will illustrate these points from the ideas and practice of N. R. F. Maier, a well-known American psychologist.

According to Maier (1965), people who are not functioning properly should be approached in much the same problem-solving manner as poorly functioning machines. Even with the "human factor" in production the cause of the disturbance must be identified and eliminated. To accomplish this in the human, as well as in the machine, says Maier, it is necessary to understand the mechanisms by which the disturbance is caused (p. 36). With humans it is a fundamental assumption that the disturbance is conditioned either by the situation (S) or by the organism (O). Where one begins in the elimination of the disturbance is, however, a question of costs. If, for example, the disturbance is found to occur among 5 percent of the workers, then it is more rational to begin treatment with the "organism." But when, for example, 90 percent of the workers are affected, it is better to alter the situation (pp. 33ff.).

Owing to the central opposition between the interests of management and workers, which is based in the irreconcilability of the aims of management to attain greater profits and the aims of the workers to gain higher wages, better working conditions, more vacation, and so forth, conflicts and disturbances necessarily arise if preventative measures, particularly under the guidance of psychologists, are not taken.

An essential prerequisite for the resolution of conflicts, according to Maier, is a recognition of the fact that the conflict is rooted in the different standpoints of labor and capital and that therefore questions of right and wrong do not arise. "In order to preserve the economic system which permits development of such opposed interests," Maier explains, each party must recognize the specific point of view of the other and must accept, on the basis of general tolerance, the behavior expressing the respective differing interests, and thus get along with each other (p. 39).

From this, Maier derives a general strategy for the avoidance of conflict, which, for capital, has two sides. The representatives of capital must become conscious of the fundamental opposition of interests between labor and capital and thus develop an "understanding" for the situation of workers, who are not mere elements of production, but subject to frustration (that is, display "psychic," especially emotional reactions), in order to be prepared for and to check possible aggressive reactions.

Among workers, on the other hand, the idea of the common interest of capital and labor is to be encouraged, which amounts to asserting the dependence of the workers for their well-being on "their workplace." Since management has the broader view and thus knows better what is good for industry, including the workers, the latter should leave matters confidently in the hands of the managers and not, by making extravagant demands, provoke conflict that could, in the final analysis, work harm for all. The production of a feeling of community, of a "harmonious atmosphere" of tolerance and freedom (p. 137) – against the background of fundamental dependence – is, according to Maier, the central precondition for workers' accepting and carrying out the requirements that are made of them. An effective method of securing this feeling of community or for production of an identification with the workplace is, according to Maier, to create the idea of the possibility for influence through codetermination in minor questions.

From this explanatory framework follow Maier's ideas about the "emotionality" of workers and how to deal with it. For Maier emotionality is opposed to reason, that is, to the recognition of the existing relations of power and the aspiration for arrangements on this basis. According to Maier, it is in "emotional reactions" that aggression brought about by frustration is directed unilaterally at the managers or at the economic system they represent. Emotional arousal is thus, as such, by Maier's understanding of reason, unreasonable and irrational.

According to Maier's views it would be a cardinal error to bring the "emotional" workers into any discussion about the causes of their arousal. This would violate the principle that there can be no right or wrong in conflicts between labor and capital and would only worsen the conflict. Instead, Maier recommends that provocation be avoided, discussions sidestepped, and aggressors allowed to "run themselves out" as long as they don't question decisions, existing relations, and the interests that stand behind them. Discussion is in order only when the opponent has "cooled off" or "come to his senses," that is, is reconciled to the reality of differing interests and existing relations of power and on this basis is seeking a "rational" resolution to the conflict, meaning that he is ready to adjust his attitude instead of demanding changes in the basic position of the other side or the actual conditions (p. 108).

In his explication of such conflict avoidance strategies, Maier speaks, as does Volkelt, of the need to consider the "logic of the emotions" (pp. 60ff.). But by this he means just the opposite, namely not emotion as a guide and first step toward knowing, but rather a certain operation of emotionality in the *obstruction* of the knowing process.

The avoidance of discussion, the appeal to so-called common interests, and the warnings about the threat of conflict, are supposed to obviate the dangers that stem from learning and its resulting self-confidence; that is, the knowledge of the individual's situation is to be obscured and emotional engagement and readiness for action are to be weakened.

The "understanding" for the situation of the workers and (as Maier expresses it) the "regard for emotion as a fact" (pp. 179ff.) do not come out of any immediate interest in the subjectivity of the other, but are simply means for recognizing and controlling the dangerous resisting tendencies of the workers, and the emphasis upon the commonality of interests is only a method for the better use of "human resources."

Thus a state of affairs is revealed in which subjectivity, the "human factor," is itself exploited for the purpose of making people into objects and then subordinating them to alien interests.

Maier sees it as an essential task of the psychologist as an advocate of "understanding" the worker from the side of capital to facilitate the latter's passage from emotionality to "reason" through the application of well-aimed measures. The principle behind these measures is to provide free expression for emotion in the absence of the actual opponent and thus without conflict, that is, without bringing it to the point of concrete demands or actions and without the experience of a massive counterreaction and the irreconcilability of interests that that would reveal, and, by means of an effectless elimination of emotional reactions, to bring about a subjective relief or emotional "tranquility'' and, as a long-term consequence of the experienced ''tolerance'' and ''understanding,'' a positively altered attitude toward objectively unchanged living conditions and power relationships. An essential role in this connection, according to Maier, is played by the ''counselor,'' a professional psychological ''adviser,'' with whom workers can express and vent their emotional arousal – in total confidence – through aggressive verbalizations against their supervisors and thus in safe and inconsequential ways be brought to ''reason,'' that is, to appropriate behavior (p. 113). For the same purpose, Maier recommends the introduction of a punching bag on which the workers can vent their aggressive feelings. He says that he has observed how, after a session with the bag, people return ''quietly and satisfied'' to work (p. 110).

If the *theoretical* isolation of negatively defined emotions from cognition and action in fact conceals within it the suppression of a *real* connection between emotion and the actions resisting the interests of capital that arise out of the ''evaluational'' knowledge contained in the emotions, then one can see in the practical application of bourgeois conceptions of emotion a certain *negative confirmation* of our interpretation of emotions as instances of mediation between cognition and action. If emotions were in fact only free-floating subjective phenomena and did *not* constitute assessments of cognition as a precondition for action, then it would not be necessary, following Maier, to reject taking cognizance of the causes of emotional reactions or to steer the resulting impulses to action into ''safe'' courses. In a certain respect the Freudian theory of repression, according to which instinctual energy can be separated from the instinctual idea and become available (through sublimation or symptom formation) to other ideas, finds here a consciously manipulative application: The repression processes are more or less directly forced or directed into the ''measures'' described by Maier; impulses to action that are critical or directed against existing relations of authority are ignored or diverted onto substitute objects, and discussion is resumed only when the existing authority structures are recognized and the causes of the impulses to action are completely repressed, that is, when there is emotional tranquility.

The crude procapital partisanship of the psychologist in the workplace seen in Maier's writing appears to contradict the seemingly ''neutral'' formulations of the cognitive theories of emotion described earlier. It should have become clear, however, that with respect to the nature and function of human emotionality both positions are based on the same premises of the immutability of relevant life conditions and abandonment of the individual to authority. The ''partisanship'' is therefore not based on the judgment of the psychologist, but is rooted in the basic theoretical conceptions themselves. Identification with the standpoint of authority, which is part and parcel of this kind of psychological theory and reflects its societal function, is sometimes concealed by what claims to be a basic scientific, neutral stance, but in others the connections to the class struggle in production are very clear.

Oppositions like this between seemingly pure "scientific" neutrality and crude partisanship in favor of capital are also found in other important psychological theories, such as those of Kurt Lewin, a father of modern social psychology, and Abraham Maslow, the founder of "humanistic psychology." These will be dealt with briefly here (a more complete analysis of the ways in which Lewin and Maslow represented ruling authority in their "purely scientific" claims will appear in the volume, *Motivation III*, to be published).

Similar to Maier, though in somewhat different and more diffuse terminology, Lewin (1920) speaks of the fundamental, and thus in principle irreconcilable, opposition of interests between "production" and "consumption," or between "work consumers" and "output consumers." Work consumers are, by his definition, those who "consume" work, that is, essentially the producers, the workers in immediate production, whereas by "output" consumers he means consumers "in the ordinary economic sense of the word" (p. 12). "The interests of production and consumption are," Lewin explains, "doubtless opposed in many ways" (p. 15). There would be no problems, Lewin believes, if all unpleasant work could be transformed into work "of value to one's own life" (p. 15), if work were done not on the basis of economic compulsion, but out of an inner calling. "Since this, however, cannot be achieved at all, or only in an infinite process . . . , since for the present we must reckon with the existence of unpleasant work, on the one hand, and with idlers and professional hedonists, on the other," we are stuck with compromise solutions.

It would be, however, altogether "unreasonable to demand that . . . work improvements should be introduced without *any* consideration for production, that is, for the interests of the remaining members of the community, the 'consumers' in the ordinary sense of the word, who are here designated as output consumers in contract to work consumers. . . . On the other hand, whereas the work consumer must look after his own interests, the output consumer has to share in decisions about the economic deterioration of work for the purpose of increasing its consumption value, whether by direct representation or through the mediation of the state" (p. 21).

If one assumes it to be naturally given, as Lewin obviously does, that some take on or carry out the "production work" under, as he admits, hardship and coercion, while others benefit from the possibilities that have been thereby produced, then less exploitation of workers necessarily means the narrowing of the basis for existence for the beneficiaries of their work to the point even of threatening their very existence as beneficiaries. Thus Lewin, for example, speaks of the *danger* stemming from the "union of output consumer and work consumer in the same person" (p. 21), which, in plain English, can mean nothing other than the "danger" that those who produce the social wealth will also have control over this wealth or, conversely, that the "idlers and professional hedonists" will be deprived of their economic security. For Lewin, it is therefore right and just, that is to say, "fair" and "democratic," if the people thus threatened have a voice in the extent to which the exploitation of the others, who are the very foundation and precondition for their own life possibilities, might be transformed so that those others will have to sacrifice less sweat and fewer years of life creating the very things they enjoy. This consideration for the "work consumers" is all the easier, Lewin assures us, because it follows from the necessity of securing one's own existence, since the "reckless exploitation of the individual in the service of production with the consequence of more rapid aging, requiring the highest possible output as the average output of work, whipping workers to more intensive exertion with all available means, degradation of work through extreme division of labor without consideration for the spirit of the workers, in short, the "use" of the worker in the service of production according to depreciation and amortization schedules that apply to machines . . . should not be done even from a human economic point of view" (p. 17) and can only hurt production.

A further need for improving working conditions can be derived from the fact that it usually results in an increase in the productivity of work and is therefore an "essential factor of good business" (p. 18). Another reason is that there is "presently a strong current among workers" that increasingly emphasizes "the interests of work and occupational consumption as opposed to those of production" (p. 24) and cannot easily be ignored.

Although not explicitly concerned with emotion theory, these conceptions of Lewin express the same understanding of the nature and function of emotional concern for workers that we found in Maier. Here, too, the "understanding" for the worker is seen in the context of the constellation of forces, and emotional concern is seen as necessary when rebellion or resistance threatens. We are dealing only with a variant of the general bourgeois psychological tendency to make subjectivity over into an object. Even Maslow, the founder of "humanistic psychology," emphasizes the need of management to develop an "understanding" for the situation of the workers in order not to provoke them irresponsibly into unwanted, even organized, opposition. This understanding is easily obtained by imagining oneself spending the rest of one's life in the position of the worker.

If the "managers" and "bosses" would only realize that, in the situation of "slavery," "anonymity," and "expendability" that he thinks forms the fate of the workers, they would behave themselves even more like "vandals" and "rebels" than do the workers who have become used to such an existence and are only partially rebelling against it, then they would "almost automatically" have understanding and sympathy for the emotional reactions of the workers. What's more, this understanding would cost little or nothing yet could lead to essential improvement in the industrial situation (Maslow, 1972: 47–48). Empathy for the situation of the workers, as Maslow understands it, does not have the goal of improving their objective situation; rather, it serves to prevent improvements, that is, to recognize the danger of the revolt in order to nip it in the bud. An essential way of preventing workers from rebelling against what Maslow vividly describes as slavery, anonymity, and expendability and from forcing an improvement in their living conditions is to acknowledge the "dignity" and "self-esteem" of the workers in their "unfortunate" situation, that is, to retain them in their inhuman situation by the use of humane treatment and thus not provoke them by incautious behavior to emotional outbreaks that can no longer be controlled (p. 48).

But to prevent any misunderstanding of his "empathic" description of the workers' situation, Maslow emphasizes that "understanding" of management for subordinates is possible only if its own supremacy is acknowledged, which for Maslow is usually based on and justified by – at least in the United States and the "free world" – a natural superiority (pp. 103ff.). If the power based on this natural superiority is doubted, then the relationship must be clarified by firm action, such as authoritarian management or "cracking the whip over fearful people." "Authoritarian characters," confronted with the principles of humane management, would, Maslow believes, consider the managers to be "weak in the head," or at least sentimental and unrealistic. An authoritarian person "has to be broken a little" before he comes to appreciate friendliness and generosity or to take orders (p. 34).

In another place he makes the following recommendations regarding "authoritarian" persons: "The correct thing to do with authoritarians is to take them realistically for the bastards they are and then behave toward them as if they were bastards. That is the only realistic way to treat bastards" (p. 72). In order to make clear what he means here, Maslow draws upon his university experience, which has taught him that the best way in which to handle "authoritarian" students is "break their backs immediately," "to make them jump," that is, to set one's own authority against them, "to clout them on the head in some way that would show very clearly who is boss in the situation." When this is clear, "then and only then could [he] become slowly an American and teach them that it is possible for a boss, a strong man, a man with a fist, to be kind, gentle, permissive, trusting, and so on" (p. 72). In short, the people whom Maslow designates as authoritarian are those who demand authoritarian treatment, that is, the firm action of the true, naturally superior authority. They do this by rebelling – in misjudgment of their own position in life or subjective limits – against and disputing existing authority, that is, genuine authorities like Maslow.

The contradiction between empathy for subordinates and the oppressed and the objective identification with the oppressor is resolved by Maslow by interpreting the subordination as a regrettable fact of nature. "The fact . . . that great superiority is unjust, undeserved, and that people can and do resent it and complain of injustice and unfairness is of course," as the humanist Maslow concludes, "an extremely difficult problem, a profoundly human and existential problem" for which there is no solution, "because the fact is that fate *is* unfair . . . " (p. 149).

Meanwhile, Maslow cannot allow the acknowledgment that fate is "unfair" to stand because by doing so he would have to concede the "naturally given" existence of conflicts and tensions. Fate, he continues, assures that each person is destined for a particular occupation through which he can find complete self-actualization, and fate assumes responsibility for the fact that its "call" reflects precisely the radical inequalities in developmental and life possibilities associated with existing class relations.

Developing this idea further, Maslow says that "each task would 'call for' just that one person in the world most uniquely suited to deal with it, like a key and a lock, and that one person would then feel the call most strongly and would reverberate to it, be tuned to its wave length, and so be responsive to its call. There is an interaction, a mutual suitability, like a good marriage or like a good friendship, like being designed for each other" (p. 10).

But if someone denies this unique responsibility, does not follow his fate, or cannot hear its call, then intrinsic guilt feelings arise, feelings of "unsuitability," "like a dog trying to walk on his hind legs, or a poet trying to be a good businessman, or a businessman trying to be a good poet. . . . It just doesn't fit; it doesn't suit; it doesn't belong. One must respond to one's fate or one's destiny or pay a heavy price. One must yield to it; one must surrender to it. One must permit one's self to be chosen" (p. 10).

But if everyone would recognize his own specific abilities and inclinations, would be sensitive to his calling and find the occupation that matched it, if for every task there would be only volunteers, then, in Maslow's opinion, a "feeling of brotherhood and colleague-hood" would bind all people together, and, with everybody knowing that all belong to the "same army," the "same club," or the "same team," and depend on the contribution of others, mutual regard and gratitude would emerge.

Maslow reminds us that we owe special recognition and gratitude to those whose developmental limitations and exploitation make possible our own privileges. This gratitude has the function of keeping these people subjectively tied to their generalized subjection. "That means," Maslow explains:

. . . in principle, that if there aren't enough "mesomorphs" [people with a sturdy body build], then the "ectomorphs" [people with slightly built bodies] like me would have to do the work of the "mesomorphs." But since I am an "ectomorph," I can't do the jobs of "mesomorphs" very well and I wouldn't like them anyway. They would be a miserable duty for me, although a great pleasure for the constitutional mesomorph. Therefore, if I have any sense, I should be very happy about the fact that there are mesomorphs in the world, and I should be very grateful to them for being constitutionally equipped so as to desire to do the jobs that I don't like doing, but which must absolutely be done. If I correctly appreciate this, then I will love the mesomorphs according to the same principle as men and women who understand themselves as mutually completing one another, who are able to love the other sex instead of being antagonistic. . . . Thus the lawyers should be grateful that there are doctors in the world and the doctors should be grateful that there are machinists in the world, etc., etc. If all this goes deep enough, we come to the point even of being grateful for the morons in the world, people who are willing to do the garbage collecting, the dirty work, the repetitive work, etc., the work that must absolutely be done but that we would hate to do. (pp. 255ff.)

Before this ideal situation of mutual dependence and love can become reality, Maslow believes, the concepts of rivalry and competition would have to be redefined against a background of "colleague-hood." The improvement of the conditions of life is not sought in an active alteration of those conditions but rather in their reinterpretation, that is, a change of attitude. The central precondition for such an attitude change, however, is the acceptance of the existing relations of authority as the natural order and the lack of one's own development as a naturally given limitation. The acknowledgment of the existing power structure is all the easier for those disadvantaged by fate as it becomes clearer to them, on the one hand, what their assigned position is, that is, the more thoroughly they are purged of expectations that exceed the position that suits them, and, on the other, the more humanely and kindly they are treated in their "unfortunate" situation. Of course, this humanity and warmth is more easily generated by master-types like Maslow as they become conscious of the dependence of their own life-style on the concrete existence of the others, the "lower-class people," and become less ambiguous in the acceptance of their "equality of rights."

Whereas it is only implicit in most other theories, Maslow makes it particularly clear that the function of "emotionality," "love," "respect," "humanity," and so forth, is to sweeten existing relations of dependency and limitations to development and to cover up the underlying violence. On the one hand, feelings are opposed to reason insofar as they refer to existing developmental obstructions; on the other hand, they *replace rational arguments* when it comes to defending prevailing relations or the power of authority. Therefore, the claim that decisions made under the guise of loving one's neighbor are in the interests of those not taking part in the decisions must satisfy the latter in order for them to submit themselves to the resulting actions without critique or reservation, and we can expect "understanding," "respect," and the consequences thereof only if there is this "trust" in principle, that is, only if all experiences that contradict this "trust" and all the resisting tendencies to which they might lead are suppressed.

The contradiction in presumably best serving one's own interests by negating them, even when not clearly conceptualized, is still experienced. The immediate experience of violating this trust "in one's own interest," that is, giving in to prevailing conditions under the pressure of immediate need, thus affirming one's own lack of development and giving up further prospects, is an essential precondition for individual disorientation and confusion, which can develop under certain circumstances into overt disturbance that is then reflected in bourgeois emotion theories as the "generalized human" characteristic of emotionality, a prerequisite for mental disorder. I shall return to this topic in the next chapter.

7 Action Potence, Education, and Psychotherapy

Ute Holzkamp-Osterkamp

Theoretical absolutization of the situation for people whose relevant living conditions seem unalterable, leaving only psychological modes of adjustment, must surely occur in other areas of practical psychological application. This is certainly the case in education, which, in the ruling interests, must also serve to reproduce the attitudes that make it possible for adults to accept or at least tolerate their alienated existence in production. I shall present some ideas of Kurt Lewin's as an example.

Isolating the Subjective Situation from Its Objective Causes as an Educational Strategy of Conflict Avoidance for the Preparation of Children for Self-Management Within Dependence: Lewin

The basic concept of Lewin's famous "field theory" is *"life space,"* that is, the world that is for any particular person psychically real and effective. It is distinguished from the objective world, which is regarded as psychologically irrelevant. Lewin developed a complicated, partly mathematized model of forces, vectors, attractions, zones, mental limits and barriers, psychic locomotions, and so forth, within the life space, from which particular constellations of motives, attitudes, and behaviors of the individual and their changes were supposed to be derivable. The idea that the individual's relevant life conditions are unalterable is thus implicit in the theory. Only the psychic movement of an individual within a given life space is taken into account, not the individual's influence on it. The objective relations that determine the life space are excluded from the concern of psychology from the outset, so their alteration cannot be understood as a psychological problem at all. This was formulated by Lewin as the distinction between "quasi-physical," "quasi-social," and "quasi-conceptual" facts as psychically effective elements in life space and the objective physical, social, and conceptual facts, which are irrelevant for psychology (cf. Lewin, 1936/1969).

134

Among the various applications of the Lewinian life space model there are detailed explanations of techniques for raising children. I refer here in particular to the recommendations stemming from the *function of punishment as a means of training*, as described in his essay on "the psychological situation in reward and punishment" (1931). Lewin expressly addresses the question of how a behavior that does not correspond to the child's actual interests can be trained, one that, as he puts it, does not contain a "natural teleology." Lewin explains that reward is normally to be preferred over punishment for directing child behavior because with punishment there are several risks for the trainer. An essential disadvantage of punishment is, in his opinion, that it creates a situation in which "child and adult are hostilely opposed"; that is, "the situation achieves for the child the character of a 'situation of struggle' and . . . in struggle the child will use means naturally and spontaneously that it would perhaps not use in an atmosphere in which it was not confronted by an adversary" (pp. 35ff.). A further risk of punishment is that the child "comes to know the actual degree of unpleasantness of each form of punishment" (p. 29). The child then weighs the "actual unpleasantness of the task against the punishment . . . and becomes, as one says, 'hard-boiled' with respect to the punishment and thus less sensitive to the threat of punishment" (p. 29).

But a more important consequence of punishment, according to Lewin, is a "revolutionizing of ideology," a "reassessment of values" by the child. The adult usually presents punishment as something "morally" disparaging, in which the "fear of punishment," that is, fear of – where possible, public – moral incrimination of the child, is the main educating element. But if by being punished children lose their timidity with respect to the whole area of punishment, if they begin their reassessment, the morally disparaging in punishment may disappear. "Behind the threat would then stand only the special unpleasantness of a particular punishment, and no longer the fear of the whole realm of punishment. The child 'no longer cares' about being punished" (p. 30). It could happen that the task would be seen as so aversive that the child would prefer the punishment, see the punishment as the "lesser evil" or even as something positive, and could try taking the punishment as a "way out," thus putting the authority of the adult into question (p. 31).

The Lewinian view that the fear of punishment can in certain circumstances be more effective than punishment itself has been confirmed in numerous investigations and observations (for example, Aronfreed, 1968; Seligman, 1975). In this connection the finding of Beech and Liddell (1974) that compulsive neurotics were seldom or never punished during childhood or in school is interesting. The authors offer the explanation that compulsive neurotics obviously feared punishment so much that they did anything to avoid the experience, which got them into the vicious circle of decreasing contact with reality that led to the neurosis. Evidence for this thesis is also provided by many observations on conflict avoidance, not only of compulsives, but of all psychically disturbed persons (see below).

It will have become clear even in Lewin's theory that leaving the active alteration of one's own life conditions out of the account and isolating the subjective situation from objective relations, when translated into practice, become advice for *producing* an appropriate life circumstance; the child *shall not* be given any chance to test its resources in open dispute with adults or to learn about possibilities of acting on its own, thus questioning the authority of adults, and the child *shall not* be given experience regarding the objective composition of punishment *so that* its capability to be manipulated by the threat of punishment will not be destroyed and the controlling influence will not be lost through a questioning of authority. The threat of punishment as an existential threat of exclusion from the community of adults, which is effective only as long as the individual is dependent, leads, then, to a *blockage* of thought and action for the sake of avoiding realistic experiences of the superability of existing dependency relations and the discovery of alternative life possibilities in order avoid disagreement with the authorities and at the same time maintain inner "stability" under existing conditions.

The lack of real experience that comes from the fear of the risks and real conflicts associated with development, along with the resulting generalized insecurity, keeps the individual in a dependent state. This is the subjective precondition for the generalized acknowledgment of authority; it is necessary for the general renunciation of the right to check existing life circumstances for their necessity and justness, for giving up the possibility of changing things through active dispute, and for discouraging the introduction of undistorted individual claims on life. Along with, or in connection with, a limitation of general action potence, it leads to strong feelings of inferiority and aggression toward oneself and the environment, to the capriciousness with which aggression occurs, and then, however, in order to avoid confrontation, is usually retracted, that is, internalized or only indirectly expressed, as in the form of a camouflaged refusal to produce that is then interpreted as a general inability to produce, thus leading to further insecurity and dependence.

From the similarity between the child-raising strategies presented by Lewin and those described for avoiding conflict in the workplace, both of which are based on the same theoretical premises about human subjectivity, it can be concluded that in education just those attitudes are to be acquired that lead to the acceptance of alienated existence in adulthood. Or rather, these theories are the "scientific" versions of behaviors that more or less produce themselves under existing conditions of dependence and lack of influence on relevant life processes that exist for most adults under capitalist relations.

Educators' own dependence upon the subjection to the relations under which they have gained certain possibilities of existence and thus certain external and internal stability create an immediate need to defend existing relations, and this will be all the more the case, the less their influence upon the societal developmental process and the more alienated their individual action with respect to the maintenance of societal existence.

To the extent, however, that educators themselves are excluded from conscious influence on societal developmental processes, they can't give any new perspectives to their charges, nor can they make the process of education into something that can be tested against individual requirements. They can't make education into a task in which individuals can share responsibility. Rather, education becomes essentially filtered through the personal conceptions and needs of the parents, which are, again, expressions of the special problems of their societal existence.

To the degree, however, that they carry out the parental educational measures in a natural way, that is, oriented on their unmediated, unreflected, contradictory needs, every doubt about the justification of particular demands must end up as doubt about the authority itself of parents and thus is a danger to their carefully acquired stability. The educators themselves become unfree in their reactions and respond with corresponding arousal – fear or aggression – to their own insecurity through the children and thus burden them at a purely emotional, nonconceptual, nonverbal level (for example, see the investigations on "schizophrenia and the family" by Bateson et al., 1969). Thus the unresolved problems of the parents become directly the difficulties of the children, who are now faced with dealing with them without having a hope of resolving them. The emotions of the parents serve immediately, then, to orient the child and thus acquire their expression as "argument." In order to be able to adjust finely to the moods of adults, children must take these moods on through adroit behaviors and try to make them useful to their own purposes. The instrumentalization of children by adults thus has as the immediate consequence the children's instrumentalization of the adults. Empathy as an interest in others serves, then, one's own immediate behavioral orientation and actually implies a dulling of sensitivity for the subjective situation of the other, which is taken for granted and with respect to which one takes care to develop one's own adequate responses.

The sensitive empathy for the situation of the other – above all, of the more powerful – made useful for the purpose of enriching or securing one's own existence is a central precondition for opportunistic behavior, which under bourgeois conditions of life is regarded as normal. This involves the working out of mutual arrangements on the basis of unequivocal authority relationships and is ideologically expressed as the equality of rights of all people and mutual tolerance.

The organization of education essentially around the needs of the educators or the negation or active obstruction of the needs of the children always means, on the one hand, the unacceptability of their persons, and at the same time the devaluation of their emotionality as a subjective measure of the value of objective conditions of life. This implies a central insecurity in two ways: as a general self-doubt and an individual lack of goals or goal orientations. This impedes the active grappling with the environment that serves as a basis both for the development of action potence and for the raising of self-confidence. The subjection to existing conditions to which one is brought by the active obstruction of influence over relevant life conditions has the consequence of subjectively confirming the power of the others and causing the individual to internalize existing power relations. Tendencies to revolt against the limitations then become problematic for the individual, the connection between objective facts and subjective values begins to dissolve, and the individual loses confidence in the justification and accuracy of his or her feelings. The individual is therefore action impotent in practice, absolutely dependent on external guidance and stimulation, and correspondingly thankful for it.

The Human Image of Bourgeois Theories: Adjustment to Immutable Conditions as "Normal" and the Normality of Adjustment as Precursor to Mental Disturbance

The indifference of all versions of functionalist theory to the development and welfare of the subject is even more evident when we see that the adjustment of individuals to their unyielding circumstances and the relations of power that stand behind them, such as implicitly assumed or explicitly demanded by these theories, is actually an early form of mental disturbance. We shall now examine this a little more closely.

The lack of possibilities for influencing relevant life conditions and the general orientation of individual striving toward the securing of private existence by maintaining "good relations" with the prevailing powers and authorities are the objective and subjective preconditions for opportunistic behavior, that is, behavior directed at the securing of short-term individual advantage in the immediately given situation.

As a political category opportunism is especially characteristic of the petit bourgeois, standing as they do between the two great classes of wage labor and capital; alternatively, it is a form of consciousness corresponding to petit bourgeois existence. The situation of the petit bourgeois person, through which these specific life conditions are realized, is such that, as Engels writes, they "hope to swindle their way up into the big bourgeoisie" while they are "afraid of being pushed down into the proletariat. Hovering between fear and hope, they will save their precious skins during the struggle and join the victor when the struggle is over. Such is their nature" (Engels, 1870/1968a: 98).

"In a progressive society and from the pressure of their circumstances," writes Marx, "the petit bourgeois will at one time be a socialist, another time an economist, that is, he is blinded by the glory of the great bourgeois and has pity for the suffering of the masses. He is bourgeois and masses at the same time. Deep down in his conscience he flatters himself as being impartial. . . . Such a petit bourgeois idolizes contradiction because contradiction is the kernel of his being. He is himself merely the social contradiction in action. He must justify by his theory what he is in practice" (Marx, 1870/1968: 30–31).

The petit bourgeois, according to Marx, is "continually tossed back and forth between capital and labor, between political economy and communism" (Marx, 1968: 30). He is "made up of on-the-one-hand and on-the-other-hand. This is so in his economic interests and *therefore* in his politics, religious, scientific and artistic views. And likewise in his morals, IN EVERYTHING. He is a living contradiction. . . . Charlatanism in science and accommodation in politics are inseparable from such a point of view" (Marx, 1870/1968: 33).

Petit bourgeois consciousness is not limited to individuals in the economic situation of the actual petit bourgeois as "self-supporting"; it occurs in one form or another everywhere as a blind reproduction in consciousness of class position where individuals are, on the one hand, dependent upon the power of capital but, on the other, able to imagine themselves distanced from the interests of capital, as well as from those of the proletariat, because they enjoy a preferred, privileged, leading, seemingly public welfare–oriented position and seek their security and advantage through maneuvering between the classes. (I shall not elaborate further on this here.)

Political opportunism is dependent upon the level of development of the societal contradiction in connection with the power relations between the classes and the degree of organization as well as the militancy of the workers. A problem that should be distinguished, if not separated, is the question about the conditions under which each individual opportunistic attitude arises and what consequences they have for the individual experience of life. The essential subjective preconditions for or characteristics of such opportunistic behavior at the individual level are being punctual and prepared in advance for events so as not to be taken unawares by them, tossed off balance by them, but at the same time being relatively open, emotionally and otherwise, that is, unattached, distanced, "precisely observant, soberly calculating . . . , reacting with cleverness and tact" (Redeker, 1963), maneuvering between the various fronts and sides in order to be able to use every possibility offered to one's own advantage. The central maxims for the behavior of the "adjusted" individual must therefore be not to allow oneself to be unambiguously pinned down, to avoid taking positions or sides, to avoid or play down debates and conflicts, to make a virtue of the necessity of being pressed into the role of observer, that is, to derive a kind of detached superiority over differences of interest and opinion from having to relinquish rights to the active shaping of relevant life conditions and keeping out of all principled opposition to the ideas and objectives of others. This can then find fashionable expression in various forms of aloofness, such as tolerance, serenity, wisdom, cynicism, and so on, and since neutrality, that is, total lack of interest, is always a fiction, it must become problematic for the individual in whatever form of appearance it takes.

The attempt to arrive at an adaptation to existing relations of dependence without conflict, that is, within the limitations placed upon individual development by the interests of others, must necessarily fail, no matter how the relations stand with those who are in principle, in the same situation or even with those who hold the power and upon whom one is dependent. On the one hand, this is because the relative advantage of one necessarily implies the disadvantage of the other, and – from the power politics point of view – the "rise" of the advantaged leads to the weakening of those "left behind" and thus to a corresponding resistance among them. On the other hand, it is because the renunciation of influence on relevant life conditions, that is, the withdrawal from individual needs in order to avoid the conflict that would arise from acting upon them, means nothing other than being drawn into the examination of alien interests. The difference among the various forms of conflict existing under the conditions of capitalist society amounts to the fact that in the single instance the conflicts become an individual and private problem that is at the same time alien. In their efforts to improve the security of existence or standard of living, isolated and helpless individuals are drawn into the discussion of alien interests without knowing enough about them to adopt a conscious position and become engaged with their content. Sometimes, however, in place of the more or less blind involvement in alien conflicts of interest there occurs a conscious consideration of long-term security and development in accordance with one's own needs. This begins to make possible the solidarity with others with the same basic interests against those who have to keep others in a state of relative lack of development in order to maintain their functionality and usefulness. The short-term avoidance of decisions and the difficulties and conflicts associated with them and the always more or less clear knowledge that individual problems are essentially unsolvable can lead to a general inhibition of future-directed thinking and action, such that the immediate living for today, holding fast to that which exists, not only is the expression of external repression, but can become an individual need reflecting one's own impotence and helplessness.

This tendency to hold on to familiar things and to prefer the accustomed to any kind of change, as a general behavioral tendency in the situation of being abandoned to circumstances over which one has no control, can under conditions of existential anxiety or lack of social integration become fixed as a completely maladaptive behavior that manifests itself as a psychical disorder.

Trying to act "correctly" in accordance with the expectations of others while being insufficiently or contradictorily informed about these expectations but knowing more or less clearly that the situation is a delicate one leads, despite the objective limitations, to a general incapacity for decision, that is, to the tendency to act only when the outcome of the action is absolutely sure, and thus to a behavior pattern that, from the start, reduces the objective opportunities to gain more comprehensive experiences with the existing possibilities and limits of action within social relations and thus also to a reliable relationship to reality as a basis for individual action potence. The existing or offered orientational structures are then no longer accepted on the basis of objective or factual grounds, but rather for the purpose of individual stabilization. Psychical insecurity is thus a central precondition for the possibility of manipulating individual thought and action, thereby making the individual culpable in his or her own subjugation. This effort to avoid risks and the reaction to it become stronger, the more fragile the relations to the community are, the more the necessity of consolidating these relations becomes the central determinant in the thought and action of the individual.

The difference between adjusted, opportunistic – that is, normal – behavior, in which people, through skillful maneuvering, successfully realize and extend their own advantages within the framework of existing life conditions, thus retaining some action potence with respect to the surrounding world, and psychical disorder is essentially a question of its degree of conspicuousness. The causes of concrete psychical difficulties beyond the "normal," that is, that interfere with immediate action potence, are extraordinarily complex and varied and must be analyzed for each individual case. A central factor giving rise to manifest psychical disorder is always, however, the renunciation of actual life possibilities, that is, the refusal to extend action potence and clinging to immediate dependence out of anxiety over sanctions or disputes with those who wield power and upon whom one is dependent. Thus the subjective necessity of submitting to the expectations of others, the neglect of one's own interests and needs in the actions of others, and the general internal and external groundlessness of existence, indeed the very striving for security, emphasize the insecurity of one's own existence and lead to traumatic effects when it is discovered just how generally useless repression and the self-inflicted betrayal of one's own interests are. Such situations frequently result in psychical breakdowns when an individual who has been convinced of the correctness or appropriateness of behavior relative to the expectations of others and has been prepared for confirmation and approval unexpectedly experiences quite the opposite; The carpet seems to get pulled out from under, orientation to both to one's own interests and the expectations of others is lost, and action impotence is revealed. This pain of this kind of experience is directly proportional to the difficulty one finds in denying one's own interests and to the amount of "sacrifice" made to secure the benevolence of others.

Psychical disorders thus presuppose a heightened sensitivity to the contradictoriness of objective relations and one's own behavior and an individual impotence that prevents struggling against these relations in order to determine one's own behavior. They always include simultaneous revolt and withdrawal from revolt, that is, knowledge of the need and possibilities for changing existing objective life conditions and the suppression of this knowledge out of anxiety over the consequences of its use.

This connection between "opportunistic" forms of coping with existence and the development of psychical disorders can be clarified and made more concrete by existing mainstream psychology without a Critical Psychological reinterpretation. As constantly stressed in recent literature (for example, Beech & Liddell, 1974; Davids, 1974), psychical disorders arise in situations of impotence and surrender only when the individuals are confronted with demands that are felt to be beyond their ability, when a significant decision seems at least partially dependent on them, but they are completely disoriented about what to do and lack any trust in the possibilities for dealing with others.

Such an overtaxing situation, that is, one of simultaneous disorientation and pressure to act, ordinarily expresses itself as a heightened state of general physiological arousal, an "inner unrest" that demands immediate relief. There appear to be several ways of coping: direct reduction of the inner tension, indirect reduction through present external conditions, or redirection into substitute actions. On the other hand, sensitivity to external stimuli can be reduced either automatically (Delius, 1970) or by alcohol, drugs, and so forth (Solomon, 1977). There are many different relations between general reduction and redirection of the arousal into certain substitute actions: Substitute actions like running and eating can lead to the reduction of general arousal by bringing about a general weariness, and the general reduction in information intake can lead, as Delius has shown, to further substitute actions that then support the state of general tiredness or relative indifference to surrounding events and the passive retreat from concrete demands. This then "resolves" the state of subjective incapacity for decision by producing a relatively unambiguous action impotence and accompanying reduction in responsibility. The original means for "sedating" individual responsiveness by means of demands from the environment can, under certain conditions, become addictive and thus also a distinct problem, in contrast to which the primary, more or less diffuse difficulties and anxieties lose significance, are subsumed within the greater suffering, and are relativized.

Suffering that radically undermines one's own action potence can serve the purpose of distracting from the suffering that grows out of the subjectively experienced, though not realizable, need for action, such that therapeutic efforts that attack the consequences of psychical disorders without treating their causes can encourage this process of displacement.

Just as the general reduction of individual responsiveness means a confirmation of the situation of action impotence and lowered responsibility, being "over active," being distracted by certain features of the surroundings, or even being overburdened with tasks and activities, can represent protective mechanisms against being subjectively overtaxed, that is, imply a more or less automatic, general, or partial screen against new demands. Obviously, for these defense techniques, activities are preferred that allow expression against the demanding situation and lack of support from others. The compulsion of "cleaning up" has, for instance, the advantage of redirecting the general tension and its related anxiety while, at the same time, expressing aggression against those who restricted or let one down in an irreproachable way, that is, in culturally highly valued activity (see, for example, Davids, 1974).

Since motivation always depends upon the concrete possibilities for action, the state of general demotivation or indifference can be maintained through the systematic interference with or elimination of existing possibilities of action, thus preserving the most reliable protection against suffering in a situation of general surrender to surrounding conditions. The killing of individual hopes or possibilities of experience, as contrasted with external suppression, makes one less sensitive and thus "free." It gives the person a perverted autonomy, that is, the so-called independence of a person without needs. In place of the freedom to develop the personal needs and capacities that provide the only guarantee of an active role in shaping the societal conditions of life, we get the "freedoms" of denial, modesty, humility within existing relations, the subjective prerequisites for Maslow's glorified bourgeois society in which nobody strives beyond their assigned positions.

General efforts at orientation and maintenance of action potence under existing conditions in which we are thrown back on isolated private existence, particularly in the search for certainty as a prerequisite for individual action potence, can lead to increasing restrictions on the room for action and thus to a total loss of action potence, helplessness, surrender, and retreat. On the other hand, this self-surrender can be a means for achieving support and approval and even a certain "freedom of action" in the form of a refusal of self-determination.

The tendency to seek certainty before making a decision and becoming action potent can lead, as Kelly (1955), Bannister (1960), Reed (1968, 1969), and others have clearly demonstrated, to a specific peculiarity of thinking in which, because input is overstructured or categories overdefined, one becomes totally incapable of organizing and integrating experiences for the purpose of anticipating coming events. This leads, in turn, to an even stronger tendency to seek exact and detailed information. Thus it is that through the cognitive processing of environmental information the causation of psychical disorder achieves a relative independence. Insofar as the individuals have no superordinate goals, no ideas about what they want to achieve, do not know what is and is not relevant, have no criteria for selecting the essential from the inessential information, but are trying to move safely, there results a kaleidoscopic disintegration of the world into smaller and smaller unconnected bits and pieces, such as is typical of neurotic compulsive or even schizophrenic thinking.

Thus Kelly, without going into the conditions that give rise to such a reaction, speaks of the minute pseudomathematical exactness with which neurotic compulsives attempt to anticipate events. Irrelevant information is either reinterpreted or avoided. They get into situations only for which they feel totally prepared. Kelly calls this "constriction." Neurotic compulsives must, Kelly writes, keep control at all costs. In their search for absolute security they break down their world and their routine tasks into ever-smaller parts that must remain absolutely constant in order not to give rise to any disturbance and further withdrawal from reality. If something happens to what remains of the workable "constructs," that is, of the interconnected behavioral demands or plans, they will have nothing left to hold onto and will be confronted with the disintegration of their whole system. Mental collapse is inevitable. The lack of match between idea and reality therefore does not lead neurotic compulsives to extensions of their frames of reference through the processing of information about the development of relevant skills and knowledge, or to an active exercise of influence upon circumstances in order to produce the match as would be possible in a secured development untroubled by existential anxieties. Rather, because of general insecurity and being thrown back upon immediately individual efforts to secure an existence, which is characteristic of mental disorders, it leads to defense against the affecting area of reality and thus to a reinforcement of the isolation and its related anxieties.

When individuals proceed further in the fragmentation of their systems, they can be led, as Bannister (1960) has stressed, to thought disorders found in schizophrenia, in which, according to Searles (1961), every alteration, even in the smallest details is experienced as a metamorphosis that destroys the continuity succeeding perceptions. An essential difference between compulsive and schizophrenic behavior is obviously that neurotic compulsives are still motivated to retain some orientation and therefore also the capacity to communicate and act, that is, to check out plans and ideas against the world and to gain clarity, even if these efforts at self-assertion become increasingly reduced in scope and more and more under the control of security needs. By contrast, the schizophrenics appear to completely give up any claim to control over their surroundings. The barriers between them and the external world are, at least in advanced stages, seemingly eradicated. They cease to confront the world as "conscious" actors with goals and needs and seem to dissolve themselves into unity with it; that is, they can no longer separate themselves from the world, and this inability leads to the typical symptoms in which one's own impulses are experienced as alien influences, as when sexual arousal seems equivalent to an externally applied electric shock. Searles (1961) suspects that the fragmentation and failure to differentiate in schizophrenic thinking serve a defensive function: the prevention of negative emotions arising from possible association of present experiences with overwhelming past experiences.

These examples will suffice to substantiate the alleged connection between the situation of "normally adapted" opportunistic behavior in bourgeois society and that of mental disorder. The subjective causes of disorder lie in the lack of possibilities for influencing relevant life conditions, in the state of abandonment to the whims of others, and in the isolated, unconscious, half-hearted, reserved protest that grows out of the immediately experienced restriction on individual development and the inability to articulate and represent one's own interests and needs with respect to the restrictive world on which one is existentially dependent. On the one hand, the inability to recognize and represent one's own needs, to discover existing oppositions of interest, and to arrive at a structured world are consequences of individual insecurity and at the same time represent a defense mechanism against eventual suffering. On the other hand, the unconscious protests that result from a subjective evaluation of the experienced developmental possibilities and barriers and the individual's inability to resist – due to the individual's not understanding the problem and not wanting to take risks – express themselves in a form that, owing to the subject's lack of action potence, appears to justify the external decision of important issues. Thus in their willing submission to existing circumstances individuals share responsibility for their own impotence and surrender. The less clearly the external barriers can be objectified, that is, the more they are experienced as protection justified by one's own dependence and helplessness, the more complicated and incomprehensible the circumstances become.

Under certain conditions, especially when control over one's own development seems impossible, the seeming detachment of the emotions from the objective circumstances of which they are an evaluation can lead to the apparent autonomy of "inner" and "outer" realities because individuals distort the external conditions in accordance with their wishes and needs or shut themselves off from the consequences of their actions, which allows current needs to become the measure of actions, and place themselves more or less outside of society by disregarding the external barriers and not doing anything about them or questioning their justification.

The Critical Psychological conception of psychical disorders as gained from the reinterpretation of pertinent mainstream theories and findings will, of course, have to be worked out in greater detail and empirically tested. Especially we will have to work out the conditions under which "normal" opportunism becomes a generalized disposition to manifest psychical disorders and, in turn, becomes the circumscribed patterns of symptoms that we know as "compulsive neurosis" and "schizophrenia." What is needed now is to move beyond the mere reinterpretation to new formulations and investigations of the problems based on the position of Critical Psychology. Here the analysis of the therapeutic process must serve as the basis of a more detailed and verified understanding both of the psychical disorders and of the prospects and means of overcoming them. We have already made an initial approach to such analyses in connection with retrospective investigation of a course of therapy (Holzkamp & Holzkamp-Osterkamp, 1977). Thesis research is currently being conducted on therapeutic activities based upon Critical Psychological premises (for example, Fanter, 1978; Boetel, Gerhardt, & Scheffler, 1978; Gross & Harbach, 1978). We cannot go into this work here.

The current state of analysis, however, allows us to describe more concretely certain of our ideas about the basic direction for further work on a Critical Psychological approach to therapy from which the position we are trying to develop in contrast to traditional approaches becomes clear.

Consequences of the Analysis of the Connection Between "Adjustive Opportunistic" Dependency Arrangements and Psychical Disorders for the Concrete Development of a Critical Psychological Conception of Therapy

The distinguishing feature of the Critical Psychological conception of therapy is that emotional circumstances are used not as a means of control over the individual, but rather as an expression of the subjective necessity to improve the relevant life conditions or surroundings. This then becomes the guideline for therapy. Such a psychotherapy cannot consist of regulating emotional arousal while maintaining or reinforcing its suppression by the individuals' objective life circumstances. Rather, we have to consciously grasp the real connection between cognition – its emotional value – and the subjective needs for action that grow out of it in specific social relations. This is what must determine our actions. Individuals must learn to recognize the objective knowledge content of their emotions and allow that to guide their action.

An essential function of therapy is therefore to break down the isolation of individuals, that is, to make it possible for them to recognize their own and others' needs without reservation and to feel obliged by them, that is, to represent them actively and learn to translate them into action so as to become better oriented to the world. Since dependency relations are not accidental or temporary but have the function of stabilizing the position of whatever at the moment happen to be the dominant relations, all efforts to expand one's action space or to free oneself from direct dependence will elicit direct counterreactions, anxiety, and aggression that, to the extent that individuals are not prepared, can become a threat to existence, which then leads to an adjustment involving the giving up personal demands.

A central component of therapeutic work must therefore be to prepare individuals for the inevitable resistance that accompanies the breaking out of existing dependency relations, to show how these are related to objective conditions so that they can be dealt with, to dissolve the apparent harmony, and, on the basis of a clearer articulation of interests, to arrive at a new definition of relations and a corresponding reorientation of action.

In view of the close connection between cognition and possibilities for action, individuals will generally be capable of actively representing their own interests to the extent that the anticipated difficulties can be made objective and known to be surmountable in principle or when individuals are able to control and withstand the objective and subjective insecurity that comes from the active clash with the world. This capacity to recognize and withstand conflicts in the struggle to expand individual life possibilities is an essential countermeasure against spontaneous repressive tendencies that must be developed in the therapeutic process. This does not mean, as it is occasionally asserted, that Critical Psychology is just a general conflict strategy, that we advocate the provocation of conflicts willy-nilly or urge people to learn to cope at the cost of others. Rather, conflicts are objectively present, and as an essential prerequisite to their being dealt with, they must be made conscious and we must adopt an appropriate attitude toward them so as not to be caught unprepared. We do not want to give up our developmental demands or fall back on merely adjustive behaviors that might be evoked by existential anxiety associated with not having more adequate strategies. The development of individual possibilities for living and experiencing stands in the absolute forefront, and conflict plays a role only insofar as individuals have to learn to actively use it in their opposition to developmental obstructions. These should not be accepted out of a general shyness about conflict, which would only contribute to limitations on life possibilities and to self-deception.

It thus becomes clear that it cannot be the task of the therapist to satisfy the immediate needs of the client. It is more important in therapy to promote the conditions under which it becomes possible for clients themselves to fight for their own concerns, needs, and interests and thus regain control over their own lives. The immediate satisfaction of needs by others does not lead to their elimination, but rather to the masking and consolidation of the general dependence, surrender, and resulting anxiety.

As can be deduced from these considerations, the therapeutic support of clients' active representation of their needs does not mean promoting individuals' forcing through their own advantage over others. Rather, the basis for one's own possibilities for action includes consideration of the interests of others with whom one knows oneself to be bound. On the other hand, "modesty," putting one's own needs behind the interests and ideas of others, does not, in itself, mean that one is behaving socially. It is more likely an expression of helplessness and impotence and thus also of having been thrown back upon one's own immediate state of need, which always includes a certain egocentricity and a generally hostile attitude to the surrounding world or the turning to the world for the purpose of securing one's own immediate existence. Orientation to immediate short-term individual use is thus, as we have said, precisely an expression of general abandonment to the demands of the surrounding world. Only on the basis of real existential security and control over relevant conditions and clarified relations to fellow human beings will individuals be able to grown out of immediated ego-centeredness. Only on this basis will they develop an interest in the surrounding world and fellow human beings as a part of their own possibilities for living and experiencing.

The extension and improvement of social relations as a basic prerequisite for individual possibilities of action is not developed therapeutically through the direct practice of so-called social skills, empathy, and so forth, but rather only by extending individual action potence, the ability of individuals to represent their interests and needs consciously. The objective quality of social relations can be seen in the concrete support or obstruction of one's own efforts at development by others. Understanding this makes a critique and improvement possible. In place of a superficial harmony with the immediate expectations of others and an absence of conflict stemming from indifference and resignation, there must (insofar as there are no antagonistic interests) be a genuine connectedness that promotes mutual development and is alone reliable and lasting, a connectedness that can arise only through clarification of interests and complete consideration for the needs and problems of others. The words of Karl Liebknecht apply here: "Not 'unity' but clarity above all . . . through an unrelenting exposure of the differences between principled and tactical unanimity, that's the way" (Liebknecht, 1958: 112).

Clarity in the setting of goals as a basis and condition for personal stability and of general engagement, which can be developed only through active representation of needs in the extension of individual possibilities for action, is thus also the central prerequisite for openness toward other people and therefore also for the openness of unequivocal and reliable relations as a basis for the full realization of possibilities for human life and development.

It follows that therapy cannot take place mainly in the "therapy hour" either as conversation with or "treatment" of clients; it consists in the extension of individual spaces for action in the struggle against objective and subjective obstructions to development or in creating the objective and personal prerequisites for carrying on the struggle against individual isolation and for openness and reliability in social relations.

This extending of relations to the surrounding world, overcoming individual isolation, and intensifying interpersonal relations also cannot be achieved through so-called group-dynamic forms of therapy. The therapeutic function of "group therapy" in the usual sense is only to make clients recognize that their problems are shared by others, to generalize this experience and see problems no longer as the fates of individuals alone. It leads, however, to nothing more than a casual abreaction of individual frustration, a mutual confirmation of the state of general lack of development and a short-term recuperation from the trials of everyday life, which will only permit a better adjustment if the knowledge gained does not translate into goal-directed action for the improvement of the concrete conditions of life. The actual goal of therapy must therefore be to get beyond the relatively accidental grouping of individuals with common complaints, which are always abstracted from particular conditions, and to develop as quickly as possible clients' social relations in specific life and work contexts, in consideration of the real commonalities and differences of interest, and in realizing existing objective possibilities for action under whatever particular conditions. The aim is, in short, not just to relieve present suffering, but to create the objective and subjective prerequisites for consciously attacking the causes of the suffering, not to retreat from the concrete world, but to deal actively with it.

Learning to recognize one's own interests and to act accordingly is a complicated process. In the effort to understand and articulate needs and to overcome the objective and subjective barriers to this articulation, "exaggerated" emotional reactions can and must occur because it is often the case that only by clarifying one's subjective suffering in existing conditions can barriers to thought be overcome. Thus, a certain detachment from the surrounding world and concentration on the subjective situation without concern for its "acceptability," a full playing out of emotional reactions, is an essential step in the acquisition of knowledge. In general, however, such an abandonment to emotion and intensification of one's experience of the world can only occur when, depending upon the subjective state of security and action potence with respect to the expected counterresponses, the associated risks can be taken and compensated for.

Emotional clarification of the insufficiency of existing relations is therefore an essential prerequisite for the acquisition of knowledge, just as the intensification of experience means giving up the noncommitedness of behavior and actualizing concrete impulses to action, which also means a commitment to action. Rebellion against the limiting and painful conditions of the surrounding world, that is, the concrete recognition of the general suppression of individual interests and needs, can go on to become a general rebellion, a conscious screening of the demands of authority, that can temporarily cause overshooting of the goal and unnecessary difficulties. Such a general rebellion will occur if clients have not gained enough security and distance to represent their own needs relative to those of others and to attribute their behavior and interests to the objective conditions of their existence and thus recognize their mutability. This general rebellion, however, gives way to goal-directed representation of interests when clients acquire enough inner freedom to be able to enter into the needs and conceptions of others, or at least to begin to do this without having to be afraid of being "sucked in" to betraying their own needs and aims.

This temporary screening against the demands and conceptions of others is objectively necessary to the extent that other people will be interested in bringing their others "into line" as quickly as possible for the sake of their own psychical stability. This means making the others' behavior "predictable," thus preventing them from discovering their specific interests. Individuals must actively defend themselves against their own tendencies to give in to expectations, which only contributes to the maintenance of their generalized insecurity.

If, therefore, in therapeutic activity conflicts are not dealt with for the sake of the individual's presumably well-known interests, the client is actually prevented from arriving at an appreciation of his or her circumstances that would help the client to recognize where the real oppositions of interest lie and on which side he or she stands. This makes it more difficult for individuals to come to an unequivocal emotional engagement with those who have objectively the same interests and therefore also to acquire a secure and clear basis for individual development and fulfillment.

It must be kept in mind that in the active struggle with the surrounding world in which opposing interests sharpen and collide there is a real danger of a subjective overload and developmental regress. But this cannot be handled by holding back the claims of the individual. Rather, it is to be dealt with by preparing clients for the intensity, shape, and causes of the conflict, by helping to create the objective and subjective conditions that allow them to represent their own requirements with respect to others in a comprehensible way, and occasionally by teaching them how to get their way in the face of external resistance.

Since admitting the existence of discrepancies between needs and the lack of opportunity to satisfy them implies the recognition of one's own weaknesses and insecurity, and since this recognition is a subjective burden that can be taken advantage of by others, there is little danger that clients will plunge head first into the fray. Given a particular shyness regarding conflict that cannot be gotten over from one day to the next, it is more likely that clients will admit their own interests only to the extent that realizing them implies no demands and appears aggressive only in such a way, or in such situations, as allow a circumvention of concrete dispute. The more likely task of the therapist therefore will be to encourage the client to take up his or her dispute with the surrounding world rather than to discourage any exaggerations in extending his or her possibilities. Generalized aggressiveness normally comes about only when individuals have not learned how to assert themselves or how to eliminate the causes of their aggressiveness.

As plausible as they may sound, the policies of "measured" procedures, "modest but realistic goals," and so forth, often described as attempts to protect the client from negative experiences, rest on an approach that is false because it is not oriented toward the client's development. It represents a decision on the client's behalf as to what is in his or her interests. This representation of a client's interests and aims by the therapist is always a pretentious evaluation of those interests and aims that is usually limited by the therapist's own restricted state of development and is diametrically opposed to the therapeutic goal of extending the possibilities for action and knowledge as a necessary prerequisite for the independent representation of interests. This kind of interest representation is more likely to prevent the overloading of the therapist than that of the client. It represents an active inhibition by the therapist of clients' efforts at development.

To what extent an overload of clients occurs depends in no small measure on the ability and willingness of the therapist to actively support their struggles to improve their circumstances, that is, to prepare them for the expected conflicts and, in times of trouble, to take their part, to put "starch in their backs,'' instead of retreating from achievable goals under the pressure of resistance or ''for the sake of peace.''

Generally speaking, actual ''overloading'' of clients and their social surroundings (including the therapist) cannot be avoided. Indeed, it may be necessary in order to enable clients to recognize their own reactive behavior patterns, which detract from more long-term aims and are associated with immediate adjustment and submission. It may also be necessary in order to break through the ideological gloss of the demands and behavior patterns of others, to make visible the objective and subjective barriers hidden behind the pretended reasons for their behavior. In general what is significant here is not so much the concrete overload as the question of the extent to which one can draw the right conclusions from the circumstance of overload, that is, the extent to which the situation of surrender and helplessness appears in the future to be avoidable or surmountable. The overload only becomes traumatic when the client has no opportunity to analyze the situation for its determinants and thus do something about it.

Refraining from presenting clients with the aims of their action does not mean that they are to be shown no ways of acting, given no direction, and offered no interpretations. It does not mean making no effort to stimulate, assist, and systematize the clients' own initiatives and to bring these into therapy. What is essential is that the testing of aims and requirements, the immediate experience of their subjective value as the basis for further-reaching decisions, be left to the clients. It is important that they not be committed to concrete goals by the therapist in their presumed own interests, which will only cause them to be increasingly reluctant to bring their own needs and interests into therapy. This, of course, would make therapeutic progress impossible.

Therapy's ''chances of success'' are thus always immediately connected with the objective conditions of development and are accordingly low when the alternatives available to the client are even less attractive than the concrete disorder. Nevertheless, if, with the aid of the therapist, clients learn how to deal consciously with objective developmental obstructions as they affect their subjective situations, the analysis of the situation from their standpoint can lead to an essentially changed situation when they see themselves taken seriously in the emotional assessment of their circumstances and are not, in addition, made responsible for their own suffering. Under these conditions, the experience can provide them with renewed subjective motivation for development.

In order to avoid misunderstanding, it is important to stress that it is not our opinion that class consciousness arises out of the immediate experience of resistance and contradiction in concrete reality. ''Class consciousness'' is an objective category reflecting the general state of societal development and knowledge (that is, it does not arise out of individual subjects, but is given to them at a particular stage of societal development as a possibility for knowing, as a part of societal knowledge), to which individuals can relate more or less consciously, depending on their concrete objective and subjective situations. Our primary concern therefore is neither the development of class consciousness nor its appropriation by the subject. It is more generally the question of how subjects' objective possibilities for knowing are realized, repressed, or distorted, depending on the anticipated consequences of action and the objective and subjective possibilities of coping with them.

Traditional Psychotherapy as a Means of Securing the Therapist's Existence at the "Therapeutic" Expense of Clients

An essential condition for the ability of individuals to break down their screening and rigidity, that is, to overcome their mistrust of the surrounding world, and to articulate their needs, which also makes them vulnerable, is the absolute reliability, that is, openness and trustworthiness, of the therapist as revealed in his or her willingness to support clients without reservation in their struggle to extend possibilities. The therapist must take clients' problems seriously and not subject them to superficial or unreasonable censure tailored to the coincidental expectations of others. Just as no conscious determination and therefore no unambiguous action are possible on the basis of unclarified emotions, the analysis of emotions only makes sense if the knowledge acquired can be translated into practice and tested. It is precisely this support of clients' practice that must be an essential function of the therapist.

When psychical disorders are the consequence of a particular sharpening of negative factors characteristic of the situation of a large part of the population in bourgeois society and associated with individual impotence and surrender, then it must be assumed that since they are in principle no different from other people (no matter how they may view themselves), therapists will be in the same situation of impotence and surrender (even if not in their "pathogenic" forms) as their patients. This means that therapists will generally have just as little influence and insight as other people and will be maintaining for themselves a small area of action potence within generally incomprehensible and unyielding relations as a prerequisite for a secure individual existence. One must therefore consider whether and how the specifics of the situation, the function of therapists, and the conflicts that grow out of these can affect clients and their possibilities for development.

It must be noted that the problem of the petit bourgeois consciousness maneuvering among the great class conflicts must become generally more acute for the psychotherapist because in capitalist society this maneuvering is part of the therapist's job. This is not just because of his or her economic position (as a small business person or as a wage earner in a special relationship between dependency and privilege), but because of the way in which society defines his or her function. The psychotherapist is usually called for the purpose of avoiding and resolving conflicts or difficulties that arise in the adjustment to existing circumstances and is taken into service by those who have a particular interest in the restoration of their functional efficiency under existing conditions or who have the means to purchase these services and want for their money a corresponding benefit and certainly not additional problems.

Insofar as the psychotherapist wants to do this assigned job properly, he or she will have to look into the clients' psychical problems, but only to the extent that these interfere with expectations and demands placed on them and have become a cost factor. This is also the case where clients engage the therapist and are bearing the expense: Their problems are precisely an expression of their "willing" submission to alien interests. So at first they expect therapy to make them functionally efficient again within the framework of existing dependencies and without giving rise to contradictions with those in power. Thus it is a danger for the therapist that, if these expectations are not fulfilled, the client will withdraw or be withdrawn, which will not only prevent the client's interests from being realized, but will threaten the economic basis of the therapist's existence. The petit bourgeois characteristics of holding "socialistic" and personal economic concerns simultaneously and doing good within existing circumstances become especially clear in the specific function of the psychotherapist.

The goals sketched out in our earlier discussion, to support clients without interrupting the development of their practical insights into the subjective necessity to do away with the state of surrender as a prerequisite to a genuine resolution of problems, will, in bourgeois society, always threaten the therapist with insecurity. A therapist unprepared for this may react with panic or defense mechanisms that will interfere with the clients' developmental strivings.

The individual defense against conflict is generally subsumed in whatever theory or form of therapy is being used by the "societal" assimilation of the therapeutic situation, so that the situations in which the main interest conflicts, risks, and anxieties can be experienced directly are avoided from the start, making it possible for the therapist to earn a living in a way that is "unburdened" and free of conflict. Since, as Marx observed, the petit bourgeois must always "justify in theory what he is in practice" (Marx, 1865/ 1968: 30–31), the various psychological therapeutic approaches will always have to be examined for the extent to which they are in fact oriented toward the development of the client or just toward securing and facilitating the therapists' existence. It is also of interest to know the extent to which these possibilities for securing therapeutic existence are important factors in the success and popularity of certain theories and techniques.

Ignoring objective societal conditions, tracing all disorders to conflicts in early childhood, confining therapy to the therapist's office and to the merely verbal level, role playing, free expression of emotions independent of the clash with concrete surrounding circumstances and obstructions to development, as is typical of psychoanalysis, nondirective therapy, and similar conceptions, or limiting the client to externally set (sometimes accepted) goals, eliminating or training away symptoms, removing "deficits" to improve functioning in existing circumstances, as is characteristic of behavioral and similar therapies, all of these should be analyzed from the point of view of securing the psychological-therapeutic existence.

Even the various discussions of the therapist–patient relationship, the problems of rapport, transfer, fear of change, the therapist's inability to satisfy the needs of the patient and related guilt feelings, and so forth (cf. Searles, 1961), can be seen as derivative of this general strategy of conflict avoidance, in which the possible development of the client is prevented by the therapist because of his or her own capitulation and anxiety, and which essentially has the function of distracting from the real involvement of the therapist in the problems of the patient by fixing upon less explosive side effects and marginal phenomena. We cannot go further into this matter here.

It may be possible for certain professions to remain aloof from active politics, but this is surely not the case for psychologists whose "natural" function in capitalist society – as we have said – is to arbitrate conflicts, remedy difficulties of adjustment, liberate "human resources," and so forth, and whose work is directed at the active justification of existing circumstances, which is always thoroughly political. One cannot get beyond this general adjustive function by good will, commitment to socialism, or the dedication of one's work to "the service of working people." It is more important that general consciousness about existing obstructions to development and the psychical problems that stem from them be transformed for the psychologist in his or her everyday psychological practice.

The alternative to the relatively difficult path of unreservedly supporting the development of the client in the expansion of his or her objective conditions, which first means breaking down existing dependency relations (which are later, when possible, to be changed into cooperative relations) and their ideological disguises, and which in this phase of conflict intensification can have threatening consequences for both the client and the therapist, is just to talk either about generalized reconciliation and subjugation or about an all-embracing love of humankind, of generosity to the suppressed, that is, making exploitation under existing conditions easier to take. This is found in rather crude form in Maslow's humanistic psychology but is widespread among psychotherapists. It was analyzed by Marx and Engels as a typical petit bourgeois function in capitalist society, namely to serve as conflict manager and priest of "reason" and to find in existing conflicts assurance of external material existence and "inner" fulfillment.

The height of this general attitude of "doing good" under existing conditions so as to threaten neither the powers that be nor one's own existence found expression in a program shown on German television in the late 1970s, in which the father of a concentration camp doctor told why a doctor should be willing to undertake such a job: Nowhere in the world can he do as much good as in a concentration camp because there he had the possibility – naturally within the given framework – to be more "generous" than others in the selection of prisoners for medical experiments. That only a cruel postponement of murder could be achieved by this did not even occur to him; at least he did not say so. Instead, as a proof of his humanity, he pointed to the doctor's mental anguish in doing the job, which made it necessary to bring his family to the local village so they could give him mental strength for his difficult work. This may seem an exaggerated example that is not appropriate here. But the question is to what extent the fear of "exaggeration" in such cases signifies a fear of recognizing possible long-term consequences of present relations that would require some anxiety-producing alterations of behavior to change, and whether it is not hiding one's head in the sand that is the greater problem, owing to its widespread practice.

The fear of extremes, which Marx and Engels found to be characteristic of petit bourgeois consciousness, that is, the tendency toward mediocrity and remaining inconspicuous (which in the psychotherapist's situation must work negatively because real solutions to clients' problems require deviation from "normal" practice), does not affect only those who try to support their clients. The anxiety that bourgeois theories and therapies encourage us to circumvent through avoidance of conflict only becomes fully effective in materialistically conceived therapeutic efforts to extend the abilities of the client to take on and work through conflicts. Here it must be carefully controlled to prevent a retreat by the therapist to individual or even societal defenses that may become barriers to the clients' developmental efforts. The general danger here is that even the politically conscious psychotherapist may allow the therapy to be guided by his or her own interests and anxieties when a client's developments begin to move out of his or her control, become less predictable, and the therapist begins to be threatened with being drawn into the client's disputes. The therapist may ascribe his or her own efforts for security and success to the client and avoid conflict in the client's seeming interests. He or she will keep emancipatory efforts to the minimum and orient toward the immediately "practicable," which may be limited to existing developmental possibilities or obstructions. In this kind of pragmatism, taking steps that are only as large as the therapist can subjectively handle and that are guided by the "reason of adjustment," what tends to get lost is the central therapeutic goal of developing the possibilities for influence and thus also for conscious coresponsibility of clients for their concrete surroundings and the concretization and representation of their own needs and interests.

The way out of this situation, however, does not lie in a general admonition to be less anxious. The specific problems, limitations, and anxieties of the therapist must be drawn fully into the therapy, but not so that relief and change of attitude are sought in a general discussion of them, and not so as to add the therapist's problems to those of the client, but to try to change them by changing their objective causes. By pursuing the objective causes of their own subjective problems, therapists can possibly serve as examples for their clients. In any case, by actively expanding their own action spaces, they extend as well their therapeutic qualifications and will be that much more helpful to their clients.

Efforts should be directed at creating real conditions in which therapists are objectively less existentially dependent, in which they can control their anxieties by improving their possibilities for action and cooperative relations, and in which they can consciously deal with the danger of being subjected to existing conditions, with its resulting consequences for their clients. In our knowledge of the interconnections presented here, it is important to get rid of individual therapeutic practice (including the usual "group therapy"), which is a reinforcement for individual impotence and its related reactive tendencies, and to develop countermodels and alternatives in which the possibilities for real change in the circumstances of clients, the central component of therapy, will be improved through an organizational amalgamation that brings together social workers, jurists, and so forth, by moving therapy outside the office into the real familial and occupational situation of the clients, and through alliances with progressive forces, such as labor unions. In realizing such a model the described difficulties will not be done away with and the unhindered development of the client or therapist cannot be guarantied, but at least a broader and more stable basis for confronting the world will be created, along with the prerequisites for a greater preparedness for risk for both the therapist and the client.

We have discussed the problematic of "theoretically" safe strategies for avoiding conflict and their effects upon therapy and its eventual success. An apparently contrary solution to the dilemma of the psychotherapist in bourgeois society that is sometimes recommended by politically conscious psychologists is the systematic separation of concrete psychological theory and practice from "progressive" or "revolutionary" political activity. But on closer view this "solution" is, despite its "radical" clothing, simply a more consistent form of the strategy for avoiding individual conflict than the ones already mentioned.

The separation of the professional and the political work of psychologists has the necessary consequences that under the pressure of the immediate demands of psychological work, even that which is socialist minded, the techniques used are those that are available. This means that psychologists allow their practice to be defined by the prevailing economic interests while their socialism remains confined to their hearts or their tongues. In this way, as is typical of left opportunism, one's own "capitalistic" practice is justified: Faced with the impossible demand for all or nothing, revolution or reform, one opts for nothing, that is, for that which exists, for capitalism. Thus concrete action and intentional effort to improve the situation of the client is replaced with a general lamenting. This actually misuses the client materially and ideally for one's own private purposes. What Engels had to say about the abstract opponents of philosophy, who thought of themselves as so superior that philosophy was too superfluous for them even to bother disputing it, applies as well to psychology: "And those who grumble most about philosophy are the very slaves of the most vulgar remains of the worst philosophy" (Engels, 1925/1968b: 480). The separation of "higher" political consciousness and spontaneous, unreflected psychological practice necessarily leads to an emptiness of the political phrase and to conservative or reactionary practice. And because of its resulting lack of perspective and ineffectiveness of action, the consequence is shallow and inconsistent engagement in both political and psychological activity.

The conflict arising from the desire to avoid, where possible, endangering either the client or the therapist while also wanting not to take the short-term route to adjustment has no easy solution. What is essential is that we are conscious of the problem and treat it as an object of systematic scientific analysis in order to be able to translate our general knowledge about the effects of capitalist class reality on the development of personality and everyday activity into the right kind of practice.

The two variations we discussed regarding the danger of slipping into conflict avoidance strategies by politically conscious psychotherapists can be understood as special cases of a more general right or left opportunism in the political movement.

According to Engels, "forgetting the main points about the immediate interests of the day" is the central problem of opportunism, whereby, as he describes it, "this wrestling and struggling for momentary success without regard for later consequences, this betrayal of the movement's future for the sake of its present . . . [can] have honest intentions: . . . but opportunism is and remains what it is and honest opportunism is perhaps the most dangerous of all'' (Engels, 1891/1963: 234). On the other hand, the "true socialists," who are concerned in the struggle for socialism (owing to their privileged position and their freedom from day-to-day concerns about existence), "not with practical interests and results but with eternal truth," and for whom every instance of political progress, because it is useful to the bourgeoisie, is an evil, have made "the most revolutionary claims that have ever been put forward into a protective wall around the morass of the German status quo" and are thus "reactionary through and through" (Engels, 1847/1971: 41)

The general problem, that in capitalist society the individual's possibilities for action necessarily exist "abstractly," that is, are real but generally quite limited, and a basic orientation of the individual life toward consciously assumed goals on the basis of knowledge and its subjective value is effectively prevented (a situation that is particularly clearly manifest in an increasing joblessness that begins to be felt in the earliest stages of individual development), cannot result in general resignation, but, more sensibly, in the struggle to eliminate the conditions that obstruct development. In this struggle psychotherapists must use their special knowledge of the destructive effects of general lack of perspective and surrender to existing conditions and translate it into appropriate political demands and direct political engagement. In this, the possibilities for development that do exist under present circumstances should, in the interest of the individual, be fully utilized. A spontaneous incentive to political struggle to eliminate the conditions obstructing development and the necessary strength and endurance to do so will grow out of the direct experience of the constraints.

It is thus important to combat the objective limitations to individual development on two levels: first, at the level of the extension of possibilities for influence and life claims of all clients, which presupposes a cooperative extension of influence and security for therapists so as to help them overcome their own isolation, impotence, and related submissive tendencies, and second, at the level of the knowledge required for the political movement and ideological struggle having to do with the manifest forms of societally conditioned suppression of individual possibilities for development and its effect upon the subjective state and personality of the person.

8 Personality: Self-Actualization in Social Vacuums?

Ute Holzkamp-Osterkamp

Despite its widespread use in psychology, the concept of personality is immensely problematic. This is true of both its definition, which varies from author to author, and its function, which is normally given little or no theoretical attention (cf. Holzkamp, 1985).

Personality is usually conceived as a totality of behavior, a typical "response syndrome" that has developed out of the interaction of innate and acquired individual dispositions and environmental influences and specifically mediates the effects of momentary influences on individual behavior. The concept "personality" encompasses the more or less imposed programming of behavior that lends the individual a certain degree of independence from or resistance to momentary influences. Approaches to personality in general psychology are largely concerned with the determination of "personality traits," such as anxiety, aggression, extraversion/introversion, frustration tolerance, and so forth, and the investigation of the interplay of disposition and situation in the emergence of individual behavior (in order to influence it in desired directions through specific interventions from either the subjective or objective side). In contrast, therapeutically inclined approaches (especially psychoanalytically oriented) are mainly concerned with the subjective consequences and costs of personal fixation, that is, "character formation" resulting from adjustment to societal conditions. ("Character" is an older term for what we now call "personality.")

To approach personality from a Marxist standpoint means more than developing just another abstract structural model using "materialist" categories like "labor" or "activity" and then holding it up to human subjects as a norm of development. On the contrary, our analysis must begin with that which is concretely given in the contradictory and repressive reality of bourgeois society, that is, with the contradictions, discontinuities, and ambivalences of empirical subjectivity and personal becoming within the class realities of capitalist society. Methodologically, this means "working through" bourgeois theories in which certain aspects of "personal" existence in capitalist society

160

are reflected and ideologically generalized (just as Marx "worked through" the theories of the bourgeois economists). Only in this way will it be possible in the end to achieve abstractions that can preserve the concrete nature of human subjectivity, that is, that do not bypass real experiences, suffering, ambivalences, and illusions of individuals in a "normative" way. We need to relate to these consciously so as to create a real extension to life's possibilities.

Since I can realize such a project here in only a selective and fragmentary way, I will consider only those bourgeois conceptions of personality that base themselves on a subjective standpoint and thus, however inadequately, at least recognize what I consider to be the crucial problem in defining personality, the relationship of individuals to their subjective situations, their emotions and their needs. The conceptions to which I refer are the concepts of personality associated with psychoanalysis and other recent therapeutic approaches, especially humanistic psychology.

Such approaches – as will be demonstrated – deal, though deficiently, with central problems of personal existence in bourgeois society or at least raise them as questions in a way that is of interest to a Marxist analysis. In such an analysis, we must avoid reproducing the ideological partiality of these approaches, but we do not want to lose sight of the conceptual clarity they have attained on subjectivity in a class society.

The Psychoanalytic Conception of "Character" as a Form of Permanent Defense against Socially Unacceptable Subjective Manifestations: Insufficient Reproduction of the Mechanisms of Ideologically Binding the Subject to Bourgeois Society

According to Freud, personality develops in the individual's gaining control over drives. How this occurs depends on the individual's ego strength. It can occur through direct gratification, which involves the individual's overcoming or denying possible social barriers, or through the ability to sublimate impulses that are dangerous for society and thus not tolerated, that is, directing them from their original critical goals onto socially "valued" ones and achieving in such a cultivated way a somewhat less satisfying form of drive reduction, which, however, strengthens the individual's social integration and recognition. What Freud said about the objective and subjective conditions of such a sublimation process indicated only that it was not accessible to everyone. Lacking the internal strength for the one or the other, the individual's own drives would become a danger to him or her as a consequence of punishment resulting from their manifestations. As Freud understood it, individuals try to ward off this danger by taking sides with the powerful, that is, taking sides against impulses critical of the given circumstances and thus against themselves. As a reward, individuals are treated benevolently by those upon whom they are dependent and are spared aggressive reprisals. According to Freud then, the individual wards off the external danger of social exclusion (the exclusion from societal life possibilities by those who control them) by fighting the internal danger, that is, by repressing the impulses that could lead to external danger. This process of withdrawing the individual opposition from external restrictions and turning it against one's own "improper" impulses is systematically encouraged in society. The main mechanism by which individuals are bound into the existing social order – as derived from Freud's analysis – is as follows: All possible opposition to the existing power relations, whether conscious or not, is prevented from arising in the first place by shifting the focus to the integrity of the person. Individuals are made to feel guilty about their "improper" feelings and impulses, and criticism is seen as ingratitude, since they are after all, whatever their shortcomings are, being given treatment that is benevolent. Securing existence through the unquestioned internalization of the dominant norms is found, Freud claims, only in the "better-off" classes; the "masses" in general respond only to external compulsion and are not prepared to sacrifice their drives "voluntarily" for the preservation of culture (see, for example, Freud, 1968: 333).

It is characteristic of "good behavior" as a precondition for the illusion of individual autonomy and self-determination that the compulsion behind the self-restraint remains invisible, since we automatically do what we are expected to do. This self-restraint in turn provides the foundation for that assumption of what Lerner (1979) has called surplus powerlessness, in which subjects actually keep themselves in a state of dependency and powerlessness over and above that objectively required because they are afraid of freedom, autonomy, responsibility, and so forth. A central cause of our developmental restrictions, it is said, is therefore our own anxiety and unwillingness to take risks and make efforts, which prevents us from taking advantage of objective life possibilities. It is not surprising that this thesis seems plausible to the subject because, under conditions of alien determination and inability to adequately foresee or accept the consequences of our actions, our initiative is in fact quite restricted.

The "autonomous" repression of impulses that society punishes with resulting restriction of individual development meant for Freud the internalization of external compulsion, in which the impulses to act, together with the underlying cognitions and experiences, become overly powerful, owing specifically to their repression, lack of gratification, and exclusion from consciousness, and begin to determine actions against the person's will. This appears, in retrospect, to justify external regimentation. Internalization of the external compulsion becomes the basis of increasing self-rejection and insecurity. This is so, first, because, as Freud discovered, nothing is more painful than realizing that one is not "master in one's own house," that is, being helplessly subject to one's "drive impulses" and feelings, being driven against one's will and better judgment. A second reason is that "impulse defense" generally weakens individuals, causes them to be "cautious" and to avoid everything that might, if only slightly, remind them of the suppressed cognitions and impulses and make conscious the restrictions imposed by outer reality. Freud stated that this defense can begin to take effect independently of real danger. The task of therapy, then, is to eliminate this superfluous defense and the maladjustments associated with it, which are costly both to the individual and to society. In this way the energy that was bound up in repression can be set free and become available for coping with everyday tasks and enjoying the possibilities that do exist. The conscious censorship of needs should take the place of the uncontrollable repression, the consequences of which are extremely problematic. These needs can then either be satisfied in accordance with the increased possibilities for "impulse control," subject to dominant norms and interests, or consciously rejected when the individual realizes that they are not suitably realizable.

Defense against taboo drive impulses and the experiences and cognitions that actualize them can, according to Freud, become solidified into certain neurotic character formations that only prove by their compulsivity and resistance to experience to have their origin in anxiety or the defense against anxiety-evoking "drive impulses" and cognitions.

According to Freud, personality formation is the general programming of individual behavior vis-à-vis the respective "authorities" as representatives of societal power, on the one hand, and one's own needs, on the other. It is essentially completed by the end of the child's fifth year and is crucial in shaping his or her adult life. It is based on the internalization of external compulsion, which, in turn, is based on the fear of risking the loss of social integration and the vital recognition associated with it as a result of expressing socially unacceptable impulses; that is, it is also based on the promise that by being submissive toward the interests of the powerful one will be protected to some degree from their aggressions and punishments and will be able to participate in the possibilities for life and power that they grant. But it is just this active binding of oneself to existing relations, the mixture of being oppressed and actively participating in power and oppression, and having to turn to those who cause anxiety for its relief, that makes it extremely difficult to keep a critical distance from these authorities, since this would also involve taking a critical distance from one's own "good conduct" which is, from the defensive point of view, necessary for coping with anxiety.

Freud's conception of character as a form of permanent defense against socially unacceptable drive and action impulses was developed by Reich as a central part of his theory. In opposition to Freud, who assumed that drive repression was a necessary and ubiquitous requirement for social existence, Reich limited the connection between repression of drives and sociality to capitalist society. Despite his aim to extend psychology by giving it a Marxist sociological dimension, supraindividual sociality, that is, the responsibility of the individual for this "society," not just as a lived experience but as a transcendent reality, slipped more and more from his reach.

According to Reich, character structure is a "crystallization of the sociological process of a given epoch," written into the infant psyche and remaining there "without much change" (1933: 16). It hampers the adaptation to changing social conditions necessary later in life. As in all theories that assume an aggregative relationship between subjective and objective reality, the individual is seen here as a "flow-through basin" [Durchlaufbecken] in which early impressions and determinants are deposited that, to one degree or another, hinder the individual capacity to cope with the demands of the present situation. Social structures are anchored in the character, says Reich, by the sexual oppression practiced in petit bourgeois families, which brings about a general dependency on and subservience to authority. Reich maintains that character, since it is based on the avoidance of dangerous situations, involves a certain internal strength and stability. At the same time, however, it also involves an individual restriction, rigidity, and detachment, not just with respect to internal "drives," but also against external influences. Every frustration, says Reich, contributes to a strengthening of the character's "armor" through which individual need gratification is hindered far more than is demanded by society. Too much repression of drives, however, can cause a "drive stasis" [Triebstau] that, in turn, weakens the character armor, making it vulnerable to penetration. There is a "complementary opposition" [ergänzender Gegensatz] between the starting point of character formation, defense against actual dangers, and its final function, defense against the dangerous drives and "stasis anxiety": the more the real anxiety, that is, fear of external threat, can be avoided, the greater the fear of one's own drives and the breakthrough of those dammed up, that is, "drive anxiety" (1933: 183). Depending on the individual's ability to adjust to current circumstances, Reich distinguished between a "fit" [realitätstüchtig] character, which is assertive and strong enough to satisfy its needs within the given situation, and a neurotic character, which, as a result of its excessive obedience to the dominant norms, is unable to produce the required adjustment. The causal question about individual differences in dealing with external oppression and obstacles to subjective development is answered by Reich in a way similar to traditional psychology by ascribing different inborn or socially produced psychic dispositions to it, thus leaving the question unclarified. Reich's conception of personality or character reproduces a fundamental mechanism for the ideological integration of the individual into bourgeois society based on entanglements of guiltlessness and blame and uses it to define the function of psychoanalysis. We are, on the one hand, made responsible for the social conditions, since we reproduce them with our behavior, but at the same time we are relieved of that responsibility by the assumption of a "faulty developmental adjustment" [*Fehleinstellung*] forced upon us in early childhood. We are consoled by the promise that with the help of psychotherapeutic treatment, at least as long as the faulty adjustment is not fixated, we can become constructive members of society automatically contributing to the good of all and affirmed accordingly by living "spontaneously" and "immediately" according to our "natural" needs and inclinations.

Reich and Freud describe important mechanisms by which subjects are taken in by bourgeois relations. On the other hand, the bite is taken out of such analyses when current restrictions on development are made to appear as mere psychic, self-perpetuating reactions to oppression in early childhood. The contradictoriness of capitalistic class reality, the real exploitation oppression, and competition in all spheres of life, hidden beneath the illusion of freedom, equality, and charity, that, more or less unconsciously, individuals have to consider in their behavior, remain unclarified with respect to their effects on the subjective situation of the individual, as do the effects of the adaptation to this existence and the rigorous realization of individual advantages under the pretense of propriety and altruism.

Theories of Self-Actualization: Flexibility and Internalization as Magic Formulas for the Personality's Illusory Autonomy from Society

In Freud's and Reich's theories the fact of social oppression is present – however "naturalized" or "displaced" – as that to which "character" is a subjective reaction. By contrast, some currently popular dynamic–therapeutic theories (especially in the area of "humanistic psychology") deny or "discuss away" the restriction of personal growth through oppression. It is assumed that individuals can fulfill themselves under any social conditions and that the oppositions and threats encountered in society are challenges that, if anything, provide opportunities for personality to grow.

A very successful variant of such "self-actualization" theory is that advanced by Fritz Perls, the founder of Gestalt therapy. Under the motto of the unhindered development of "natural" dispositions, the "character" theory of

Freud and Reich is robbed of its remaining critical potential under the pretense of its radicalization. This is the result of Perls's thinking of character as being like every other form of restriction, whether determined by one's own or other's needs and interests. It is presumed to be a subjective obstacle to development that limits the individual's possibilities to react to current societal demands. Furthermore, Perls declares that the real threats, seen by Freud and Reich as causes of individual submission and consequential "psychic" compulsions, are mere projections and products of fantasy. According to him, dangers and trauma are essentially lies that serve to justify our unwillingness to "grow" and "mature." It is not external forces that hinder our development, but our own timidity and whininess, our craving for recognition and security. If we were not so soft with ourselves and others, the world could do us little harm. He states that character formation can essentially be traced back to "blockages," that is, objectively overtaxing situations in which, instead of mobilizing our own potential, we learned to play weak and thus manipulate others into doing things for us. The biggest favor we could do someone would be to frustrate their wishes for security and provision, to refuse to help them, so that they could revert back to their own strengths and possibilities, become independent and learn to take responsibility for the obstacles to their development, instead of blaming others or society for them. Taking responsibility for one's own life means, as Perls clearly articulates in a maxim shared by other "humanistic" psychologists like Maslow, not just taking responsibility for one's own weaknesses and restrictions, but also refusing to take responsibility for others and their restrictions, and not allowing our enjoyment of life to be disturbed by the situations of others. "Self-actualization" is the art of taking the world as it is, of making the most out of everything and not complaining about horrible and unpleasant things in life, but accepting them as the price or foil for the beautiful things in life. An important element of self-actualization is being able to change "means activities" into "ends activities," that is, to carry out an activity not for a certain external reward/purpose/goal, but to enjoy it for its own sake.

Perls maintains that society functions, like the individual, in a self-regulating way. As long as this harmonic process is not interrupted by arbitrary interventions or directives, the most pressing need will spontaneously manifest itself and determine the further development. The functioning of societal development depends on the functioning, the "responsibility" of individuals, that is, their willingness to respond directly to the demands of a given situation. Confusion can occur if society confronts us with demands that appear to stand in the way of our self-actualization. This confusion sorts itself out, at least in a progressive society such as the American (1976: 39), if we only stick it out and live according to the maxim "it is as it should be, and it should be the way it is" (p. 79).

Where Perls maintains that we are hindered in our self-actualization, that is, in the maximal use of available opportunities, mainly by our own anxiety and whininess, and that nothing would stand in the way of our enjoying life if we could only stop ourselves from thinking about possible dangers and feel that we are responsible for the lives of others, Gruen, in a book that was highly praised by *Der Spiegel*, claims that it is precisely our inability to accept anxiety and suffering (also of others) that hinders our personal self-actualization. Autonomy, says Gruen, is not based on the assertion of our importance, but on a congruence with our own feelings, whereas a lack of autonomy is based on the defense against our sensitivity to and isolation from our feelings. Gruen puts this defense down to our "general tendency to abstract," which is characteristic for the history of our civilization in general and is mediated to the individual through the socially conditioned inability of parents, especially mothers, to respond adequately to the needs of their children. Whether a child grows up as autonomous or dependent is determined very early in life. A break in autonomy and a consequent massive disturbance in the development of personality occurs when the child, as a way out of an anxious or desperate situation, does not endure the situation and develop from it, but begins to strive for power (over others), that is, learns to identify with the powerful, to despise any form of weakness and at the same time to suppress all desires for autonomy in him- or herself and others, and thus actively contributes to the process of dehumanization (1984: 24). In explicit contrast to Freud, who assumed that adjustment to an unquestioned society was necessary, Gruen emphasizes just the opposite, that in view of the "pseudosocial" reality, maladjustment and associated pathologies are not abnormal but rather signs of individual and personal growth. The truly strong characters are not the powerful, who, in his opinion, strive for power only because they can't endure powerlessness, anxiety, and suffering, but those who demonstrate their humanity precisely in their powerlessness (1984: 145). "Dangerous things" in Gruen's opinion, "are not the external dangers, but rather fear of the terror of loneliness, chaos, and insanity" (1984: 141).

In the theories of self-actualization that I have described here, society appears as a general framework in which individuals are confronted with demands and limitations, which they avoid if they can and with which they comply, thus paying the price for conceded freedoms. Societal regimentation is said to be compensated for by private freedom – a freedom to do what one wants in the private sphere because the existing power relations cannot be touched there. The utilization and cultivation of conceded freedoms in social vacuums are "sold" as development of the personality, in which impotence, as a release from responsibility for societal relations, appears as "freedom."

"Self-actualization," as an exoneration from the responsibility for social conditions – be it through ruthless assertion of one's own interests or withdrawal into self-preoccupation – implies a "critical" toleration of the conditions that one becomes less willing to question, the more one profits from them or believes oneself to be doing so. Such "self-actualization" is not autonomy. It is an impotence, which is not a condition of our humanity, but the objective prerequisite for the lack of humanity and self-actualization among individuals. It is a requirement for behavior that, despite all semblances of "freedom," is defensive and egocentric, directed only at the preservation of one's own advantages. It is therefore asocial and, in the final analysis, opposed to one's own interests. It is the prerequisite for one's own stunted development.

The theoretical concentration on immediate self-actualization means fighting against the effects instead of the causes of oppression. It implies taking sides with the powerful by making individuals directly responsible for their own subjective situations – as in the popular ideology that "people are the architects of their own fortunes." Relations of oppression are not conceived as a condition for, but rather as a result of, individual unreasonableness and instinctivity or – as in "progressive" theories of self-actualization – as a result of individual craving for authority or submission, fear of autonomy, freedom, and self-determination. These subjective tendencies, fears, and feelings are not related to the conditions and contexts of their societal origin, but are treated as mere personal phenomena for which individuals are responsible and with which they have to deal in any way they can.

Being abstracted from the responsibility for societal relations and being shielded from the perception of human suffering, anxiety, and feelings of insecurity (as recommended by Perls and bemoaned by Gruen) are two sides of the same process. I can tolerate my critical impulses and cognitions only to the extent that I can realize them in my actions. Insofar as the realization of my feelings and cognitions in concrete action would have consequences that burden me and endanger my societal integration, I would experience a spontaneous tendency to distance myself from them and thus from myself.

Access to our feelings and cognitions, as well as the possibility of "freeing" ourselves from them, depends on our real, subjectively recognized action potence, which is always mediated through the relationships to our fellow humans; that is, it depends on our power. It is precisely this way of exercising influence over the process of societal development as a precondition for the conscious determination of the way in which we live, feel, and act that is denounced as personal striving for personal power, as an unconscious letting out of pent–up aggression, and so forth, in all theories of self-fulfillment, no matter how they differ in detail. They thus blindly reproduce the objective contradictory demands that constantly confront people in capitalist relations and contribute to their feelings of insecurity. For overcoming the behaviors and needs they criticize or censure, they recommend the very conditions that brought them about in the first place. In other words, they torment individuals with entreaties to reform themselves, but at the same time conceal the objective possibilities for such reformation and thus contribute to increased feelings of subjective insufficiency and insecurity, which are felt as a lack of inner freedom, for which they claim to be offering remedies, and so on.

By extolling inner freedom, defined as adjustment to social conditions or even as a subjective feeling of being above them, theories of self-actualization come to a number of false alternatives that systematically obstruct solutions to the problems of determination by others and lack of being one with oneself. "Security" becomes opposed to "growth" only in conditions in which one's existence is determined by others, that is, when, for fear of losing the affection of others, people allow themselves to become an executive organ of the interests of those on whom they are dependent, and when they repress or deny all cognitions and impulses that contradict this function. However, when we see growth and development not as mystical forces, but rather as an extension of the possibilities for life and development through our conscious determination, then security is not in opposition to development, as theories of self-actualization claim, but identical with it. Security is a precondition for development, as well as its result. Freedom, self-determination, autonomy, and so forth, do not evoke anxiety as such, as theories of self-actualization claim, but only when there are real dangers threatening us when we overstep the limits conceded to us. Humans are not hostile to development as such. They are hostile, however, when changes in their living situation are made behind their backs and become a threat to the integration for which they have worked so hard. The alternative to limiting and disciplining oneself out of anxiety is not openness, but rather the orientation of one's behavior according to one's own developmental interests and goals. Openness under conditions of dependency is not an expression of freedom, but a precondition for flexibility, the ability to adjust ourselves to changing social conditions and, at the same time, a defense against understanding the social function of our acting or not acting and our consequent effects on the situations of our fellow human beings and our own existence. Taking ourselves seriously is not a hindrance to individual autonomy, as theories of self-actualization claim, but its absolute prerequisite. Only when I take myself and what I do seriously and correspondingly commit myself, will I do justice to my social responsibility. Only then will the fatal thesis that we are mere cogs in a machine that functions according to some superordinate plan lose its power to convince (this thesis being at the root of theories of self-actualization). Superficial concern for oneself alone, which is generally criticized, results precisely from the doubts and lack of self-assurance about one's importance that are typical in social relations in which the value of individuals is measured by their exploitability for ruling interests.

Theories of self-actualization that presuppose life conditions over which individuals have no control gain an appearance of authenticity (and thus achieve resonance in broad circles) because – at least in part – they vividly describe and critically reflect the self-restricting and self-destroying effects of typical experiences and behaviors that have developed in response to capitalist class reality and because, at the same time, they offer "solutions" that spontaneously present themselves anyway under the pressure of such conditions. They thus remove any doubts about the appropriateness of one's conforming behavior and have an immediate reassuring effect. This path of least resistance, conformity as an immediate reaction to oppression, is portrayed as an especially "thorny" and dramatic affair, such that, for example, it is not the retreat into inner life that is seen to be an escape from social responsibility, but quite the opposite: Political activity appears an escape from the drama of the confrontation with one's "inner depths." Although for Freud the range of human happiness extended from normal misery to the neurotic suffering of a conforming existence, he demonstrated indirectly that a precondition for human happiness was to overcome alien determination (which, however, he rejected as utopian). In theories of self-actualization, however, such a necessity is no longer implied, since internal independence is divorced from external independence. If we consider the political implications of these theories in all their varieties, it becomes clear that, unlike Freud's psychoanalysis, in which individuals are helped to realize the few life possibilities still remaining to them in the face of massive social oppression, the subjects here are called upon to search for and find "the happiness of being a personality," either by ruthlessly asserting their own interests or (if in so doing they encounter massive resistance) by cultivating their "inner riches" and their capacity for suffering. It is therefore certainly not a coincidence that, despite their often "radical" or "progressive" appearance, such theories, with their denunciation of striving for security and their praise of limitless "flexibility" and/or satisfaction with inner values, can be appropriated by the present neoconservative offensive in West Germany.

It is also not surprising that the idea of retreat into an inner life as a truly human quality is not just found in certain forms of self-actualization theories, but (under certain favorable social and political constellations) sets the tone of conservative expressions of bourgeois "public opinion."

The political function of such conceptions is to relieve individuals from any responsibility for social relations and to mystify the interests behind them. This was very clearly demonstrated by Helmut Peitsch's work (1983) on West German biographies of the postwar period, focusing on how the so-called internal emigrants came to terms with or repressed the fascist past. The main defense against the accusation that they had supported fascism through their passivity and conformity was to demonstrate how they had preserved their personal integrity and sensitivity despite their conformity to the inhuman reality of the time. From such a position of individual humanity, says Peitsch, fascism in general seemed to be a tragedy in which all – fascists and their victims – were equally entangled, whether or not culpable. According to the thesis of collective responsibility, all concrete differences vanish, as does the question of individual guilt. The mystification of guilt and the glorification of suffering are thereby closely linked, as Peitsch demonstrates. Suffering is stylized, as it were, into the source of purification, which compensates for any guilt. People who suffered inwardly cannot be made responsible for their actions since they had already experienced punishment. According to this conception of "inner" humanity, all people, whether fascist or antifascist, have their good and bad points. The implication is that everyone should begin with self-criticism and stay there. Blaming the social conditions and demanding their change appear from this angle as a mere rationalization, an escape from the necessity of personal moral purification, a purification that disqualifies itself. This way of dealing with one's own "withdrawn" existence in fascism, which, at the same time, conceals the true – objective and subjective – causes of fascism, has been, as Peitsch shows, systematically encouraged in literary circles. Reports which, instead of revealing the causes of suffering, glorified it by interpreting it as a test of worth and a condition under which personalities mature and grow, were highly praised by literary critics. On the other hand, authors were generally criticized who refused to view fascism as just a disastrous human fate, who analyzed its societal causes and refuted the doctrine of universal culpability by differentiating between those who profited from or hoped to profit from fascism and its true victims. Many of these authors had demonstrated by their own actions that it was indeed possible to resist under such inhuman conditions.

The idea of individual humanity (in abstraction from its social and political dimension) was the spontaneous result of the justification of conformity to fascism and was systematically encouraged by literary and general public policy. As recommended in theories of self-actualization, it was manifested as an individual ability to make the best out of a given situation, to be open for the good and beautiful things in life, wherever they may be, and to see these as compensation for the mean and evil things that should be avoided if possible. If one does not achieve this external distance to the negative and evil things in the world, then according to these conceptions, one still has the possibility of inner distance, that is, of inwardly keeping clear of things and cultivating one's own personality and humanity in areas that are safe from harm (cf. Peitsch, Kühnl, & Osterkamp, 1985).

The Theory of Herkommer et al. on Personality Development in Modern Capitalist Societies: Spontaneous Domination of the Ideology of Self–Actualization in Social Vacuums as a Result of Economistic Distortions of Marxist Analysis

The ideological pitfalls of bourgeois conceptions of self-actualization and autonomy are not easily avoided in attempts to develop concepts of personality based on Marxism. On the contrary, a comprehensive appropriation and development of materialistic dialectic must be on constant guard against the distortions of unrecognized elements of bourgeois ideology. A clarification of the problems of personal existence in bourgeois society is impossible if the basic understanding of the Marxist fundamentals from which it proceeds is limited or one-sided. An example of this is found in the work of Herkommer, Bischoff, and Maldaner (1984). Their Marxism was confined to the sphere of production and thus economistic. This creates a kind of "empty space" that is quickly filled by currently popular ideologies, such as that of self-actualization in social vacuums.

The point of departure for Herkommer et al. is the contradiction between the production sphere, which is highly alien determined, and the sphere of leisure time, which, depending on the size of salary and the amount of free time available, "offers manifold activities ranging from the great variety of hobbies and club activities, trade union and political work, to holidays and family outings" and thus presents space for individual development (1984: 211). According to them, personality develops through utilization of the conceded private spheres from which individual workers return to production "as more capable, more sensitive, and richer in needs and, as such, developed personalities." This then allows workers to make changes in the process (p. 194). "The development of a 'leisure-time cultural life-style' in the recent-development of capitalism" has not just "brought about a personal and social self-actualization of all classes in society – albeit to various degrees – but has also brought back the values of communication and creativity into the production process. Initially one worked in order to create and enjoy a leisure time cultural life-style for oneself, family, and others; finally this life-style changed into a new evaluation of the contents and conditions of work" (p. 195).

According to their argument, social changes are brought about just as they are in theories of self-actualization. Individuals develop into personalities rich in needs in their leisure-time activities and pleasures and, as such personalities, initiate greater degrees of freedom in the production process. Alien determination, it seems, still exists, according to this conception, only because we have not yet developed a sufficiently strong need for independence. Herkommer et al. conceive subjectivity as a complicated and contradictory relationship permeating all areas of life between the societal determination of the individual and the "active forming of relationships in society as is possible within certain limits" (p. 130). We are not determined just by the process – largely alien determined – of production, but also by other spheres that are not subject to "real subsumption" by capital. The various spheres of life do not influence individuals directly but are mediated through the traditions and values of the specific groups they belong to, and they condense within individuals into personality structures that then reproduce the social relations through which they were produced. "That which repeated activity has made into an experience," a dictum of Marx's taken out of context, becomes an integral part of individual personality (p. 215). Individual appropriation of the respective spheres of life is doubly determined: through the compromise between the tendency towards social conformity and social imitation, on the one hand, and toward individual differentiation, the emphasis on personal uniqueness, on the other. The totality of individual appropriation, imitation, and differentiation activity is organized through the "habitus" that ensues from the interplay of influences from the various social spheres and the respective temperament of the individual, and which at the same time determines the character and distinctiveness of individual appropriation. "Personality" develops out of compromise between conformity and differentiation, that is, from the personalized adaptation to the various spheres of life in opposition to and excluding others.

According to this view, compulsion is limited to direct regimentation of behavior, which is strongest in the sphere of production and is less strong, even nonexistent, in the areas of life not subject to "real subsumption" by capital. Childhood is defined not, as in psychoanalytic theories, as a time period in which individual autonomy and resistance are broken and in which the basis is laid for the general submissiveness to authority, but explicitly as a period in which regimentation and drill are limited. The dimension of internalized compulsion – self-oppression in order to secure the benevolence of those on whom one is dependent, with resulting participation in power and oppression – passes completely out of view, as does the consequent subjective problematic that comes into the foreground in the form of real feelings of insecurity, generalized fears and self-doubts, and the need to demonstrate to others the worth of one's personality. A consequence of this is the harmonization and justification of the existing social relations, which offer individuals more and more leisure time and thus an abundance of possibilities to embellish their individual, that is, their private, lives or personalities.

The dependency of the development of personality on "social vacuums" provided for individuals is a feature of other theories that I cannot describe here in detail (cf. Hoff, Lappe, and Lempert, 1985); according to such conceptions, the action possibilities are more or less imposed on individuals.

Restrictive situations lead to restrictive behavior; open situations lead to an extension of individual ways of acting. The need and possibility for struggle against the restrictive living and working conditions that obstruct development are not discussed. Thus human relationships cannot be comprehended in their subjective quality, but only at the instrumental level at which the respective private interests are pitted against one another.

Conclusions from our Critique of "Personality Theoretical" Reflections of the Bourgeois Ideology of Personal Withdrawal and Private Spheres: Toward a Framework for a Marxist Theory of Personality

The quintessence of the theories we have discussed can be summarized in the following way: If one excludes the social responsibility of humans as a crucial determinant of personality, subjectivity is degraded to an embellishment of the individual person in contrast to and/or to the exclusion of others and to the forming of private relationships. The numerous conditions imposed on the "free development of personality" and the many limitations and burdens placed on private relationships in capitalist society are either seen as a mere consequence of wrong or insufficient behavior or are left out of the analysis altogether.

The result of all these theories is the simple assertion that those with the most money and free time are the most developed personalities – a thesis that can be easily turned into the claim that money and free time are not the basis, but rather the crowning, of personality development; that is, "strong personalities" automatically rise to take up the top positions in society, whereas the weaker personalities remain at the bottom (cf. Maslow, 1972).

By reducing our understanding of alienation to external regimentation and thus idealizing the conditions in the "private sphere," a central aspect of human suffering is omitted, and with it the absolute necessity of societal change: the self-degradation and consequent self-enmity that ensue from conditions of individual dependency that one has oneself helped to consolidate, and the more or less conscious involvement in the oppression of others, which massively disturbs the relationship to others and undermines potential resistance to every form of exploitation. Suffering in capitalist class reality does not come primarily from externally imposed discipline, but from one's ambivalent attitude toward fellow humans and oneself and the resulting insecurity these social relations force upon us. Self-insecurity is usually compensated for by a more or less subliminal self-adulation, the demonstration of individual virtues and capabilities, but also by personal suffering that makes all the suffering and harm one has inflicted on others appear to be insignificant or even self-sacrifice.

The task of a personality conception concerned with the development and emancipation of humans would have to reveal these forms of suffering for what they really are, that is, clarify their objective causes, connections, and consequences, so that one could deal with them consciously instead of taking up a defensive position that helps consolidate the very social conditions that give rise to this insecurity and make people manipulable for ends that are opposed to their own interests. Instead of totally avoiding the subject of anxiety, as Herkommer, Bischoff, and Maldaner do, or playing it down into a product of fantasy, as Perls does, or portraying the endurance of anxiety as a true personal quality, as Gruen does, it is necessary to reveal the critique of society that is contained in the anxiety, that is, the threats reflected in it, and to remove with its causes the anxiety itself, in the knowledge that anxiety prevents us from achieving our human possibilities, restricts our thoughts and actions, and allows us to become our own enemies.

Instead of selling the utilization of conceded private spheres as self-actualization and declaring "unpretentiousness" or satisfaction with what one has been conceded as the highest virtue, it is necessary to expose the incorporation of one's actions into the ruling relations and interests. That means exposing the objective asociality of "resignation," as well as the "cowardliness, self–disdain, degradation, and submissiveness" that underlie the retreat into inner life, and providing incentives to fight against the objective and subjective degradation (cf. Marx, 1847/1971a: 200). One must not, says Marx, grant a person "one moment of self-deception and resignation"; rather, "the real pressure must be increased by making him conscious of it; the humiliation must be made more humiliating by publicizing it" (Marx, 1844/1970b: 381).

"People must be taught to be shocked by themselves so that they become courageous" (Marx, 1844/1970b: 381); that is, they must be confronted with the consequences of their behavior so that they cannot close their eyes to them, so that they stop concealing their degradation and its causes, as well as their active participation in consolidating the relations of oppression, and begin to fight against these. Instead of celebrating the variable realizations of "private spheres" [*Freiräume*] as proof of individual autonomy and societal freedom, the point is, as Marx said, to elucidate the "conceded existences" that are bound up with "petty antipathies, bad conscience, and extreme mediocrity," "mutual ambiguity and distrust," and "narrow-mindedness" (Marx, 1844/1970b: 380), that is, to take up the fight against "modest egoism," which "asserts its own limitations and allows them to be asserted against itself" (Marx, 1970b: 389). Instead of concealing one's handicaps and their objective causes in order to avoid a bad impression, oppressive conditions must be revealed. A more defiant slogan must be adopted and turned against all forms of extenuating oppression: "I am nothing but should be everything." What is essential in the development of personality is not the private spheres conceded to us, but in whose interest it is that we act. What is essential is the extent to which we lead conceded existences, ones that are subject to the ruling interests, that is, conform to social relations in order to preserve individual existence. What is essential is the extent to which we resist such a conceded existence in the knowledge of its asocial function, that is, resist every form of resignation and coming to terms with the existing obstacles to development. What is central for the development of personality is therefore whether we strive to gain influence over the conditions of our existence by means of submissiveness, denial, and censure of our own "unreasonable" demands, or by trying to extend our action potence so as to fully realize our needs and interests. Not by utilizing, but only by rejecting, the social vacuums within which freedom exists only so long as we function according to ruling ideas and interests can a personality develop that stands up for its convictions and is not distracted from them by bribery or threats. Nelson Mandela demonstrates the strength of his personality by rejecting – in full awareness of the political consequences – the "freedom" that would be granted to him in exchange for giving up the fight against apartheid and replacing it with an internal struggle for his own humanity (cf. the remarks on Luther by Brendler, 1983).

Mediation between individual and society is thus not a "habitus," the bundling together of societal influences and/or the particular appropriation by individuals of the knowledge and capabilities necessary for them to master the various spheres of life, but rather the social responsibility of human beings for their social conditions, their conscious relationships to existing living conditions and their own needs, recognizing how these came about and how they can be changed. People's consciously relating to the conditions of their existence and to themselves is in turn determined by their societal action potence, that is, through their relationships to their fellow human beings, where powerlessness means not exoneration from responsibility, but the duty to make oneself action potent vis-à-vis conditions that restrict development. The "genuine subject" is not, as Marx stated, to be grasped "as a result" but rather in "his objectification" (Marx, 1844/1970b: 224). Instead of defining ourselves through our past experiences and sufferings and making these responsible for our present limitations, despondencies, and indifferences to societal conditions, we must define ourselves through our demands on life and our goals, through what we stand up for and what we accomplish. We must comprehend ourselves as social forces that are partially determined by our past but mainly determined by our relationships to our fellow human beings.

The attitude of young people is determined not primarily by their specific experiences of socialization, but more by their present experiences of feeling unimportant and useless, by their real powerlessness and dependency. The willingness of workers to strike, as an investigation by Bosch (1978) shows, crucially depends on their current possibilities for action, the willingness of other workers to strike, and the chances of achieving their demands. Personal factors only become determining for behavior to the extent that the general action potence, for instance, the strike-front, crumbles and individuals are once more isolated, powerless, and thrown back onto the defensive maintenance of their own existences.

According to Gramsci, "culture" is not an accumulation of knowledge and capabilities, but rather the "discipline of one's ego," which is directed to one's own goals. The "possession of one's own personality" can be achieved not by repressing one's rebellious impulses, needs, and cognitions, but only by resisting any censorship and repression of these subjective experiences and evaluations of objective reality. For Gramsci, personality is the development of a higher consciousness. This higher consciousness involves the idea that human beings comprehend themselves in their collectivity, that is, recognize themselves as a social force and so comprehend "their own historical value . . . , their own function in life, their own rights and duties" (1967: 21) and develop a "greater consciousness of their power, their ability to take on social responsibility, to become arbiters of their own fates" (1967: 31).

At the same time, the "conquest of a higher consciousness" means that people do not allow themselves to be absorbed by reality, but learn to control it (p. 31). It means that they do not remain bound "egoistically and without logical continuity" to a "system of defense against exploitation" and to "pussyfooting and sham subservience" (p. 35), but create the "necessary conditions for the complete realization of the ideal" (p. 26). The development of personality is not achieved through directly "working on oneself," one's feelings, needs, and so forth, in accordance with ruling interests; rather, it involves the struggle against all conditions in which the human individual is a "humiliated, enslaved, abandoned, and despised being" (Marx, 1970b: 385). This struggle for objective conditions in which unobstructed subjective development can take place is also, as Gramsci emphasized, a fight against "degrading servility," that is, against every form of covering up or glorification of this servility – as personal freedom, individual autonomy – in bourgeois ideology and psychology.

Perspectives and Difficulties of Elaborating the Marxist Outline of Personality Theory

In the basic definitions derived from our critique of bourgeois theories we have indicated the contradictory poles of subjective existence under bourgeois conditions, which must not be ignored or separated again in a Marxist theory of personality. At the same time we have emphasized the need to be constantly on guard against unwittingly incorporating elements of the bourgeois ideology of personality. We have thus presented only the basic requirements for a Marxist psychological conception of personality, but not its concrete definition. Much of the preliminary work for such a concrete outline for a Marxist theory of personality has been done by Critical Psychology, especially through its elaboration of the concept of "restrictive versus general action potence," with its implications for the contradictions in cognitive, emotional-motivational processes, their social connections, and their ontogenetic laws of development in bourgeois society (cf. Holzkamp, 1983). The problem of individuality as a "site" of personality-specific formation, integration, and continuity/discontinuity of psychical functional aspects has, however, only been touched upon. A major part of our future work will be concerned with the clarification of such matters by working through psychological, literary, and artistic portrayals and manifestations of human individuality as it is shaped by various forms of society.

What about existing Marxist theories of personality, especially the ones developed in Soviet psychology, the cultural historical school in particular? Hasn't the task we have set ourselves already been carried out? Can't we simply adopt these view instead of starting out on our own?

In answer to these questions, we should first acknowledge that the works of the cultural historical school have provided the essential foundations for the development of a Marxist psychology in bourgeois society. Critical Psychology would not have been possible without the ideas of A. N. Leontyev in particular. His objective definition of the psychical as a signal-mediated life activity, his "genetic" approach to the object of psychology, and much else still make up the categorial-methodological essentials of Critical Psychology. However, as Critical Psychological research became more concerned with the specifically human social characteristics of the psychical, especially with the contradictions of individual subjectivity in bourgeois society, we found that Leontyev's conceptions became less useful; indeed, we became quite critical of some of them (cf. Holzkamp-Osterkamp, 1976; Keiler, 1985; Maiers, 1985).

The general problem here is whether concepts and findings of psychology in socialist societies can be transferred to bourgeois society. First, it must be kept in mind that psychology, not only the science itself but also its "object," the individual subject, must be seen to be historically determined by concrete societal conditions. It follows that the categorial determinants of the psychical at the level of "people in general" must be made conceptually (and methodologically) specific so that we can grasp concretely those aspects of individual subjectivity that are historically determined by specific societal relations. A simple "downward concretization" of the basic categories worked out by Soviet psychology (activity, appropriation, and so forth) would be subject to the same error as that of the bourgeois economists criticized by Marx for "forgetting" the historically specific feature of work and production in "proving" the "eternity and harmoniousness of existing social relations" (Marx, 1857–8/1974: 85). If we simply transferred those concretizations of concepts and procedures developed by Soviet psychologists to refer empirical subjectivity under socialist conditions to the subjective situation of individuals in bourgeois society, then the conceptions – especially those of personality theory – would function for the latter individuals as abstract norms unconnected to their real problems of life, ones that they in principle cannot meet because the required societal conditions are not available. This would further contribute to the increase of feelings of irritation and insufficiency of individuals, which would then converge with the bourgeois conceptions of personality about powerlessness and the sovereignty of the isolated individual.

A further aspect of the problem of transfer has more to do with the history of science: one has to keep in mind that psychological conceptions do not develop in a vacuum or in direct relation to the object, but out of concrete scientific and political-ideological discussion. This is true not only in bourgeois society, but also under socialist conditions. The characteristics and direction of psychological approaches and findings only become sufficiently comprehensible when the ideas they are trying to overcome and interests they are defending are taken into account. This precludes their simple incorporation into the scientific-historical context of psychology in bourgeois society (of which the Marxist theory of personality in this country is also a part). We must not forget that Soviet psychology is not a mere accumulation of correct findings but progresses as a living science by way of intense debate. There are no superordinate concepts that can indicate to us which of the multiple and contradictory expressions of Soviet psychology or personality theory existing at a certain point in history we should adopt for our situation, so the problem is extremely complicated.

I have not been able to describe adequately, let alone solve, the problems of transfer here. On the contrary, it must be admitted that these problems, for example, the difficulties for Critical Psychology in relating to Leontyev's work, have until now asserted themselves in our everyday scientific work in an unreflected way. Their systematic and critical reappraisal remains to be done. There has not yet been a comprehensive discussion among all parties concerned. It should have at least become clear from my critical comments that whatever this discussion might bring about in detail, the concrete task of psychologically working out a Marxist sketch of personal existence with respect to individuality and personality development in bourgeois society still lies, in any case, ahead of us.

9   The Concept of Attitude

Morus Markard

As explained elsewhere in this volume, Critical Psychology demands a fundamental critique and revision of psychology's basic concepts and, to that end,
employs an historical reconstruction of the development and differentiation of
the psychic as a means of investigating the *formation* of basic concepts. The
new method of concept formation made possible by this historical approach
begins with an analysis of already existing concepts to determine their precise
object reference, their limitations, and their mystifications, so that their potential scientific value and status in the conceptual system of general psychology
can be established. The operational version of this Critical Psychological
principle of the unity of critique and further development is called *reinterpretation*. The classic example is Ute Holzkamp-Osterkamp's (1976) reinterpretation of Freudian concepts in the development of her "conflict model."

The critical result of reinterpretation should not be that already existing concepts (what Holzkamp has called preconcepts) continue to exist eclectically,
side by side with the newly developed concepts, regardless of their incompatible theoretical and methodological origins, but that the epistemological value
of the old concepts is preserved and becomes incorporated into the new ones
through an appropriate transformation. Determining the value of existing concepts can be done either by an analysis of the historical development of the
object itself or by a reconstruction of the history and development of the concept within the discipline. The latter form of analysis is usually secondary;
that is, it is used as a preliminary or follow-up to the first.

It should be clear that concepts in the old system will not necessarily re-
emerge in the new system with "equal rank." Indeed, the concept will re-
emerge at all only to the extent that "within the categorial reference of the
preconcepts the psychological object is grasped in a limited, one-sided, mystified way, but is not totally misconceived" (Holzkamp, 1983: 518). The *kind*
of reinterpretation that is possible, that is, whether its universality is totally
repudiated or it is subsumed within a more comprehensive concept, depends
on the actual object reference of the concept concerned.

180

This chapter presents an analysis of the concept of attitude using the second of the two approaches described above, that is, reconstructing the history and development of the concept within the history of psychology (see Markard, 1984, for a more detailed analysis).

The Many Definitions of the Concept of Attitude

The impetus for this analysis was the contrast between the immense popularity of the concept and its conceptual indeterminacy. As early as 1935 Allport remarked that no other concept appeared as often in the psychological literature. He also found that the term meant different things to different authors; its meaning was not fixed. Katz and Stotland (1959) referred to attitude as an "orphan child" and reported that it had "rather contradictory functions for opposed theoretical positions" (in behaviorism, for example, it was used to gain flexibility, whereas it had a stabilizing function in field theory). As for popularity, Cialdini, Petty, and Cacioppo (1981) reported a renewed interest in attitude research and Fisch and Daniel (1982) identified attitude research as one of the five top research areas in social psychology. Smith (1980), comparing the quantity of research activity to the increase in knowledge gained, remarked sarcastically: "Pages accumulated; what else?" The arbitrariness of definitions will be obvious to anyone who has recently examined a pertinent textbook or collection of papers.

In view of such a desolate situation, our first question must be whether this concept really has a determinable object. Can we solve the problem of the indeterminacy of the concept by listing all the distinguishable aspects contained in existing representative definitions? The answer is surely No! On the one hand, such a jumble would contain moments that are mutually exclusive, whereas, on the other, an attempt to establish a lowest common denominator would exclude important aspects or even constitute a new object (such as "affect"). If we tried to complement the lowest common denominator by adding aspects that were felt to be missing, we would merely be reproducing the standard procedure (see Allport, 1935, for a classic example). *What is wrong with approaches like this is that they try to resolve the problematic situation with the very procedures that have created and maintained it.* They lead merely to a proliferation of aspects and do not get to the root of the problem. The limitation of such a method of forming concepts by *combinatory conceptualization* is its lack of criteria, other than that of the convergence or divergence of concepts, for judging whether the definitions make sense. The nature of the problem demands that we retrace the "sequence of definitions" itself, investigate how it is connected to social and psychological problems, and determine the extent to which the currently existing definitional state of affairs is itself a product of conceptual differentiation. Such are the questions I addressed in my *concept-historical reconstruction of attitude*. It should be noted, however, that the concern will be with the development of understanding of the concept in "historical description," without any claim to a history-of-ideas *explanation* of the concept. Nor am I claiming to carry out its materialistic reconstruction "out of the actual context of material societal processes" (Holzkamp, 1973; 39). Where passages of the latter sort appear in what follows, they should be taken simply as indications of obvious connections.

Attitude as a Category of the "Subjective in its Social Context"

The *sociological* or *social psychological* concept of attitude has its origin in its systematic development by Thomas and Znaniecki (1918–1920/1958; cf. Allport, 1935, and Fleming, 1967) in their monumental study of the Polish peasant in Europe and America. Through a theoretical clarification of the problems of "assimilation" of Polish immigrants in America, they tried to show how more general social issues could be resolved, given appropriate sociological conceptions. They took the conflict between the immigrants' situation and their traditional way of life to be *typical*, albeit extreme, for the members of contemporary society. "Modern" society no longer had at its disposal traditions and moral values handed down over the centuries that were unquestionable and binding on individuals. On the contrary, *development* and *flexibility* in the face of ubiquitous social change were the determining aspects of personal societal existence, and it was these that theory had to explain. In view of the massive social problems of the time and the consequent trend toward the establishment of workers' movements, it was surely the idea of the reform (or reformability) of bourgeois society, with its growing contradictions, that gave impetus to a *social scientific* formulation of the problems. What was needed was a theoretical conception that could optimize social control in view of permanent social change, such that no real threat to the maintenance of existing dominance relations could arise. This could only be done by including as objects of control the subjective relations of people to these processes. From a social scientific point of view, this meant overcoming a subjectless sociology and an unsocial psychology and developing an approach that could adequately grasp the individual–society relationship.

For Thomas and Znaniecki the categories of social value and attitude would provide the key to an understanding of this relationship. By "social value" they understood any datum having an *action-relevant meaning* for members of a group; "attitude," on the other hand, is "the process of individual consciousness which determines real or possible activity of the individual in the social world. . . . [It] is thus the counterpart of the social value; activity, in whatever form, is the bond between them. By its reference to activity and thereby to individual consciousness the value is distinguished from the natural thing. By reference to activity and therefore to the social world the attitude is distinguished from the psychological state'' (pp. 21ff). Thomas and Znaniecki's elucidation of the content of their concept of attitude is wide-ranging. It includes cognitive, emotional, and motivational factors, as well as short-term and long-term aspects, physiological-biological deficiencies, complex conscious phenomena, ''internal drives,'' and expressions of behavior, but *the relationship of all these factors to one another is not defined.* They want to set their term *attitude* off resolutely from the existing psychological concepts and point out regretfully that they nevertheless had to describe their *attitude* with the terminology of the contemporary *asocial* psychology: ''to use for different classes of attitudes the same terms which individual psychology has used for psychological processes. . . . The exact meaning of all these terms from the standpoint of social theory must be established during the process of investigation. . . . It would be therefore impractical to attempt to establish in advance the whole terminology of attitudes'' (pp. 22ff.). This is the task of the *social psychology* that is yet to be developed and that, as they later point out, must become ''precisely the science of attitudes.''

Leaving aside the problems arising from the subjectivistic definition of the relationship between social value and attitude, it becomes clear that Thomas and Znaniecki considered attitude to be a *basic concept* of a future social psychology that itself had to be worked out together with the basic concept. The aim of this social psychology would be to displace the existing psychology, which they rejected because it lacked the social dimension needed for investigating the ''subjective in its social context.'' Thus attitude in its original conception proves to have been a category in the sense in which Holzkamp uses the term to characterize *basic concepts of a scientific discipline.* According to this view, categories are concepts with which the object of investigation of a particular scientific discipline can be contrasted with that of other disciplines and with which the essence and internal structure of that object can be grasped (cf. Holzkamp, 1983: 27). They take precedence over both theoretical *and* empirical concepts by indicating what parts of the empirical totality are to be observed.

At a conference of the Social Science Research Council, in 1938, on the topic of ''The Polish Peasant . . . ,'' Blumer (1939) made a presentation that was highly praised by Thomas, in which he said that the methodological scheme developed in connection with the complementary categories of social value and attitude, namely that that ''the cause of a value or of an attitude is never an attitude and a value alone, but always a combination of an attitude and a value'' (Thomas and Znaniecki, 1918–1920/1958: 44), was valid insofar as it referred to the methodological necessity of giving consideration to the general connection between them, but not if taken as a definite law involving precise and invariant relationships. In the terms of our analysis Blumer was in effect making an issue of the status of these concepts as categories. At the same time, criticism of Thomas and Znaniecki's attitude concept for its lack of precision was only justified in that they did not themselves consider their attitude concept to have the status of category, but were using it simply as a generic concept and not as indicating a program for future concretization.

According to these considerations on the origin of the attitude concept, what is significant is only the quasi-programmatic *category* of attitude as the *subjective in its social context* that must become theoretically and empirically substantiated in its manifold and various aspects (and only thus empirically rich in its content). By contrast, the theoretical and methodological content is lost if attitude is misunderstood as simply a singular variable.

From this point of view the further history of attitude research appears as the *formulation of the misunderstanding of a category as a variable*. This confusion of the categorial and variable levels is the dominant theme that emerged in my work on the psychology of attitude.

The "Variabilization" of the Category "Attitude"

The psychological reception of the attitude concept was bound up with the controversy surrounding the function of the subjective in social psychology (cf. the dispute between Bain, 1927/1928, and Faris, 1928, 1931) and the eventual domination in *social* psychology of the experimental method understood as "variable psychological" analysis. The fact that opponents of mainstream S–R psychology could not produce a positive conception of the subjectivity that they accused S–R methodology of ignoring, accelerated the "variabilization" of the category "attitude," which had been accepted at the beginning as a category, although in contradictory ways. Divorced from its original categorial intent, theoretical occupation with attitude was largely reduced to *unending attempts at definition*, the more elaborate of which distinguished attitude from other concepts, such as habit, disposition, stereotype, prejudice, and interest. It was this method of developing concepts that, as we showed earlier, produces definitional indeterminacy. This indeterminacy is clearly illustrated by the fact that the same definitions often applied to different concepts. For example, Faris (1931: 8) defined *attitude* in a way that was identical to Dewey's definition of *habit*, which he intended to distinguish from *attitude* (Dewey, 1922: 40ff.). Such confusion made questions, such as whether or not motivational force must be attributed to attitudes, *as unanswerable as they were uninteresting*.

It is obvious, however, in those definitions that are committed to the three-component model of cognition, conation, and emotion, instead of emotion being limited to one or two of these dimensions and emphasizing the temporal and structural hierarchical organization of attitudes, the original breadth of the concept is still apparent, without, however, its categorial and methodological status being taken into account. The definitional battles had to prove themselves fruitless. With increasing breadth, the definitions became vague; with increasing narrowness they became amorphous, lacking a definite line (for example, Thurstone [1967a] reduced attitude to an affect).

In view of this desolate situation, how is the indisputable popularity of the concept and the apparent ease with which we are able to communicate about attitudes in the everyday context of research to be explained? The answer to this question is indicated by Campbell's (1963: 96) observation that the multitude of definitions of attitude stands in contrast to the similarities in procedures used to study it. The success of the attitude concept has almost nothing to do with the indecisive and unending competition among rival definitions; it has, rather, to do with the fact that attitude is also an everyday term, so that despite the categorial indeterminacy and conceptual chaos, there is a general consensus as the what "roughly" it meant (cf. Murphy and Murphy, 1931: 624, 632). In short, the meaning of the social psychological concept of attitude cannot be determined by examining attempts to define it because these have only an epiphenomenal status as compared with its practical application. We must proceed on the assumption, then, that the operationalization of the commonsense notion of attitude serves as a substitute for its theoretical clarification. If we want further information about attitude, we shall have to test this hypothesis against the actual use of the concept, that is, against its operationalization (especially in attitude scaling as the most developed and dominant form), and then analyze the implications of this practice for the social psychological concept.

The Effective Disregard of the Problem of the Categorial Indeterminacy of Attitude Through Quantification of Its Commonsense Meaning

We are not concerned here with the quality, mathematical or other, of the scales, but with what is required of subjects by way of data production when they respond to the scale items. Surely if anything is "missed" at this point of the procedure, it cannot legitimately be interpreted back in later.

If I refer here mainly to the early pioneering, "classical" scales, this is because no really fundamental change in the issue concerning us here has been introduced by more recent developments in scaling and because the origins of our taking the measurability of attitudes for granted had in earlier times still to be legitimized (for example, Thurstone's "attitudes can be measured," 1928/1967a).

What is demanded of the respondents is first indicated by the instructions. For example, in the pioneering "social distance" scale of Bogardus, which purported to measure attitudes toward people of other races, national groups, and so forth, the instruction reads as follows: "According to my first feeling reactions I would willingly admit members of each race (as a class, not the best I have known, nor the worst members) to one or more of the classifications under which I have placed a cross" (1924/1925: 300). The classifications ranged from "marriage" to "would exclude from my country." Whereas Bogardus's definition of social distance, which draws upon a definition by Park, contains both a cognitive and an emotional aspect, and the intentionlike formulation of the items (for example, "Would you marry a member of this nationality?") contains a conative aspect, the instructions demand an emotional response only. Any cognitive reflection is regarded as an extraneous factor, and its inclusion is explicitly contrary to the instructions. In the separation of the emotional and cognitive "components," which becomes clearer as the history of scaling continues, emotion actually comes to be taken as opposing cognition. Emotions appear to be unrelated to objective reality and are, in this sense, regarded as nonrational.

Of course, there is no way of knowing whether respondents did in fact blindly obey the instructions. But this is unimportant because the reduction expressed by the instructions is accomplished by the procedure, which takes the respondent as exemplifying social distance as an object-detached relationship. What is essential about the type of judgment required of the respondent is that from a few members of a group a representative has to be extrapolated: *the* Bulgarian, *the* Hindu, *the* Turk. It hardly requires pointing out here that such "typical examples" are fictitious. On the other hand, it must be conceded that the unfoundedness of this judgment, that is, of classifying humans as specimens on the basis of fictive traits, does not alter the fact that such judgments are easily produced with the help of the scale. The procedure derives its existence directly from the indeterminacy of its relationship to its object. The failure of social science to question the everyday practice of ascribing traits to certain groups is a prerequisite for attitude scaling. The possibility of scale production stems from its *re*productive character, that is, its capacity to reproduce the everyday thinking in which such fictions are familiar figures. (Rehm, 1986, ascertained from an examination of the pertinent literature that the psychology of prejudice also was unable to specify the referent object of its central concept, although it is defined as "*distorting* reality.")

Although it refers to a definite object, the scale of social distance in fact measures attitude toward a fiction. It does not critically examine everyday categories but necessarily reproduces them. The procedurally determined detachment of attitudes (social distances) from the life situation of the respondent, who is reduced to a mere "bearer" of attitudes, finds its counterpart in the similarly procedurally determined separation of emotions from cognitions. The more or less "free floating" emotion is separated both from its objective causes and from cognition of them. Emotion is thus an abstract internal feeling that is externalized by the questionnaire without altering its status of mere inwardness. The Bogardus scale (Bogardus, 1924/1925) provides therefore a good starting point for our analysis because it is precisely in the reference to its object of "social distance" that the fictitiousness of the object and the unreasonableness of the judgments demanded of respondents are most easily and clearly seen. That this is not unique but typical of scaling altogether can be demonstrated by an examination of the scales that have generally been used in the study of attitudes, namely the Thurstone scales.

For Thurstone (1931/1967b) the everyday notion of attitudes does not function as a link between the category and the variable. Rather it is the very basis of the scientific concept, whose breadth of meaning must be reduced to that of "affect." Its definition is guided by one clear criterion: *measurability*. This sets the standard for both definition and theoretical potential. Assuming that Thurstone did not recognize that definitional indeterminacy was the result of confusing a category for a variable but did recognize that a mere accumulation of definitions could not advance knowledge in this field, the only remaining criterion for a credible definition, and thus also for a reduction in definitional indeterminacy, was one based upon the reduction of the object to a procedure. The *primacy of method over object*, which is characteristic of nomothetic psychology and has been roundly criticized by Critical Psychology, serves the function here of eliminating the definitional chaos caused by inadequate analysis of the object. Thurstone's definition is an expression of the procedural approach to the object, not of the object itself. His statements make it clear that the object of attitude measurement is not a relationship of cognition and emotion, but a relationship that is affective and devoid of meaning.

Before proceeding to illustrate this for the case of the method of paired comparisons, it will be necessary to deal with the relationship between the object "attitude" and *its* object, since attitude is always thought of as an attitude toward something in particular. Without this relationship the whole phenomenon would disappear and with it the relevance of the concept.

The methods of paired comparisons, whose implications for the study of attitude we shall be examining, is concerned with determining a common denominator for the purpose of comparing two objects. If the comparison is to be relevant, the common denominator must represent a dimension that is appropriate to the objects being compared and stems from an analysis of them. As such, this dimension belongs to the object side. Only if this is the case can the *subjective* evaluation *as such* be discerned. In the example of paired comparison of criminal acts, which Thurstone uses for demonstrating the possibility of ranking attitudes, it can be shown that, by excluding important considerations such as severity of act and motive of the perpetrator, a mass of comparisons was made (or had to be made) by respondents, thus constituting standards that can only be understood as reflecting technical considerations having to do with measurement. The procedure forced respondents to arrange potentially noncomparable items on a single scale. Since respondents were systematically deprived of any objectively based standard for comparison, they had to seek one "in themselves" and were thus thrown back onto affect. Procedurally, this proves to be an amorphous continuum that can be *projected* onto any object. The projective character of this operation arises from the fact that the respondent is thrown back onto bare affective appearances, deprived of any factual reference, and thus prevented from making a subjective judgment in the sense of an evaluation of objective reality against the standard of his own subjective situation. Attitude thus becomes an amount of affect residing in the individual, divorced from its object as well as from the individual, divorced from its object as well as from the individual's subjectivity, one that can be projected onto object at will. Following the logic of the scale, there is nothing preventing us from comparing Greeks, abortion, tomatoes, and the pope: Taken two at a time, which do you prefer?

The question remains, however, how the possibility of interindividual scaling is to be explained if it is inner affectivity that is mobilized. The answer is to be found in that everyday consensus by which an understanding of object contents is possible, even though they are unclear: One simply knows roughly what is meant. The minimal consensus between respondent and researcher required for scaling is provided by ordinary commonsense notions that, when taken out of the context of our everyday lives, are no longer meaningful. The inner aspect to which scaling appeals, then, is internalized everyday consensus. To detach oneself from these "popular instincts" is equivalent to refusing to participate in scaling.

Although scaling can only be accomplished on the basis of this everyday consensus, it must at the same time fall short of it. Under the coercion of affective projection, the respondents are prevented from using their practical, everyday rationality, which – for the very sake of survival – demands at least a rudimentary, but always realistic, relation to an object, a vital context that provides criteria for comparison and judgment.

That individual scale items are being made available for affective projection can be seen clearly in the construction of scales of equal-appearing intervals à la Thurstone, in which the researcher, in selecting his items, has to make explicit what is only implicit in paired comparisons by respondents: the constitution of the attitude dimension. Items that are problematic with respect to affective projection are eliminated as "irrelevant" (Thurstone, 1928/1967a). The separation of cognition and emotion is given an especially ideological formulation in the common instruction that there are no "right" or "wrong" answers to the questions (for example, Murphy and Likert, 1938/1967: 14; Schiffman, Reynolds, & Young, 1981: 27), in that in this instruction the distinction between an attitude questionnaire and a performance test is mixed in with the separation of cognition and emotion. Every object content is treated as a matter of personal taste and thus robbed of its objective basis. The respondents are forced to deny their reasons for their judgments and the facts behind these reasons.

The instructions to the effect that respondents should not worry about the consistency of their answers points to a further aspect of scaling: the total isolation of each item from the others on the scale. The ensemble of items does not form an object-related unity but a series of disconnected points. Faced with such a hodgepodge of items that must "somehow" relate to "some kind" of reality, the respondent finds it necessary to create some kind of structure. Considering that reality exists as a network of connections, the isolation of the items, the fundamental exclusion of connections, can be seen as an aspect of the object detachment that we have already demonstrated. This procedurally induced elimination of real connections does not permit *contradictions*, which are, of course, a special form of connection. A contradiction can only appear here as a *logical inconsistency* and thus as an extraneous factor. This, again, falls short of everyday rationality. The everyday practice of weighing matters, "on the one hand" against "on the other hand," must here yield to "either–or."

All this points to the *stupidity* of the tasks demanded of respondents. The scales demand that they carry out tasks that are potentially relevant to their everyday lives, but with the connections to everyday life eliminated. This stupidity, which reaches a peak in every similarity scaling, has a methodological dimension to the extent that it is necessarily both part of the procedure and, albeit unclarified, part of the results. Subjective stupidity is, as it were, the subjective correlate of a method that divorces judgments from their objects and relations and eliminates both the subjectivity and everyday context of the respondent.

These reductions are, however, ignored in the *interpretation* of the data and reified as descriptions of the respondents or even of the objects of attitudes (cf. Thurstone, 1931/1967b: 16). In reality, the fact that "attitude" is defined with respect to an object is not accounted for by the logic and practice of scaling. Since the object has not been analyzed, it remains unclear at all what the measured attitude refers to. In view of this, the *designations* of the scales are obtained under false pretenses. They are interpretations of the respondents' affective projections on the basis of the researchers' assumptions of plausibility. Thurstone himself (1931/1967: 23ff.) gave a lecture to the Midwestern Psychological Association in which he admitted that anticommunist attitudes did not have to be based on any knowledge of communism. To the extent that the researcher confines himself to the collection of measurements, he is relieved of the need to establish what it is psychologically that he is collecting. With scaling, this "theoretical relief" is built in. Moreover, the procedural elimination of nonpsychic matters, such as "the world" and "objective reality," prevents the understanding of the *psychic* processes related to them. The characteristics of the scales we have described cannot be improved by new forms and techniques. They are, as they stand, general *requirements* for scaling. More elaborated techniques of this sort would not lead to more insight into psychic processes, but only to a greater illusion of insight on the part of attitude researchers.

The Irrelevance of the Attitude Concept for the Prediction of Behavior

The theoretical, procedural distortion of the everyday phenomenon of attitude caused by the variabilization of the concept became especially evident in the attempt to relate it to real human action. The implicit expectation of relevance and therefore also of potential for social control (for example, the intent of social control found already in the work of Thomas and Znaniecki) found itself confronted with inconsistent empirical findings regarding the assumed consistency of the attitude–behavior relationship. It became an increasingly central theme of attitude research as efforts to correct the recurring inconsistency in this relationship intensified.

We shall first look at some attempts to approach the problem theoretically. DeFleur and Westie (1963/1964) tried to solve it by distinguishing between "latent process conceptions" and "probability conceptions" of attitude. Whereas the latter limits itself – realistically – to determining the probabilities with which a behavior will occur ("attitude is equated with the probability of recurrence of behavior forms of a given type or direction"), the former assumes that behind the probabilities there lies a "latent variable" (p. 21). This assumption is supposed to be responsible for the "fallacy of expected correspondence" (p. 26). Thus the concept is adjusted to the contradictory empirical data in such a way that the notion of a life context, which is implied at least in an elementary way by the expectation of consistency, is conceptually negated. Thus the problem is simply conjured away. Rokeach (for example, 1980) ends up with much the same result, but in a different way. He distinguished between "attitude(s) toward situation" and "attitude(s) toward object." In his view, behavior is "always a function of at least these two attitudes" (1968: 135), which he arranged into a relatively elaborate system of beliefs and values. Rokeach's critique was directed against the isolation of individual attitudes from the hierarchical system of attitudes and values (1980). But in doing so, he returned the discussion to the very level from which it was meant to be freed by operationism, namely that the indeterminacy of definition (especially clear in 1980: 262). Rokeach has simply taken uncritically the available concept of attitude and, in a kind of reversal of the variabilization of the concept, blown the variable into a surrogate for a theory of personality. The question is no longer whether or when attitudes and behaviors correspond, but which attitude corresponds to which behavior. The concept appears to be saved, but its practical relevance is obtained by false pretenses since attitude and behavior can, by definition, not be separated. The effect is the same as achieved by deFleur and Westie: The inconsistency is not explained; it is explained away.

Ajzen and Fishbein (1977, 1980) do not base their argument directly upon the lack of consistency between attitude and behavior, but upon the assumption that the consistency is lacking in definition. They suggest limiting the expectation of consistency such that attitude and behavior would be related to one another only in precisely specified dimensions (action, target, context, time), since the "classical" expectation of consistency, operationalized as the prediction of *particular* behaviors from *generalized* attitudes, has proved to be unrealistic. In their model (Ajzen & Fishbein, 1980; the book is titled *Understanding Attitudes and Predicting Social Behavior*), attitude is abandoned as a central variable. The immediate determinant of behavior is intention, which is itself determined by attitudes to pertinent behavior and by subjective norms, that, in turn, are a function of "behavioral" and "normative" beliefs. The existence of further variables is not denied, but they are said to have an effect only through the ones just mentioned. Among these further variables is the classical object-directed attitude. By trivializing its relevance for predicting behavior and by marginalizing it as a concept, Ajzen and Fishbein draw the pragmatic conclusion from a desolate situation: They effectively eliminate the variabilized category of attitude.

The majority of researchers, however, have stuck to the traditional concept of attitude and *in principle* to the associated expectation of its behavioral relevance and try to save both by controlling additional variables, which are introduced in an ad hoc manner (for example, Ehrlich, 1969, and the critical response by Tarter, 1970). The original hypothesis, "If attitude A, then behavior B," remains, but it becomes qualified by additional variables. The list of these variables is long (for example, Brannon, 1976) and not at all unified. They vary not only from author to author, but also according to current preferences among psychological researchers. Wicker (1969) observes critically that "the arguments for the significance of each factor are often plausible anecdotes and *post hoc* explanations." He does not, however, raise any fundamental questions about the strategy of maintaining the behavioral relevance of attitudes by bringing additional variables into play. Instead, he calls for a precise operationalization and examination of these variables. But implementing this recommendation by defining the relative importance of the additional variables can neither lead to a determination of the theoretical significance of the attitude concept nor eliminate the theoretically unrestricted generation of more and more additional variables. As demonstrated in the course of further research on the topic, it leads only to a procedurally more elaborate and empirically better confirmed expression of the dilemma that the unlimited qualification of hypotheses regarding the behavioral relevance of attitudes neither yields a theoretical clarification of the concept nor adds to its behavioral relevance. The question whether the concept of attitude has any theoretical value *at all* cannot even be posed within the context of such a strategy because it *specifies* attitude as the central variable from the very beginning. With many of the selected variables, it is not at all clear that they could not be considered as central variables, with "attitude" being taken as an additional variable. If one takes this ragbag of variables seriously, it can only have the consequence of marginalizing attitude, we have seen with Ajzen and Fishbein, whose central concept of intention is no less secure.

The real mediating connection between attitudes and behavior, according to Blumer's critique (for example, 1955/1956), is captured neither theoretically nor methodologically. Without this connection, only the categorially unclarified "poles" are compared, leaving only an inexplicable, accidental miscellany. Following the logic that led to the elimination of this mediating connection, an attempt is then made to compensate for its loss by adding variables that are supposed to systematize the accidental relationships between the "poles."

According to our analysis of the attitude concept, the question of its behavioral relevance is precluded. Since, as we demonstrated earlier, the relationship of the subject to the object has been rendered "unreal" by the method of scaling, the behavior must also have been made unreal and therefore cannot be regarded as in touch with the objective social reality of everyday life. Thus the contradictory findings regarding the behavioral relevance of attitudes cannot be understood in terms of the actual contradictory nature of efforts to cope with reality. The inconsistency of research findings on attitude represents an entirely different kind of contradiction than the ones characteristic of everyday social existence.

The Aggregative Character of the Concept of Attitude and the Impossibility of Its Reinterpretation

We have tried to demonstrate historically that the concept of attitude used in traditional social psychology represents a "variabilization" of a category of the "subjective in its social context," the categorial value of which has not been clarified by the pertinent empirical research. The question remains: Can the concept be *reinterpreted?* In attempting to answer this question, it should first be noted that in the Critical Psychological categorial analysis of the psychological object of investigation no aspect emerged that could be identified as "attitude," so the concept will have to be examined against categories that appear to be "thematically close" to attitude, such as emotion and cognition. Second, individual theories of attitude or attitude change will not be touched by our considerations to the extent that they are informed by assumptions that are independent of attitude (learning theory, dissonance theory, and so forth) and thus require a separate analysis.

The possibility of basing a reinterpretation on the original categorial version of the concept contained in the work of Thomas and Znaniecki is ruled out not only because this would overlook its variabilization but also because it would shift the content of the category onto the most general theoretical and methodological level of the individual–society relationship.

A further possibility is offered by the practical concept, which we worked out as an implication of the scaling method, with its characteristic "reduction of responses to blind affect" and "detachment of the judgment from its object." But here we must take into account that, as part of her general analysis of the category of emotion, Ute Holzkamp-Osterkamp has demonstrated that emotion signifies the *evaluation of objective environmental factors against the standard of one's own subjective situation as an instance of mediation between cognition and action* and is, as such, both "objective" and "subjective" (1975: 154ff.). From our analysis in the section on the effective disregard of categorial indeterminacy, it follows that the attitude concept radically lacks a general definition and that in the reductions forced upon it by the scaling procedures there remains nothing to reinterpret. In its variabilized form, which finds its tersest expression in scaling, the attitude concept is simply *uninteresting* from a theoretical point of view.

Finally there is the possibility of recourse to the *"components"* contained in the definitions of the attitude concept, that is, to cognition, emotion, and conation, which, taken together, are reminiscent of the original category that was misconceived as a variable and was reduced by scaling to blind affect. With regard to these components (leaving aside the squabbles over their definitions and the fact that actual research only deals with "affect"), *attitude appears as a concept without an object, but one in which essential functional aspects of human subjectivity have been brought together in the development of the concept.* This aggregative character precludes the kind of *direct* reinterpretation that would subsume attitude under another concept because the indeterminacy of the aggregation would simply be thereby reproduced. On the other hand, to investigate the components singly would amount to a change of topic.

"Attitude" as an Aspect of Everyday Coping from the Point of View of a Critical Subject-Science

The conclusion that the social psychological concept of attitude proves inaccessible to reinterpretation brings my concept-historical analysis to a close. That attitude is untenable as a scientific concept does in no case mean, however, that its *object*, the everyday phenomenon that we designate as attitude, is irrelevant. Moreover, an important aspect of the analysis of the dominance and spread of the concept would be missing if the *ideological* character of its special way of conceiving the object were ignored. I should like to finish up with some comments on these two points.

In order to determine the ideological function of the concept in bourgeois society, no *additional* analysis is needed. Rather, what is needed is to inquire of the existing results of analysis what functional needs of bourgeois democracy are served by the various characteristics of the concept. The ideological critique derives from the epistemological one. The ideological functions of the concept or, alternatively, their bourgeois partiality are revealed as aspects of its epistemological limitations.

We have demonstrated that a central element of the concept is the object detachment of its empirical referent, which, in turn, leads to a judgmental structure in which the distinction between truth and error is suspended in favor of mere opinion (as opposed to knowledge) based upon a generalized form of personal taste. When we unravel the ideological contents of this kind of relationship to the world, what we find is that when social relations become a field upon which object-detached opinions are to be projected, the inevitable result is that the *normative force of the status quo* prevails over the indeterminate plurality of opinions. By contrast, any claim to true knowledge about societal processes must appear as antipluralistic and antidemocratic, whereas object detachment and lack of commitment pose as "freedom." In the concept of attitude is compressed a notion of democracy from which the objective judgmental capacities of the members of society have, for all practical purposes, been eliminated. This understanding converges on that of Fleming (1967), who concluded that the development of the attitude concept corresponded to a "historical need" to find a name for "the incorporation of the masses into public affairs" that was "neutral and invidious in tone" but at the same time effectively disputed their competence to take part in public affairs (p. 358). Thus *attitude* can be seen as a timely word for a timely mass psychology whose goal was to maintain *control* over the members of society, but in a way that *appeared democratic*.

From the point of view of the ideological critique, the attitude concept appears to be a *specifically psychological version of a seemingly liberal pluralism concept*. The suspension of objectivity in relation to the world in the guise of freedom and democracy is in fact a prohibition against any fundamental critique based on the claim that objectively and scientifically founded decisions can be made with regard to societal planning. Object-detached pluralism of mere opinion is the enforced generalization of objectively unfounded bourgeois domination. In this respect the social psychological concept of attitude belongs to the collection of ideological means of maintaining bourgeois hegemony in a democratic-appearing way.

With this we come to the final problem, namely, to show that the scientific untenability does not imply the irrelevance of the phenomenon we call attitude. To the extent that the social forces and relations are unable to neutralize the blind ideological effects of these ideas, world- and self-confrontations of the type implied by attitude must appear as obstacles to the conscious direction of life and in this sense must become an object of subject-scientific investigation. Apart from theoretical analyses of certain "contents" of attitudes (for example, hostility toward foreigners [Holzkamp-Osterkamp, 1984]), empirical research on attitudes from a subject-scientific perspective can only mean an analysis, carried out with people who are working out their possibilities for action, of the conditions and premises that underlie the projected object-detached relations to the world and thus contribute to making these relations fully conscious.

10 Client Interests and Possibilities in Psychotherapy

Ole Dreier

This chapter is concerned with the function of psychotherapy in relation to client interests and possibilities. The other party in the psychotherapeutic endeavor, the therapist, will be mentioned only to the extent that it is necessary for this purpose. Consequently, this will not be a systematic account of professional psychotherapeutic action and thinking (cf. Dreier, 1987b, 1988a, in press).

There are two sets of presuppositions on which this work is based. First, psychotherapeutic practice should essentially be directed at mediating more extended subjective possibilities for clients. They experience themselves as stuck at particular problematic points in their life contexts, both individually and with others. This deadlock is reflected in their negative subjective state and may take on an explicitly symptomatic form. They may turn to a psychotherapist, or be referred to one, with the aim of creating possibilities for themselves that do not seem to exist in their everyday lives. Faced with such demands, therapists search among available theoretical concepts for the means of defining concrete possibilities for action in order to help their clients realize the possibilities that exist under existing conditions and to create new, extended possibilities. Therapists, for their part, turn to available concepts, especially when they feel stuck with respect to the action possibilities in their concrete practice under existing conditions or when they have doubts about their success. Beyond that, many therapists, especially the critical ones, expect not only to define existing possibilities, but, more important, to establish a basis for extending them. Moreover, this extension should apply both to their present case-related professional action possibilities and to their societal development.

Second, it is presupposed that understanding and taking care of clients' interests and needs must be of central concern to therapeutic practice. This is related to the first presupposition. Difficulties in therapy, such as lack of motivation, stagnation, resistance, and relapse, are especially likely to occur when clients' needs and interests are not being met. The very definition of

196

these needs and interests is already a difficult matter. At the start of therapy they are, in any case, unclear and contradictory. They are not immediately given or, when they are, they appear in forms that must be analyzed as part of the problem.

How, then, can clients and therapists determine these interests and possibilities during the course of therapy? How can therapists ascertain whether they are acting in the interest of their clients? What demands does this place upon therapeutic practice, and how should the therapeutic process be shaped accordingly? These are the questions that follow from the stated presuppositions and that will be addressed in this chapter from the point of view both of immediate therapeutic practice and of Critical Psychology's subject-scientific approach.

Answers to these questions basically require that the client's psychic problems be comprehended within the concrete relations among the following factors (Holzkamp, 1983). First, the meaning to clients of their present objective possibilities and restrictions of action must be understood. Then clients' subjective relationships to this range of possibilities must be analyzed, that is, the structures of their subjective grounds for action as grounded in their relationships to the meanings of their present conditions taken as premises. Moreover, the problems of their action potence and its subjective conditions must be understood, that is, their own experience and appraisal of the relevant prospectives, the objective possibilities, and the subjective prerequisites needed for their realization. Finally, the problems associated with their various psychical functions – cognitive, emotional, and motivational – must be understood.

This kind of analysis of mutually interrelated factors is aimed at reconstructing the problematic subjective processes as aspects of clients' concrete life situations. Their subjective grounds for action and their psychical states are not reduced to being only objectively determined by their conditions, nor is their clarification sought by abstractly looking inward. On the contrary, to do either would be to engage in the form of self-delusion in which clients put themselves, or imagine themselves to be above, beneath, or outside of existing relations. Subjective grounds for action and psychical states can only be clarified within the context of the subjectively problematic relationship to the existing range of possible action. Such a basis for psychological analysis implies a unitary determination of the various levels of the relationship between the subjective and the objective. Only in this way can it serve as an adequate basis for orientation to real subjective possibilities and clarify the subjective range of possibilities. It can be determined both what is possible and what can be made possible, as well as how these possibilities are related to the client's interests and needs. Broadly speaking, casework can then proceed from an initially problematic confusion about these issues to their gradual determination, that is, to an increasingly precise definition of the problem and the orientation of the work needed (Dreier, 1985a). This can lead to a clarification of clients' interest in and need for therapy, that is, the subjective functionality of therapy for them in their life situations. Finally, this makes it possible to delineate and combine the therapeutic spaces of "professional help," "self-help," and "lay help."

The general analyses, as they are sketched above, of the origin and overcoming of particular client problems form the basis of our more specific and concrete exposition of the problems of identifying the possibilities and interests of clients in immediate casework. In this, our focus will be on the conspicuous contradictoriness of interests and possibilities. Only by analyzing these contradictions can the clarification and extension of concrete possibilities and interests by achieved.

The Conflicting Nature of Client Problems

Owing to the central importance of unresolved conflicts in the emergence and maintenance of psychical disturbances (Holzkamp-Osterkamp, 1976, 1978; Dreier, 1980, 1985b, c. 1986a, 1987a, in press), contradictions are a striking characteristic of therapeutic tasks and problems at all levels. Differences between the societal conditions of classes, groups, and individuals produce different interests and hence different premises or subjective grounds for action. This leads to the emergence of contradictory goals and thus to conflict among individuals. The pursuit of one person's interests and goals often restricts the conditions under which others realize theirs. It is done, in other words, at others' expense. Thus, conflicts are based primarily on contradictions of interests, on mutually contradictory partial interests – in contradistinction to general interests, where the actions of the individuals concerned are, at the same time, beneficial to all others. For the individuals, a conflict constitutes a contradiction between the realization of one's own possibilities and their restriction; that is, it is a conflict around the possibilities for individual development. In that sense a conflict in general consists of forces directed for and against possibilities of individual development, respectively. Thus it is generally a conflict of development in an individual's societal life. Individual-subjective disturbance arising out of it is therefore a disturbance of development.

Individuals living under conditions of unresolved conflicts must inevitably relate themselves in contradictory ways to these conditions in order to ensure at least a temporarily tolerable existence. This makes the subjective structure of their grounds for action and of their psychical functional processes contradictory as well. In relation to their opponents, they are restrained and suppressed in a state of relative surrender and impotence. They must make compromises and postpone the realization of relevant possibilities of development to an indefinite future. Particular developments may eventually go off the rails or be given up. In reality, the individuals are being used for purposes not their own and of which they may or may not be conscious. This is reflected in contradictory subjective appraisals of their own grounds for action and mental states. The intentionality of their actions becomes unreliable since they cannot determine in advance either how others will react to them or what the consequences will be for future possibilities for action. The meaning of their own actions, as well as of that of others in the objective context, becomes an object of controversy among all concerned. This concerns their interpretation as well, that is, the understanding of their underlying subjective grounds, motives, and personality characteristics. In other words, the personality itself becomes an object of various forms of inter- and intraindividual conflict. This can mean that the real, societally mediated connections between causes and effects in the objective context of actions become personalized, and thus the premises of subjective grounds of action also become personalized. Out of this arises a conflict about the distribution of personal responsibility and guilt, based on particular personality characteristics. The development of personalized conflicts may reach a point where the individuals "lose their own threads." A basis for individual symptom formation emerges in which individuals, to some extent, no longer understand their own reactions, and psychical processes occur in them that they are no longer able to control in a conscious manner.

Bourgeois conceptions of psychology universalize interpersonal and individual conflicts by assuming the existence of insurmountable, natural contradictions of interests and needs. They deny that conflicts can be overcome in the course of generalizing the conditions and interests of the persons concerned. Accordingly, "conflict resolution" can only consist of shaping new compromises between the parties and for individuals. In relation to therapeutic work on conflicts, this denial implies a distinct restriction and complication of therapeutic possibilities and perspectives for change (cf. the analysis of such issues in Freud's conception of therapeutic practice [Dreier, 1985c]). Therapeutic change must be directed at establishing a new, short-range equilibrium among inherently uncontrollable forces that may lead to a reestablishment of similar difficulties after the termination of therapy. At least therapy cannot be directed at any long-range stability and perspectives for development following the termination of therapy. The typical short-range effects of traditional therapeutic endeavors should, therefore, come as no surprise.

Clarification of individual-subjective contradictions must therefore be an essential task of therapy. At the beginning, clients relate themselves contradictorily to their own interests and possibilities. These may seem to them confused, and they are consequently disoriented. Their self-appraisal may fluctuate periodically or show sudden changes. They may stand unconsciously in the way of their own interests or explicitly believe that they can give them up, although in their subjective suffering they remain significant for them. They may want to behave and express themselves unequivocally (to the point of denying the existence of any conflict at all), without noticing that the positions they adopt do not meet their interests and may in fact partially contradict them. They may feel close to people, social relations, and objectives that are in part suppressing them, and in part ensure their subsistence and reward them with limited privileges for compliance. They may want therapy to provide "solutions" to their "problems," which do not question such relations, and they may vacillate between wanting and not wanting any changes at all. They may even identify totally with given associations and consider their interests to be general ones that are in total accord with their own. They may, in other words, have difficulties distinguishing partial from general interests, allies from opponents, or finding out how to transform relations characterized by a mixture of general and partial interests into ones based on general interests. And so on, and so forth.

Contradictory Alliances and Resistances

Whatever the configuration of conflicts and their subjective expressions may be, clients' equivocal and inconsistent positions imply that it is not possible for the therapist immediately to realize an unequivocal alliance with them. That is why the simple demand that the therapist should represent clients' needs and interests (through empathy or the like) does not correspond immediately with the subjective and intersubjective realities of therapeutic processes. A "cooperative psychotherapy" conceived in that way for example (Fiedler, 1981), or a community psychological orientation "according to the needs of the people" and based on an ideology of society as a social community, are one-sided denials of contradictions in the handling of client interests. Nor can progressively intended principles about "radical partiality for the client" or "absolute unequivocality of one's own actions" (Jantzen, 1980: 134–138) be directly and simply applied. These are analytical stances whose realization only becomes possible in the course of the objective and subjective generalization of client interests. Until then, clients will feel, in various ways, that the attempted one-sided reduction of their interests is making them objects of persuasion, seduction, misunderstanding, mishandling, and so forth. Consequently, they will react with different forms of compliance (often mistaken by therapists for a confirmation of their own interpretations), covert reinterpretation, resistance, withdrawal, interruption, and the like. Still, the analytical perspective of a generalization of interests is the only one by means of which mutual and self-imposed restrictions on possibilities can be replaced by un-equivocality, mutual association, and support as a precondition of more viable and comprehensive extensions of possibilities. In that sense therapy may proceed from a principal indetermination and equivocality toward increasing determination and comprehensive generalization of existing problems and interests. This generalization is only made possible by developing a consciousness about the subjective relationship to the existing conditions, differences among which are the basis of the conflicting interests and contradictory subjective reasons for action. Consequently, the subjective generalization can be realized only to the extent that relevant conditions can be generalized and individuals can unite in this perspective. Generalization is a determination of direction and foundation for unifying concrete possibilities of development. Thus, a basis for therapeutic action can be constituted neither by responding directly to immediately appearing needs, interests, and possibilities nor by maintaining a – however well intentioned – professional monopoly over their definition. It must consist in the clarification of their contradictions and generalizability.

In reality, all talk about the interests of "the" client is an abstraction. Individuals can resolve their conflicts and extend their possibilities only within their particular interpersonal relationships in the various areas of their societal life in which they have arisen. There are always others who are affected by individuals' ways of relating to their conflicting possibilities, including therapeutic treatment and alteration. And how these relate to interests of both parties, conversely, significantly influences the individual's prospects for change in possibilities. It is therefore essential to every individual, whether client or not, to learn to distinguish partial from general interests, as well as to contribute to the clarification and extension of general interests and alliances in one's own life contexts. If clients do not pursue their interests in this way, they will contribute to the maintenance of interpersonal conflict, give others good reason to oppose them, and eventually reproduce their own relative isolation and suffering.

In the history of therapeutic practice it was due precisely to these conflicting mutual influences among immediately concerned individuals that others were brought in various ways into the therapy. It was particularly done in order to take into account the otherwise threatening resistance to, restriction, or even annihilation of therapeutic progress, which could result from the interpersonal conflicts of which the individual symptoms are a part and could be further aggravated by the individualistic ways in which therapists supported their client's development. Interestingly enough, the phenomenon of individual resistance in therapy was simply replaced by interpersonal resistance (Esser, 1987). From being mediate objects of the therapeutic process, interpersonal conflicts became immediate objects. That, of course, only multiplied the problems of the therapeutic handling of interests and the creation of alliances. Based on the premise of the universality of partial interests, traditional therapeutic conceptions posed this dilemma for therapists in the form of questions like the following: With whom and against whom should therapists ally themselves? Could and should they totally balance out or conceal their partiality? Could and should they position themselves as a neutral expert, totally outside or above the conflicts? Should they, so to speak, use their partiality as a "totally impersonal" technique of therapy, thus instrumentalizing their own personality? Is it possible for them to involve themselves in the process and bypass the whole issue of partiality by being "purely humane"? Let us, however, insist on the following fact: Clients and other persons affected do not agree about the nature of the problem to be treated, what its conditions are, what or who is the cause of it, how and what can and should be changed, and which perspectives and goals of change should be pursued. As a consequence, they also do not agree about what the therapy should be used for or about which concrete function and meaning it has or ought to have. If they claim to agree on these issues and a therapeutically guided process of change is still necessary, it is because their point of view on the problems is itself a problematic one and thus cannot lead to a solution of the problem. This is because, for example, it is based on partial interests and therefore may be against the interests of others immediately affected, possibly even against the client's own interests, and will evoke negative reactions to the attempted changes.

Furthermore, let us insist on the fact that the therapist's means, actions, grounds, and perspectives are also objects of conflict. Since they are necessary conditions for the clients' processes of change, they become themselves part of the field of conflict. The only tenable conclusion that the therapists may draw from this about their own actions is that the ambiguity and its basis in the conflict must be taken into account and treated as a special, even essential, object of therapeutic practice. They must make clear the societal mediation of the immediately appearing personalized conflicts, their dependence on objective conditions as premises of their subjective grounds, and therefore also the possibilities for overcoming them through the generalization of conditions, interests, and grounds. In this respect the many versions of therapy as problem solving, such as are found, for example, in the cognitive therapy tradition, are reductive and one-sided. The general ambiguity of conflict processes does not allow for an unequivocal definition of the initial problem. This would only be possible once a complete resolution of the conflict had been achieved. Until that should happen, individual points of view on the problem would not totally coincide, and no individual contradiction could be defined more closely than as simply a contradiction. If therapy were carried on despite the contradictions, the results would be superficial, one-sided, not in conformity with the interests of the subjects.

Societal Mediation of Client Conflicts

We have repeatedly drawn attention to the contradiction between regarding conflicts from an immediate point of view and as mediated. In Critical Psychological categories, this corresponds to the distinction between the interpreting [*deutenden*] and comprehending [*begreifenden*] modes of thinking as the cognitive functional aspects of restrictive and generalized action potence (Holzkamp, 1983). In our exposition we have used these categorial definitions as a general analytical basis for addressing concrete empirical questions. Restrictive action potence and the interpretive mode of thinking are subjectively functional whenever individuals experience an inability to extend the possibilities for relevant action because of particular conflicts and, instead, reject this alternative in favor of finding an adjustment to their dependency on existing conditions. Events within the immediate life situation are then interpreted, in short-circuit fashion, as having their causes only in the participating individuals and their interaction. Responsibilities and guilt must, accordingly, be distributed among the participants. Since the restrictive mode of action is based on the continued existence of contradictory interests, interpretations are permeated with contradictions both within and among individual participants. As a consequence, the interpretive mode of thinking maintains the impotence in relation to that which can only be overcome by means of generalization. It is, moreover, characterized by a tendency to personalize, whereby individuals deny the impact of their circumstances on the premises of their subjective grounds for action. Thus they position themselves in abstract opposition to others, above, beneath, or outside of the situation. Interpretive thinking, furthermore, tends to be characterized by a static notion about existing conditions, denying precisely their nature as possibilities. This is expressed in equally static characterizations of the immediate participants and in the belief that changes must be implemented from outside, as many clients expect from their therapist at the beginning of therapy.

For these reasons, the demand on therapists can be neither to affirm immediately nor simply to negate the subjective point of view of clients regarding their problems. They must, rather, transcend the boundaries of immediacy (Holzkamp, 1983) and move toward a comprehensive clarification of the concrete societal mediation of their mental states, their conflicts, and the possibilities of overcoming them in the various areas of their lives. This task of therapists might be called a task of mediation, starting as it does from the contradiction between the immediate restricted point of view of the problem and the real societal mediation of individual existence. It is the task of revealing societal possibilities of action and getting people to think beyond the immediately observable aspects of the individual life situation. Only when this happens does individual thinking rise above the level of short-circuited "sensuous evidence" to the level reconstructing the range of individual–societal possibilities and expanding into a more comprehensive, developmental form of thinking.

This clarification of the subjective functionality and of the contradictory interests behind restrictively interpreted mental states and grounds for action can only be pursued as a part of subjects' experienced extension and generalization of their individual possibilities for action, which permit them to overcome these contradictions. It is the discovery of such possibilities that makes it subjectively functional to further clarify one's own subjective state. In so doing, clients come to understand how the existing possibilities for action relate to their problematic subjective mental state. They see beyond their short-circuited, personalized view of them and develop perspectives on what changes can be made in the range of possibilities in order to improve the subjective mental state. They understand how their mental states can be improved by extending prospective possibilities and how they depend upon these.

The generalizations that clients develop about "their" cases thus deal with their subjective range of possibilities and their interests and needs in its extension. It becomes clear to them which conditions must be present, or must be created, in order to realize relevant extensions of their possibilities, as well as what (altered) subjective prerequisites and behaviors are required for that realization. Implicitly or explicitly, they use general categorial definitions of societal mediation of individual existence to elucidate their particular subjective range of possibilities and to generalize their cases empirically into "such a case" of a "typical range of possibilities" (Holzkamp, 1983: ch. 9).

Inside or outside the therapeutic setting, and together with others immediately concerned, clients clarify the meaning that the conditions of their objective contexts of action have for their individual mental states and grounds for action. That makes it possible for them to ground their problems and demands in this reality. In this way others, too, can reconstruct them and take a rational stand on them. It becomes clear to clients and others that overcoming their problems implies definite demands on the way in which they relate to each other, since that relationship represents a condition affecting each party's range of possibilities. Likewise, it becomes clear to clients that problems are partially determined by how others relate to them and how, conversely, their problems affect their possibilities and mental states in problematic ways. Two things become clear from this. First, in principle, everybody is represented in this process as individual cases of human beings relating to their own possibilities in a context of action that each shares and that constitutes the premises of each person's mental states and grounds for action. In that sense everybody is alike in being an individual center of intentionality and an other to the others: Thus everybody appears basically generalized (Holzkamp, 1983). The intersubjectivity of the interpersonal relationship is revealed and generalized.

Second, the different mental states and ways of relating to the shared context of action can be understood on the basis of its different meanings and possibilities for the individuals concerned. In other words, the differences can be grounded and reconstructed on the basis of the shared contexts of action. Ways in which they can be maintained or transcended become apparent. Consequently, it can be determined more precisely what is in reality generalizable and what is not and how to deal with the relationship between that which is general and that which is unique.

Since therapy is a particular process of extending subjective possibilities, it demands of both clients and therapist that they think about possibilities, that they work on developmental thinking that aims at the clients' being able to determine and realize, generalize and extend the range of their concrete subjective possibilities. Thus, the therapeutic analysis of subjective, mental states does not remain (subjectively short-circuited) at a descriptive level of immediate appearances, the mediation of which is not understood and thus cannot be elucidated in a generalizing and objectifying way. Nor is the mental state explained and influenced from the external position of a therapist or some other powerful person, that is, denied "first-person" existence (Holzkamp, 1983: ch.9). Therapy does not adhere to an ideology of complete, final solutions. It is conceived as a particular support for steps in a definite direction that can be extended beyond its termination, depending on concrete possibilities. It can do no more, although some expect therapy to have some special "secret" that enables it to create a satisfying life under dissatisfying conditions, so that one may safely let things take their course and take private refuge in therapy. Therefore, therapy must be evaluated according to the way in which it supports the processing of present possibilities and their extendability.

The Subjective Functionality of Therapy for Clients

According to our exposition thus far, therapy is a particular processing of the subjective forms of conflicts found in the clients' societal life contexts. Thus, the meanings of the whole therapeutic arrangement – relationship, interactions, and the therapist's personality – can only be ascertained in relation to their status in or connection to the clients' societal life contexts. The contents and forms of therapeutic interaction cannot be determined in themselves. Most therapeutic conceptions, however, attempt to do just this. They try, so to speak, to reveal their "secrets" in the microprocesses of the immediate therapeutic relationship. This is another expression of the adherence to immediacy that is characteristic of therapeutic forms of thinking (Dreier, 1988a).

The clients' own subjective ways of relating within and toward their therapy must, likewise, be conceived on the basis of how they experience the meaning of their therapy in their life contexts.

By that we mean, first, that events and processes in the client's everyday lives, outside the immediate therapeutic relationship, decide whether, how, and for what they use their therapy in coping with their conflicts – including whether, how, and which themes from therapeutic interactions will be further processed and possibly reinterpreted. Unfortunately, the ideology of a "neutral service" has made therapists refrain from exploring which and how interchanges with, and effects on, everyday living determine the occurrence of therapeutic "success" or "failure." Had they explored that, they would have been forced to take a stance on the issue of whether therapy overcomes the real causes of psychic suffering or simply offers "other solutions" that bypass them.

Second, only within clients' life contexts can we determine the contribution that therapy really can make, that is, what the actual needs and interests are and what possibilities exist for a therapeutic response to them. It is therefore only possible to clarify the questions posed at the beginning of this chapter on the basis of the connection between life context and therapy. Though dominant ideology tells us that therapy and the therapist exist for clients and in their interests, we must, nevertheless, realize that the real meaning of therapy for clients, their experiences with this meaning, and their perspectives on an undertaken therapy remain surprisingly unexplored. We are confronted with a noticeable contradiction in therapeutic action and thinking, according to which everything is done for the clients' sakes, even though they are viewed and appraised only from the therapist's external, profession-centric perspective – and not "in first-person." This represents a violation of a supposedly subject-related practice by a form of "science of control" (Holzkamp, 1983: ch. 9). To the extent that the interest in control permeates the process, clients necessarily become unmotivated regarding their therapy. Only if they are caught up in the ideology can the therapy they are being offered appear to them as their own, that is, their own particular means of processing and overcoming their conflicts. For this to be the case in fact presupposes a democratization of the control over the therapeutic process. Influence on its definition and course must be made possible for clients in such a way that they actually discover such possibilities for themselves, that they can make use of them, and that it can become subjectively functional for them to question their own mental states and ways of relating (including to their own therapy). Only then do their needs and interests become transparent, and the therapist's understanding of them becomes less complicated by contradictory, tactical behaviors.

Clients' Position and Influence Within Therapy

To become a subject of one's own therapy cannot be achieved simply by the inclusion of individual-subjective "inwardness," as is done, for example, in "empathic" and "client-centered" therapies. Therapy must rather be developed on the basis of possibilities to relate consciously to one's own therapy as a condition for looking after one's own interests. If that is not done, a therapy, however much "client centered" it is, must finally be expected to have to deal with relatively unmotivated clients, or to try to legitimate relative therapeutic stagnation by interpreting the clients as unmotivated. All that remains then is to carry through therapeutic changes by means of persuasion, subtle pressure, outwitting, allurement, and other tricks (Dreier, 1984).

In the end, this kind of restricted realization of the subject's position in the immediate therapeutic situation leads to false interpretations of client's behaviors. Therapeutic interpretations misunderstand clients to a much higher degree than is generally assumed, and, indeed, without being discovered – except by mere accident – because the client's perspectives are not comprehensively encouraged, explored, or conceptualized (this contradiction is given impressive, empirical support by Eliasson & Nygren, 1983). On the one hand, this leads therapists to misinterpretations and imprecise conceptions of the meaning and impact of their overall therapeutic procedure and their particular reactions. On the other hand, therapists must consequently interpret their clients on the basis of the implicit assumption that the clients just "are" as they are interpreted to be. A concrete disproof of their interpretations, if taken seriously at all, often only leads the therapists to construct other interpretations about their clients. All in all, to a remarkable extent, clients are seen only from their therapists' perspectives, one-sidedly, profession-centrically, and not from their own.

That is why it has remained relatively unexplored how clients selectively use, neglect, weigh, appraise, and generalize from the present (or present*ed*) therapeutic meanings. In addition, it has remained just as unexplored how, at various points in the course of therapy, clients construct hypothetical connections that are different from those that therapists construct for themselves on their clients' behalf. Of course, clients may come to the same suppositions and results, but then often by another route or as a result of other episodes in the course of therapy, which, cumulatively processed, causes a particular connection to "dawn upon them" or be altered. The clients' points of view, their ways of relating to their therapy, and their structures of subjective grounds are, in other words, different in many respects from what their therapists suppose.

What's more, they are certainly unclarified, contradictory, and conflicting at important points, and they change in the course of therapy. For therapists it is important to understand and consider the conditions and processes of precisely these developmental steps when trying to clarify their own grounds for action. Add to this that perspectives, ways of relating, and courses of change differ systematically among individual clients, even those involved in the same case, as we established earlier from the general existence of conflicts and took into account in defining the therapeutic task.

Our exposition should have made it clear that clients include their therapists in their subjective processing in a much more encompassing and complicated way than is normally supposed. Relating to the experienced meaning of their therapy, they also relate to the experienced meaning of their therapists' actions, to the therapists' grounds for action, and to their personalities. All this they interpret, and their interpretations achieve their particular status from the way in which they relate to their conflicts and their clarification. Therapists are included in and interpreted from the perspective of their clients' fields of conflict in the latter's attempts to give their therapists a particular function in accordance with their own interests. That leads, naturally, to misinterpretations, reinterpretations, and instrumentalizations of these interpretations in the various struggles in which they are engaged. In other words, therapists become an object of struggle for the clients, and the impact of their actions is mediated by the struggle that takes place largely outside of the immediate therapeutic relationship.

Against this background it is decided for clients which means of procedures can be used for understanding their conflicts. In other words, it all depends upon the range of their conflicting subjective possibilities, including their peculiarly developed subjective-functional presuppositions. The generalization of particular therapeutic strategies and means must, consequently, be based on a generalization of their individual usefulness to clients with typical ranges of possibilities.

Concrete decisions about strategies and means should, accordingly, not be taken by the therapists over the heads of their clients. Nor should they be applied in a uniform way according to some abstract standard, as might be legitimated by the science of control. Using them in this way would lead to clients' submitting to the therapist's treatment in what is alleged to be their interests. In fact, therapeutic actions cannot be defined in terms of diagnostic or technical units based on abstract standards, but rather only in terms of the existing, conflicting possibilities for both clients and therapists. It is, after all, the clients who have the experience with the subjective conflicts in their life contexts, and therefore in the end only they can decide which analysis is suited to grasping the origin of their conflicts and eventually overcoming them.

Therapists, on the other hand, possess more or less explicit theoretical experience, generalized from other cases, about similar types of possibilities. They can use this experience to form hypotheses about how to uncover the nature of the new case and, at least tentatively, how they should proceed. The development of such hypotheses gives the therapist more systematic knowledge of the range of subjective mental states and grounds for action and of ways for getting at and resolving their internal conflicts. These hypotheses can be compared with particular individual cases to determine their generality and applicability. They can also be useful in helping to identify the pertinent details of a particular case. Under such a strategy, the aim would not be to subsume individual cases under types of possibilities; rather, it would be to use existing experience to expose the generality and particularity of each case and to advance its treatment accordingly.

Some democratically intended conceptions, on the contrary, claim that the use of such theoretical experience implies the denial of individual uniqueness and a prejudiced, reductive influence on clients that does not meet their needs or interests. It is concluded that the therapist should not be allowed to apply any definite theory, but should leave the choice to the client. Such a view surely does imply quite a different and more critical appraisal of existing therapeutic practice than the prevailing supposition of its being a service in the interests of its clients. But it is quite a different view from that stated above, that practice can serve clients' interests. It suggests that the therapist should renounce professional and theoretical experience merely on the suspicion that it is inadequate. But it is unreasonable to expect one to do everything possible to help and to give up assumptions at the same time. Why, then, after all, is a therapist there? In any case, it is doubtful whether an analysis of available possibilities and their extendability can be omitted without neglecting essential client interests, including those in therapy. So an extensive analysis of present ranges of possibilities can hardly be regarded as a reductive manipulation.

Such ethical considerations and suggestions have another background, however. Therapy enters into the interpersonal, societal conflict about individual characteristics and the interests involved in influencing them. It cannot be removed from its immediate connection to particular interests of control. The societal organization of therapeutic work is, in part, connected with the handing over and taking over of control. It is therefore necessary to clarify the societal contradiction in interests related to therapeutic action at the level of concrete casework. For therapists, this societal contradiction in their professional action corresponds in many ways to the tendency of many clients to give the therapist the responsibility for and control over their therapy. They do this because they feel powerless in relation to their conflicts or because they hope to get a neutral solution from their therapist that can be accepted by everyone immediately involved, although it remains an object of mutual struggle. The readiness to submit to the therapist's treatment corresponds to and maintains the contradictions in their restrictive modes of action, which were supposed, on the contrary, to be overcome. In this way, it constitutes a contradiction between the means – control by others – and the real objective and goal of therapy – increased determination by the subject. This contradiction stands in the way of getting clients involved in shared control over their therapy. It restricts their capacity for working with pertinent conflicts. To many therapists, such client involvement seems to contradict their own possibilities for responsible use of their knowledge. This shows that they think of their knowledge mainly as a means of influencing and controlling their clients. Conceptions and forms of practice based on a science of control as a means of handling the everyday contradictions of therapeutic practice are still widespread. The range and viability of such contradictory forms of practice has to remain limited. The most clear-cut examples of such an approach are so-called systemic therapy (Esser, 1987) and the tradition of behavior therapy (Dreier, in press).

Ranges of Possibilities for Professional Practice

We should be reminded that we are dealing with professional practice only when professionals are included. If we want to comprehend therapeutic practice, it is therefore not enough to analyze clients and their claims on therapists. We must also include the therapists' possibilities of supporting or realizing client interests and needs. It is, in other words, necessary to make an equivalent analysis of therapists' ranges of action (Dreier, 1987b, in press). This would also entail an analysis of their needs and interests. These are not immediately apparent, but only become evident from a subjective processing of their contradictory conditions. To be comprehended, they must be investigated just like their subjective ways of relating, grounds for action, and mental states. If we are not satisfied with a personalizing interpretation of therapeutic action that stays within the boundaries of immediacy and want to comprehend the therapist's ways of relating also at the level of immediate casework, then these boundaries will have to be transcended. When we talk of the societal interest of control in therapy, it is obvious to most people that therapeutic actions cannot be comprehended only in relation to client needs and interests. This is, by the way, one reason for the suspicion of professional conceptions and grounds for action mentioned above. But it does not apply only to the interests of control and the contradiction between control and help. It pertains as well to the execution of help itself. Help cannot be optimally exercised if therapists simply place themselves at the disposal of clients' needs while pushing their own range of subjective possibilities into the background or trying to forget it for the time being. That leads, on the contrary, to restricted care for client interests (Bader, 1985). Besides, it represents an illusion that denies the real influence of the therapist's own interests and of societal interests on casework and therefore mystifies the interpretations made about the clients. Clients already know that they relate to the contradictory contexts of action in which therapists execute their practice, and they interpret therapist actions and grounds within that context. They do not merely relate to the personality of the therapist as some kind of isolated creature, although many therapists believe and expect precisely that.That kind of reduced self-conception appears in many therapists' everyday forms of thinking, but even more distinctly in common conceptions about therapeutic action in which their actions are interpreted on the basis of their immediate relationship with their client. The typical conceptions are, in other words, much too restricted. Technicalizing conceptions about therapeutic action are one such expression of an adherence to immediacy in therapeutic notions about practice.

Therapeutic action is, in reality, determined by experienced, concrete possibilities, restrictions, contradictions, and conflicts, for the client as well as for the therapist. It can be guided neither by abstract-normative conceptions nor directly by immediate client needs. Its subjective grounds, generalizations, conceptions, and development must, on the contrary, be determined on the basis of an analysis of concrete ranges of possibilities. In relation to our present topic, the task is to determine the therapist's societally mediated possibilities, interests, and contradictions relating to the care of client needs and interests (Helbig, 1986). We must ask what kind of professional possibilities and conceptional means of action need be at hand if client needs and interests are to be comprehensively attended to. Practice must, in other words, be evaluated according to the possibilities of both clients and therapists. Therefore, it depends on therapists' understandings of their possibilities and how they respond to the extension of their relevant, societally mediated, professional ranges of possibilities. This sketches a long-range perspective that is capable of guiding concrete steps toward the development of professional therapeutic practice. Its execution will, of course, depend on the given possibilities. This kind of analysis of concrete contradiction and possibilities is the topic of the project "Theory–Practice Conference" within Critical Psychology (for example, Dreier, 1988c). It aims at analyzing present contradictions of the professional practice of therapists who are unavoidably caught up in prevailing conditions, with a view to sketching out possibilities of further development.

11   Play and Ontogenesis

Karl-Heinz Braun

For both historical and systematic reasons there have always been connections between psychology and pedagogy. So it is not surprising that Critical Psychology has, again and again, spoken of the implications of its concept of subjectivity for education and pedagogy. Until now, however, this has not been done systematically. This chapter represents an attempt to elaborate, in a three-staged argument, the reciprocal relationship between Critical Psychology and Critical Pedagogy.

In the first stage a *pedagogical* perspective on the theory of play based on the work of Friedrich Froebel is outlined, and guidelines for the assessment of theories of play are developed. It is also made clear that pedagogical science is an autonomous science and not a subdiscipline of psychology.

Then the theory and practice of a materialistic *psychological* theory of play is clarified in the context of a discussion of Elkonin's approach and a project directed by Feuser on the fostering of integrative play among handicapped and nonhandicapped children.

Finally, psychoanalytic approaches are considered, the critical discussion of which – against the background of the insights that we had acquired at the time – was a vital element in the development of Critical Psychological and Critical Pedagogical thinking.

Froebel's Educational Theory of Play

Certainly people have played since at least the time when societal production yielded a reliable surplus, but independent theoretical reflection has been given to this process only – at least in the European tradition – since the bourgeois revolution. What was peculiar about these early discussions was that they were guided by a unified social philosophical-pedagogical outlook. There was no segregation of particular aspects into different departments of science. The high point and conclusion of this stage of development occurred

212

in the works of Friedrich Froebel (1782–1853) (Froebel, 1965; Flitner, 1982; Günther, Hofmann, & Hohendorfer, 1973). The starting point for his deliberations was the religiously interpreted universality of the world; this he called "the spherical" (Froebel, 1965: 6), and education was determined by it:

For the determination of man it is preferable to develop, to educate, to demonstrate, first, *his* spherical nature, then the spherical nature of being *as a whole*. . . . For the development of the spherical nature of a being with consciousness means to educate this being. . . . Education of man is development of his power for knowing and knowing of and for free action. . . . The true, adequate education of man demands that he be developed out of himself all-sidedly in unity of mind and feeling, trained, raised to independent all-sided representation of the unity of his mind and feeling for complete self-knowledge.

Such a conception of education necessarily contains the perspective of unity of the objective and the subjective, of "external" and "internal," of societal and individual processes; Froebel claimed: "Man finds the external in the internal and, conversely, the internal in the external; one appears in the other and is represented in the other; thus in the external appearances of life can be seen their internal conditions, and conversely" (p. 7). The thus-intended *education for all* is also fundamentally in the interest of playing children and takes from their individual joy its crucial subjective developmental foundation. This joy is not linked to the external object of play, but rather to "what the child can represent through it, what, in and beneath the *externally* presented, he can *imagine, see,* and *think*. . . . " This is what "creates *joy* for the child in play, what effects thereby his *satisfaction*. . . . " The object with the greatest pedagogical value, then, is one "through and with which he shapes the most, executes the most, that is, that calls forth from him the most numerous and most satisfying ideas, imaginings, phantasies, these being so lively that they appear to him, if only as the most incomplete outlines and representations, really to be both inside him and outside him" (p. 103). Play is thus both a (logically understood) *stage of learning* and a *stage of life*. It characterizes the specificity of the childish world- and self-view; it is the specific way in which the child *appropriates* the world and thus realizes his or her own possibilities for development. The realization of the "temporal determination" of the child consists in this: "through all-sided *representation of his internal world,* through a lively *acceptance of the external world,* and through a testing *comparison of both,* to achieve a *knowledge of the unity,* the *knowledge of life* in itself, and the true *living according* to the demands of the same" (Blochmann, undated: 21). This merging is itself a developmental process that demonstrates its own qualities; that is, play develops as does the child. Conversely, it is a condition and form of development, an expression and possibility of the unfolding of individual subjectivity. "As . . . in an earlier time, that of childhood, only *activity* as such was the purpose of play, now its purpose is always a certain conscious goal, now it is the *representation* as such, the to-be-represented itself, that develop as characteristics of the free play of boys in advanced age . . . " (Blochmann, undated: 86). The games of this stage of development are "wherever possible, mutual, and thus develop the sense and feeling of mutuality, the rules and demands of mutuality. The boy tries to see himself in his companions, to feel himself into them, to measure himself against them, to recognize himself in them, and to find himself through them; thus games work and develop immediately for life; they awake and nourish many civic and moral virtues" (Blochmann, undated: 87).

We see therefore that Froebel did not ascribe to the child his or her subjectivity, his or her humanity in any abstract way, but assumed an inner tension between the human (-divine) quality and the development of this quality, and tried to reconstruct it. The joy in play had for Froebel its central foundation in the possibility that it arises for overcoming one's own helplessness:

This *helplessness* of the child and his striving to do something about it develops now in the child the *strength* and especially the *will* . . . ; it makes itself known in the person as a being that is destined to consciousness, on the road to becoming conscious. And thus, in that it is overcome, helplessness increases the strength and will of the child and of people altogether, and in this self-generation of strength out of one's own will the child demonstrates and reveals himself as a person; through it the person, the child, comes to knowledge of self and to *consciousness* of self, consciousness of the circumstances of his own life and of humanity's altogether. (Blochmann, undated: 20)

Just because it has to do with the process of the unfolding of human subjectivity at the child's level, the *support* of grown-ups is indispensable. At the same time, play is an essential *medium for knowledge* related to the child's subjectivity (Blochmann, undated: 17).

For the purposes of our present discussion, the following aspects of Froebel's theory of play are important. First, by means of its foundation in the theory of education (which, owing to its religious and romantic inclinations, often remains unclear) it understood play as a specific form of life for children, as a special form of appropriation of the world. It is also important for the pedagogics of play that general education (understood as education for all in both general and special abilities, skills, needs, and so forth) mediates between the existing objective universality and the possible subjective universality.

Second, all educational processes must reduce the helplessness and dependence of children and promote their independence in the context of social communities; the adults (parents, teachers) are responsible for this.

Third, all educational processes can be divided logically and systematically into two areas, *play* and *instruction,* with instruction logically presupposing play (Klafki, 1964).

In the second half of the nineteenth century the comprehensive theoretical designs regarding play began to dissolve, and from then on the various special sciences and disciplines, relatively isolated from each other, studied certain aspects of play activities. Seldom were these efforts with their resulting increase in detail knowledge brought together into an overall conception. The works of Groos (1899), Buytendijk (1934), Elkonin (1965), and Piaget (1975) are among the relevant exceptions to this tendency.

Marxist Theories of Play: Cultural Historical School of Soviet Psychology

The (co-) founder of the cultural historical school of Soviet psychology, L. S. Vygotsky, was already occupied with the problems of play; his pertinent remarks are admittedly brief but nevertheless pioneering. This is particularly so of his insight that play is not *the* determinant of overall development in preschool age, but is "only" one specific dimension. Play arises (beginning in the third year) when the child develops many needs and wishes that "cannot be satisfied immediately but continue to exist as wishes. On the other hand, the tendency is retained almost completely to seek immediate satisfaction of wishes. . . . It is here that play develops." This is "to be understood as an imaginary, illusionary satisfaction of unrealistic wishes. Fantasy is a new formation in the consciousness of the child and does not occur at all in animals" (Vygotsky, 1980; 443). From this it necessarily follows that play *cannot* be the dominant activity of the child:

In the most important situations of life the activity of the child is diametrically opposed to play. In play action is subordinated to meaning; in real life, on the other hand, action naturally has precedence to meaning. . . . Thus we have in play . . . the negative of the generally normal behavior of the child. For that reason it would be completely unfounded to suppose that play is the prototypical life activity of the child, its dominant form of activity. (p. 461)

This does not make the significance of play by any means peripheral, but clears the way to seeing its central *development-promoting* function: "In principle, the child moves itself along through play activity. Only in this sense can play be called a leading activity, that is, an activity that determines the development of the child" (p. 463).

Elkonin adopted this basic understanding and studied the matter more closely with respect to the societal historical prerequisites and the different courses taken in ontogenesis (Elkonin, 1965). From the point of view of societal history it was the growing complexity of the production process and its related work activities that were the decisive basis for the development of play. Although it was possible in the early phases of so-called primitive society for children to participate immediately in the societal process of providing a living (though participation was reduced already at the beginning of this epoch owing to the introduction of tools), it then required an evermore costly *preparation* for these activities. Not only the toy arises in this connection, but also – though historically a bit later – what Elkonin called role games (Elkonin, 1980: ch. 2). What is important here is that since productive activity as such has historically become independent of both the individual (it contains an independent quality of development quite apart from individuals) and the surplus product it assures, *play* and *labor* have been related but distinguishable processes and activities. Since this time children have developed within objectively and societally determined opportunities for play.

This development requires, however, certain prerequisites on the side of the individual. These are the ability to investigate the surrounding world of objects and to orient oneself to them, whereby the "interventions" become limited to immediate manipulation. Toward the end of this stage of development object manipulation becomes linked to the common activity of children and adults. Already, *operative* and *social* (interpersonal) moments become linked together (if only just externally). *Object-oriented play* (objects used according to their immediate use value) and *playing with substitute objects* (for example, stick for a fever thermometer) or with *playthings* (dolls, animals, cars, and so forth) then follow in a developmentally logical way. In order to define this new level of action more precisely, Elkonin introduces two central concepts. For him the *subject of play* consists of that "realm of reality which the children reproduce in their play. The subjects of play are . . . extremely varied and reflect the concrete condition of the child's life. They change, independent of the child's concrete conditions, as his point of view broadens" (Elkonin, 1980: 48). What forms the *content of play* is "what the child reproduces as the characteristic feature of the activity of adults and their relations among them in work and in societal life. The content of play expresses how profoundly the child has understood the activity of adults: Possibly only the external side of human activity becomes apparent, only that with which the person acts, or possibly the relations of the person to his activity and to other people, or even the societal significance of human labor" (p. 48).

In that the actions of the child begin to become independent of immediate objects, the prerequisites are formed for the transition to *role play*, and in this is realized for Elkonin (1980: ch. 4) (agreeing with Vygotsky) the "real," the most significant developmental aspect of play. As the result of many developmental-experimental studies, he was able to distinguish four levels of role play (pp. 309ff). First, at the core of the content of play are actions with objects that relate to playmates. The role is still determined by the character of the action; it is uniform and consists of a series of repetitive operations.

Second, the main content is still action with objects, but the agreement with real action comes to the foreground. Further, the children name the roles themselves, and the logic of the action is determined by real sequences, and violations of these are not accepted.

Third, now the execution of a role becomes the main content, and it determines the logic and character of individual actions. These roles are precisely defined and distributed, and infractions against the action logic are not accepted.

Fourth, the relations among the persons played by the children become the main content. The roles are clearly defined, and the language used takes on role character. The various actions of the persons played constitute the exact logic of action, and infractions are criticized.

These four levels of development can be organized into two main stages: levels 1 and 2 form the first, and levels 3 and 4 the second. "In the first stage (three to five years) the main content of play is socially directed, object-oriented actions that are compared with the real logic of action. In the second stage (five to seven years) social relations between people and the societal significance of their activity become the main content, which is not compared to real relations among people" (Elkonin, 1980: 315). With this level of role play, play reaches the highest expression of its development-promoting function; after that, learning assumes this task, and play becomes a feature of learning that fulfills the functions of supplementing, supporting, and sometimes even inhibiting it.

From this brief presentation of Elkonin's (and Vygotsky's) theory of play we can positively emphasize the following points. First, in agreement with Froebel, play is here understood as an independent stage of education. Contrary to Froebel, it is understood not as the determining feature of overall activity, but as the decisive feature of development. The differentiation between play and development/ontogenesis and its implied *narrower* concept of play appear to be sensible and represent an advance in understanding.

Second, play is social historically and ontogenetically placed into relation with the social process of labor as the process of specifically human, generalized provisioning and control of reality, without postulating a linear, uninspired deductive relationship between the two. This is particularly clear in the emphasis on the *distancing from*, as well as the *penetrating into*, reality, that is, the specifically childlike way of creating epistemological distance as a prerequisite to knowing reality.

Third, contrary to Froebel (or sometimes just doing it more plainly than he does), it is stressed that there is a developmental level *before* play, the realization of which provides the prerequisites for play.

Fourth, also in agreement with, or in approval of, Froebel, the essential feature of the inner merging of play and personality development is seen as the stepwise transformation of operative features into interpersonal-social features. In support of this, a great array of interesting empirical materials are presented.

Having mentioned these important and progressive aspects, some critical remarks are also necessary. However correct and important the distinction between play and ontogenesis and however interestingly the development of play processes is worked out, a concept of the *necessities of ontogenetic development* is missing. Only if these are known can we establish precisely just what development-promoting status play processes have. Unlike Elkonin, Critical Psychology has worked out such a concept (cf. Holzkamp, 1983: ch. 8). But it has until now paid little attention to play and can therefore offer only an initial hypothesis in that connection. In agreement with Elkonin, it is assumed that through the qualitative transformations that took place in the evolutionary transition from animal to human [*Tier–Mensch–Uebergangsfeld* (TMU)], fixed individual developmental sequences or phases were transformed (the pertinent physiological maturational processes are not determining for specifically human ontogenesis), out of which arose the lifelong ability to learn and develop. The reconstruction of ontogenetic developmental necessities therefore does not yield chronological steps, but rather a series of qualitative stages, each of which must be achieved in order to go on to the next, that makes comprehensible the overall development of action potence. That is, out of the specific quality of action potence is revealed the *logical* genesis of action potence by means of a *regression-logical* method (one proceeds backward from the higher form to the lower). The resulting accesses to development, in the sense of developmental-logical sequences, are (now viewed from the lower to the higher) the ontogenetic preliminaries, the move to develop a generalization of meaning, the move to a transcendence of immediacy, and finally the move to fully developed action potence. These can be characterized in the following way:

> *Ontogenetic preliminaries:* It is essential here that small children try, through probing and watching, to orient themselves in an elementary way within the material and social world that surrounds them and that they learn the immediate meaning of signals, and with them to make themselves understood by adults with respect to their immediate needs, such as eating and drinking.
>
> *Development of social intention:* Through signals small children can only orient to the external behavior of adults, which radically limits their possibilities for influence because "behind" externally equivalent behaviors there can exist totally different, even opposing, intentions. The child extends his or her possibilities for action qualitatively when beginning to exercise influence on adult intentions and, at the same time, beginning to form his or

her own intentions. In that this becomes a generalized strategy, the child develops his or her first distinguishing characteristics, and his or her intentional development acquires a stable, generalized, social character.

Development of the generalization of meaning: Relations among people are not purely social and interactive, but mediated by meaningful, objective, cooperative connections and conditions. Adults themselves form their intentions in connection with these material and personal meaning structures; the child is just learning this dimension, does not have to influence an adult in order to get a certain object (for example, a sausage), but can get it him- or herself (for example, because the child knows how to open the refrigerator). This new stage in the development of the child's interests and needs is further differentiated in itself.

Use of objects as determined by meaning: At first the child learns to deal appropriately with the objects of its immediate surroundings. He or she learns, for example, how to cut with scissors, how to hit a nail with a hammer, how to light a match. This comes about because, if the objects are dealt with arbitrarily or according to purely individual whim (for example, using a teaspoon for soup), the child notices that the results are not optimal, that there are means that better suit his or her original intention (for example, to satisfy hunger). Thus develops a relatively rigid use of objects. Only later does the child learn a use of objects that is more conscious and "reflective" (for example, to use a teaspoon for soup when the soupspoon is not available or because the child can annoy someone by doing so). Although this counts as a clear increase in power (actions of adults and educators can be questioned and criticized respecting their appropriateness), they nevertheless do not know why these objects have this or that meaning. This is revealed to them in the next stage.

Meaning-appropriate production of objects: The making of objects is now attempted in accordance with one's own intentions. In this the child gradually learns that a lot of experience has gone into available objects, that they have been constantly improved so that they were better suited for their purposes. The child learns, in other words, to recognize the meanings in objects as generalized purposes. And in that this is vitally important for the child, what directs his or her action is no longer purely individually determined purposes, but these generalized meanings, out of which then develop the child's own individual intentions as the first mediation between the objectively necessary and the subjectively meaningful. Through this horizontal extension of objective meanings, insights into the personal network of meanings are also extended; the child makes a gradual connection between generalized objective meanings (for example, a hand tool) and certain groups of persons (for example, workers). While, providing the development is successful, the cooperative aspects become ever more important, the possibilities for influence are extended, the dependencies diminish, well-being is increased, and anxieties are overcome; all this has essential limits in that it remains attached to the immediacy of the child's life world, and the "actual" societal connections do not become clear and accessible.

Development of the transcendence of immediacy: It is especially through participation in extrafamilial life processes, whether on the street, in the community, or in educational institutions, children's and youth groups, and so forth, that the pure and immediate cooperation is broken down and the partial aspects of the mediated interconnections of societal life (such as the content of the parents' work activity) become accessible. But this extends not only the needs for control, for knowing, and for stable social relations (all these needs grow gradually alongside one another and become the specifically human "productive" needs), it also allows the child (or young person) more and more to ask questions about *his or her* place in the immediate, social and comprehensive, societal processes and forces him or her to take positions. Thus arises that consciousness of self that knows that it is the self that can formulate its own goals and intentions and that it is the self that has responsibility for itself, its own deeds, its life – within the limits of existing possibilities.

Emergence of fully developed action potence: In that the immediacy is broken through and transcended through participation in practical everyday life, individual action potence is increased, and the horizon of life is broadened, dependencies can be drastically reduced – in accordance with concrete historical, societal conditions. The single individual can now take care of him- or herself within this framework and can secure and shape his or her one life through participation in meaningful societal processes of production and reproduction.

Returning now to Elkonin, we find that he gives at least a plausible account as to why there are no play processes in the ontogenetic preliminaries in which the child is appropriating the world through probing and watching. Even in the transitional sequence of social intentionality, in which the small child is extending his or her worldly stride in the social and personal realms in which he or she begins to influence the intentions of another person and thus develops personal intentions in a more "generalized" way, no play processes are to be found. *Play* belongs therefore – and this is the hypothesis – to the developmental move of *generalizing meaning*. It is in this move that the child develops the *immediate cooperation* that both promotes and is promoted by play. This especially begins to affect the ability to develop generalized intentions, wishes, and goals. Only when these are present can mental-imaginative processes of consciousness emerge, processes that make their appearance or are produced only in the *absence* of intentionally acting people or of meaningful objects. It is thus a prerequisite for the development of imagination that there develop a qualitative independence of conscious activities with respect to actually present reality. In the framework of the development of generalized meaning the child comes up against barriers again and again that he or she really cannot surmount; these are barriers to this stage of development as well as to the next. The child overcomes these barriers now *imaginatively* in and through play. Play is therefore an extension of competence, a broadening of control and possibilities of influence (including the always associated development of needs) – but all in an imaginary form. Thus the logic of the development of play lies in the logic and scale of this imaginary extension of horizon, which is characterized by the inner contradiction that a more profound *turning toward* reality is achieved by a *turning away from* the same reality. It contains as well the contradiction that play is both *necessary* and *self-contained,* that it deals with *contents* but is largely centered on *function.*

Elkonin assumes at least implicitly a development-initiating discrepancy between the societally necessary action potence of adults and the existing action potence of children (as we have already seen, Froebel also had this idea). But what remains unclear is how this *external* contradiction can become an *internal* one. The solution is made more difficult when Elkonin assumes there to be an external opposition between the *biological* and *social* features of development (cf. Elkonin, 1980: 49ff.), thus overlooking the fact that *human nature* is, on the basis of the genetic changes in the TMU and the subsequent period of hominization, the *societal nature of the human being.* This societal nature is not fixed or anything like that, but a general, nontranscendable *directional determinant* of individual socialization. Because it forms the "inner" side of the necessity and possibility for socialization, the human individual *can* and *will* become socialized. Insofar as this succeeds, the individual can increasingly reduce personal dependencies and take his or her business into his or her own hands (whereby, for the solution to societally caused developmental difficulties, the individual must combine more and more with others), and the individual's needs can become more and more sources of happiness and satisfaction, rather than of anxiety and suffering. In this contradiction between anxiety and happiness lies the subjective "motor" of personal development (this is the real heart of Froebel's considerations on the relationship between children's "overcoming helplessness" and "self-activity and developmental joy").

The theory of Vygotsky and Elkonin arose under the conditions of developing socialism in the Soviet Union. They may have assumed therefore that there were no antagonistic contradictions between the dominant societal relations, the societal values and norms that result from those relations, and the aims of educational institutions, on the one hand, and the developmental interests of children, on the other. It is, first of all, problematic that this assumption is never mentioned, that concrete historical findings from capitalist countries (for example, Piaget) are often relatively directly compared with those from socialist countries, and that from this a formalizing tendency enters into the overall argumentation. Even in psychological questions, however, for both scientific and political reasons, the greatest possible clarity regarding the *specificity of societal formation* is indispensable. But also, it would be naturally very interesting to know what effects the *nonantagonistic* (but not always harmless) contradictions of socialist society have on the individual and institutional educational processes.

A central problem of *method* is that general, human determinants (Critical Psychology calls these *categorial*) and those of the historically specific kind (called *particular theoretical*) are not sufficiently clearly distinguished. The fact is thus obscured that each kind of theoretical effort needs different empirical safeguards (categories are based historically and empirically, particular theories are based on actual empirical findings). It is therefore often unclear in discussions whether the concerns and considerations are categorial or particular or what empirical findings are appropriate. Relative to our immediate theme, it remains open whether play is a general fact and therefore the concept has categorial rank or whether it is limited to historically specific epochs. Elkonin's lack of clarity on method has certainly contributed to the fact that he has no clear answers to these questions.

The use of the concept of role or role play doubtless represents a conceptual shortcoming. The essentially real heart of the content that Elkonin and Vygotsky designate with this term is that the child is at every stage of development dealing with certain aspects of the societal positions of adults and their realization, that is, that societally produced requirements in the sense of possibilities for development and action are transformed in a child-specific way and thus made accessible (including *alternatives* of action). But the concept of role or role play does not reveal this in any pertinent way because (a) it brackets out the societal ability to produce and to change and (b) it leaves the relation of norms and values as aims of action to material society in an unclear state and robs them to some extent of their historically concrete content.

Marxist Theories of Play: Theoretical Implications of Critical Pedagogy of the Handicapped (Feuser)

We shall continue by expanding our discussion of the theory of play as it applies to the *common* education of handicapped and nonhandicapped children. In the context of critical pedagogy of the handicapped, Feuser (1984a), pointing explicitly to the parallel between his efforts and those of Critical Psychology, has presented a series of considerations based on a kindergarten project in Bremen-Huchting that began in November 1981, with the main research project beginning in August 1982 and presently nearing completion.

Following directly from Leontyev (1971), but drawing as well from Elkonin and Vygotsky, Feuser and his colleagues start with the assumption that play is the *dominant* activity of the preschool child. For this reason the kindergarten assumes a double significance: It is the first place in which, in an institutional setting, there can occur any segregation of handicapped, or handicap-threatened, children; it is also the place in which this can be effectively prevented. A practice aiming at integration must therefore have an integrative pedagogy as a counterpart, must overcome the separation of the pegagogies of the handicapped and nonhandicapped – not just on the basis of charitable and humane attitudes, but on the basis of theoretically grounded knowledge that the basic processes of personality development are in principle identical for *all* people. "Disability is therefore not a 'pathological' but a 'developmental-logical' result of the attempt of people to make the best possible adjustment to conditions that isolate them and to maintain an individual existence by means of this adjustment and the appropriation of isolating conditions" (Feuser, 1984a: 5ff.). For practical purposes, this means a fundamental relativization of the difference between handicapped and nonhandicapped children, on the one hand, and, on the other, an institutional reformation in the sense of regionalizing and decentralizing of common educational planning and the safeguarding of competence transfer as an element in the production of collective pedagogical action potence.

As far as the immediate interpersonal processes are concerned, an integrative pedagogy thus understood must ensure that adults with the relevant competencies that guarantee and support the children's developmental processes are available. This includes not only the general pedagogical and didactic abilities, but also abilities that apply specifically to the developmental needs of crippled or disabled children. Along with the work of special physical educationists, we could mention the support personnel who, within the framework of the regular kindergarten, work in the areas of medical and neurophysiological problems, diagnosis of learning difficulties, and so forth.

On the other hand, it is characteristic for a pedagogical point of view that recognizes and promotes children as developing subjects also to demand and encourage interpersonal support and safeguarding processes among the children. Out of that come important experiences regarding the *didactic of helping*. Here a certain educational intervention is necessary

> . . . to let the nonhandicapped children know that they were not to shower the handicapped children with help and other assistance. They simply imitated the function of the civil servant, the therapist, or the support personnel and thus, quite understandably, took over many tasks that, in a special facility would require additional personnel and therapists. But the children learned quickly that help is not just something that can be given to somebody, but is also something that can be asked for, something that must be analyzed and discussed. Having noted this, the children soon became sensitive to the fact that the offer of help is not identical to its immediate execution, but that the handicapped child must first be asked whether the offered help is needed. For their part, the handicapped children learned not to wait for help, as they had become accustomed to doing in the special facilities, but to request it and demand it in such a form that meets the particular need and is not just the easiest thing for the adults or the group. (Feuser, 1984a: 79)

In learning this, children are well ahead of most adults, especially their parents, and are able to explain *to them* how one should act with injured/handicapped children and what, if possible, should be avoided (the job of the parent was an essential feature of the project work). In other words, an educational strategy like this is oriented toward the comprehensive and generalized developmental interests of *all* persons – and it demands of each and everyone the same ability and readiness to develop. As even this project has shown, this cannot simply be postulated; one must consider, discuss, decide, alter, and assess concrete ways and means that can offer teachers the possibility to learn and practice something new. The project therefore correctly placed much value on the preparation, guided practice, and training of the teachers. It is to be understood as a great compliment to the project group that the director of the children's home remarked that "even if there were no handicapped children in the facility, it appears to us that the new pedagogical method would be necessary" (Feuser, 1984a: 52).

Finally, we want to bring up a problem that is increasingly occupying the project group: the continuation of this integrative education in the *regular elementary school*. It is not taken for granted – usually quite the opposite – that handicapped or disabled children (with appropriate pedagogical supports) learn with nonhandicapped children in regular schools. It was therefore necessary that everyone concerned make extraordinary efforts, both pedagogically and politically, to assure that all of the children in this day care center were accepted into a regular elementary school. This also pointed to the basic fact that the segregation of disabled and handicapped children indicates, in the final analysis, the *class character* of education, which shows up in one way or another as a qualitative inequality of chances for education, that integrative pedagogics is therefore in opposition to the fundamental ruling interests, which can be restrained only within limits in educational political disputes (see, for example, Feuser, 1984b, c).

This interim report of the project and its accompanying publications contain much significant empirical material that is also important, at least implicitly, for the theory of play. In summary, the following points can be emphasized: First, it is worked out at a particular theoretical, actual empirical level just how disabled or handicapped children need specific supportive activities and how these must relate to the general pedagogical supporting and safeguarding activities, such that – even contrary to best intentions – isolation and segregation are not reproduced.

Second, the empirical forms taken by integrative pedagogical processes are reconstructed, even at the educational political, institutional, and interpersonal-psychical levels. This has made clear *that, how,* and under *what conditions* the developments of handicapped or disabled and nonhandicapped children can be merged.

Third, there are widespread (sometimes scattered) didactic or learning-psychological considerations related to special objects or contents, including a didactic of helping.

We want to raise a few questions and problems, not in the sense of claiming to know better, but in that of pointing to difficulties and oversights that can perhaps be corrected in the course of the project's work. Three aspects seem important to us. First, it is still questionable whether play should be viewed as the dominant activity of the preschool child. This is not a quibble with words, but a concern whether the distinction first made by Vygotsky and continued by Elkonin between dominant activity and crucial moment of development allows a more differentiated and accurate understanding of the child's personality development (this is our opinion). The view represented by Leontyev and the Feuser group could lead us to the false conclusion that this way of formulating the problem already contains a concept of ontogenetic developmental necessities. This is certainly not the case – and for this reason the project group has fallen back on a biographical phase model. This appears to us – for reasons that we gave earlier in connection with the Vygotsky/Elkonin approach – as not a very satisfactory solution of the problem before us. It would be worth trying to reexamine and reinterpret the project's empirical material with the aid of the categories of the Elkonin/Vygotsky theory of play and those of Critical Psychology's theory of development. There is good reason to believe that this would open up many new perspectives.

Second, Feuser and his co-workers correctly point out that the didactic considerations leave many questions unanswered. That is certainly right – and seems to us to be traceable in no small degree to the fact that the didactic considerations were too narrowly oriented toward Galperin's theory of learning. However one may assess the details of Galperin's theory, it is undeniably the case that it is intended to encompass only a partial aspect of the instructional process and that therefore a didactic theory must go qualitatively beyond the limits of learning theory. Galperin's theory cannot or will not confront the following central issues: how the aims and contents of learning are determined; the crossing over between scientific and subject (need, experiential) orientations; relevance of exemplary learning and learning as the central feature of an education in the medium of the universal; the educational effectiveness of learning processes and their relation to the assessment of performance; and the generalization of instructional experience in the form of didactic principles. A theory of instruction must put these questions at the center of its considerations. Beyond that, more precise consideration is needed as to whether *play* processes can in fact be comprehended within Galperin's learning theoretical approach, that is, whether a learning theory can be fruitful here at all. Generally speaking, it is not a question of schematically separating learning and play. At the same time, however, we should not forget Froebel's central insight that play and instructional processes must be understood as qualitative stages in a unitary educational process.

Third, the considerations of evaluation are also still a bit vague in that it is here correctly assumed that research is to be done *with* the subjects, not over their heads, and that it must have to do with the objectification of the "inner" psychical processes and not with the purely superficial recording of external activities. Precisely because of the relatively favorable institutional conditions, it would be sensible to test the adequacy of Froebel's ideas (which, incidentally, have been taken up at least implicitly by psychoanalysis) that for adults (here, the experimenter) *games* are a medium of practice and knowledge, that children express their self- and worldviews in them that use them for dealing with their psychical conflicts, and so forth.

We shall end our discussion of Marxist approaches here and move on to psychoanalytic conceptions with the intention of reinterpreting them.

Psychoanalytic Contributions to the Theory of Play

If we survey the whole extent of psychoanalytic theorizing and research, especially the efforts to develop a psychoanalytic pedagogy, it soon becomes evident that the problem of children's play, so significant for pedagogy, has been given very little attention. At the same time there is a certain discrepancy with this in the fact that psychoanalytic ideas are at least implicitly very effective in this area, both as everyday and as scientific points of view. We will try here to put these elements into both theoretical and practical relief.

The basic position of psychoanalysis regarding children's play was presented by Sigmund Freud in a very brief but theoretically important sketch as part of the larger study "Beyond the Pleasure Principle." The main question was that of the "economic" function or gain in pleasure brought about by play. This question cannot be answered by direct observation because it is obvious that children reproduce events and situations that are certainly not pleasurable for them. The interpretation is that in the real situation the child is simply "bowled over" and that it is only in the play situation that the child is in the position, after the fact, to deal with them. At first the child is "in a *passive* situation – he was overpowered by the experience; but, by repeating it, unpleasurable though it was, as a game, he took on an *active* part. These efforts might be put down to an instinct for mastery that was acting independently of whether the memory was in itself pleasurable or not" (Freud, 1920/1975: 10). In commenting on this, Freud mentions a further aspect of child's play, namely the wish it expresses to "be grown-up." He writes:

It is clear that in their play children repeat everything that has made a great impression on them in real life, and that in doing so they abreact the strength of the impression and, as one might put it, make themselves master of the situation. But on the other hand it is obvious that all their play is influenced by a wish that dominates them the whole time – the wish to be grown-up and to be able to do what grown-up people do.

It can also be observed that the unpleasurable nature of an experience does not always unsuit it for play. If the doctor looks down a child's throat or carries out some small operation on him, we may be quite sure that these frightening experiences will be the subject of the next game; but we must not in that connection overlook the fact that there is a yield of pleasure from another source. As the child passes over from the passivity of the experience to the activity of the game, he hands on the disagreeable experience to one of his playmates and in this way revenges himself on a substitute. (pp. 10–11)

Thus for Freud these play activities fit into a larger context of the compulsion to repeat. Supported by observations in other areas of living, he comes to the assumption

. . . that there really does exist in the mind a compulsion to repeat which overrides the pleasure principle. Now too we shall be inclined to relate to this compulsion the dreams which occur in traumatic neuroses and the impulse which leads children to play.

But it to be noted that only in rare instances can we observe the pure effects of the compulsion to repeat, unsupported by other motives. In the case of children's play we have already laid stress on the other ways in which the emergence of the compulsion may be interpreted; the compulsion to repeat and instinctual satisfaction which is immediately pleasurable seem to converge here into an intimate partnership. (pp. 16–17)

Robert Waelder (1932/1973) followed up these ideas in an article first published in the *Zeitschrift für psychoanalytische Paedagogik*, in which he recognized the pleasure of functioning [*Funktionslust*] that Karl Bühler took to be the center of the analysis of play but argued that it was only a subordinate function. Drawing indirectly upon the basic psychoanalytic theorem of the central contradiction between the needy individual and the denying society, he expressed the psychical function of play in the following way:

For the mental organism just coming into life, for whom everything is still new and much still joyfully attractive, much, however, painful and threatening, excessive stimulation – trauma, one might say – is virtually a normal experience, while it is exceptional in adult life. This is surely one of the reasons why the playful abreaction (working out) of traumatic experience plays such a great role in childhood (P.57).

The assimilation of the burdening experiences can thus be carried out by various types of play.

First, the very fact that the child produces a passively experienced situation in play signifies a transition from passivity to activity. In a group of games it happens that the child exchanges in play the role that it had in reality; if in reality it was a suffering part or he was a fearful onlooker, in play it often becomes an activity part as helper or deus ex machina. In this group the move from passivity to activity is emphasized by the choice of role; the example of the dentist applies here. In another group again, the child alters the beginning of the experienced situation in play and gives it another outcome. Probably other types of assimilation can be distinguished as well. (p. 58)

By way of critique and evaluation of this conception, attention should be drawn to three of its features. First, of course, the assumption of a fundamental contradiction between individual and society is scientifically untenable; if human needs were really radically opposed to the societal process of life maintenance, it would be impossible to explain why, on the basis of subjective aims and intentions, individuals should devote themselves to society (which they do in reality, and not simply because they are somehow forced to do so, but because their needs are satisfied in this way). Reciprocally, this means that under the assumption of antagonism no human society could possibly have arisen and maintained itself. This thought can, however, claim a relative historical truth because under capitalist conditions (as in all antagonistic class societies) the *dominant* societal relations are in fact fundamentally contradictory to the interests and needs of those who are actually or prospectively suppressed and exploited. The relevance of the psychoanalytic perspective for Marxist approaches consists basically in thematizing the *necessarily internal contradictoriness* of the *class-determined individual socialization process*. This means that no working Marxist psychologist (or pedagogue) can afford to lose sight of the fact that the individual developmental and appropriation processes take place in anything but a straight and problem-free way; they require the *working through of existentially significant psychical conflicts* at all stages. As much as psychoanalysis emphasizes this fact, as much as it stands up for individual subjects (especially for children), this engagement is just as much shattered, disconnected, and limited by its complete acceptance of the superordinate bourgeois class relations. The unresolvable contradiction immanent in psychoanalysis of scientific (and practical) partisanship for individuals *and* for bourgeois society demands replacement by a Marxist conception of the problem.

Second, the assumption of a fundamental contradiction between the needy individual and a denying society removes the educational function of play – so stressed by Froebel – from the focus of attention, if it does not overtly deny it. That the child appropriates the world in part through play so as to overcome his or her dependence gradually and thus gain better control over the sources of his or her needs' satisfactions, that the child learns through play to relate him- or herself ever more consciously to his or her own subjectivity and to social reality – all this is (largely) left out of consideration by the psychoanalytic conception of play. In this connection, however, an important, historically specific problem can be thematized: that in bourgeois society the activities of adults (parents, teachers) aimed at supporting and safeguarding children represent not only the *fostering of development*, but also the *hindering* of the child's subjective unfolding. In capitalist conditions there are no unalienated niches or regions. Even the most intimate relations, such as those between parents and children, are ultimately stamped with societal antagonisms. Even here adults, depending on class position (whether they are aware of it not), reproduce in one way or another interpersonal dominance and suppression. Critical analysis of play activities cannot ignore this fact, but it cannot accept it fatalistically, either. Rather, it must provide theoretical knowledge about *these* interconnections and through it offer to adults and – according to their level of understanding – to children the possibility of relating *consciously* to these contradictions and constraints. We are particularly concerned here with the comprehensive common interest of adults and children to resist and finally overcome these repressive relations. Once again, let us emphasize: Whoever, for whatever reasons, peripheralizes or ignores the inner contradictoriness of the support and maintenance processes will, at the same time, be blind to the fact that individuals, even *as individuals,* have an elementary, objective interest in a more humane existence, whether these individuals are adults or children.

Third, a further problem with the psychoanalytic concept of play is that play processes are always supposed to be essentially directed at events of the past. Rather, we agree with Froebel that the emphasis on the *development-fostering* character of games is, at the same time, an emphasis on its *orientation to the future.* Generally speaking, this future consists in optimal participation in the relevant societal processes having to do with development and decision making and the action potence that develops along with such participation. This means that games must be seen in connection with the societal labor process. Psychoanalysis regularly excludes not only the societal and historical prerequisites of play, but also the relation that play implies between the individual and the societal production process. But despite all criticism, psychoanalytic ideas have even here a relative truth, for if these developmental processes unfold within the field of tension between fostering and hindering, education and dominance, then this becomes manifest in children as *profound conflicts in psychical development.* The child must work these through and find ways of asserting his or her interests, needs, aims, and intentions against the various forms of resistance (in whatever limited way as is possible). And the psychoanalysts surely are right when they assume that children are dealing with real-life situations in games (in essential agreement with Elkonin and Vygotsky). At the same time, it is correct to say that children can be retarded in play when they are not successful in working out significant aspects of their psychical conflicts, when they rather engage in defenses, repress, deny, and thus do not move beyond their current level of development. In these specific cases, then, games are in fact primarily concerned with the past.

From Psychoanalytic Play Theory to Play Therapy (Zulliger)

The psychoanalytic theory of play has, like other aspects of the psychoanalytic theoretical system, developed in close contact with practical therapeutic requirements and reflections. It was Anna Freud (1968, 1980) (especially in opposition to Melanie Klein) who always pointed out that psychoanalytic therapy must be modified for children because their egos and superegos were not yet (sufficiently) developed. The most comprehensive conception, however, was worked out by the Swiss Hans Zulliger (1952, 1957). He summarized his basic understanding of children's play (as an early stage in human ontogeny) as follows (Zulliger, 1957: 20):

1. In child's play lies hidden a breakthrough of libidinal drive.
2. From this arises the pleasurable character of play; to the pleasure of drive reduction comes the "pleasure of hiding," which derives from the Oedipus complex.
3. The compulsion to have a will of one's own is invested in the drive breakthrough.
4. The developed ego of the child takes part in the formation or selection of play activity by permitting a rather primitive but still masked drive satisfaction and by making play into a compromise between the drive and ego demands.
5. In that one can see a bit of adaptation to social and physical reality.
6. Play signifies a symbolic abreaction, closely related to the treatment of symptoms.
7. Economically, there occurs in play a relaxation of drive, avoidance of displeasure, and often also a transformation of anxiety into pleasure.

Emphasizing the specificity of the child's worldview and with an eye to pedagogical requirements, he writes later:

If you want to treat children psychotherapeutically, you must not only know theoretically that the child thinks "magically" (animistically, totemistically, in images), you have to know in a practical way what this means. . . . And it is good to confront the child in his thinking with the same kind of thinking so that he will understand you. . . . On this rests theoretically the "pure play theory without interpreting unconscious contents and interconnections." (Zulliger, 1957: 42)

Accordingly, the following purposes are ascribed to play (Zulliger, 1952: 86):

1. To uncover pathogenic conflict.
2. To deal with it psychotherapeutically; the conflict is dramatically and actively modified and resolved.
3. To create the possibility for the child, through play, to arrive at cultivated drive satisfactions by presenting the child with a well-dosed sequence of everfiner games or play practices. In the same way, the child can be guided to transpositions of drive, domestications of drive, and sublimations.
4. Games give clues about what in the milieu of the child must be changed; many a child shows signs of neurosis only because he or she has been *made* milieu-sick.

By way of expanding and concretizing these ideas, in another place he gives instructions for the therapeutically oriented selection of toys; he formulates the guideline "that the more primitive the toy, the more useful it is. *The toy should limit the creative imagination of children as little as possible.* It should be almost raw material or such material with a tool that leaves open to the child's creative powers the widest possible freedoms and possibilities" (Zulliger, 1952: 74).

Because, according to Zulliger, at the child's level of development the consciousness is insufficiently developed in that the conscious and unconscious are still closely connected, play therapy does not require much interpretation; it is enough that the analyst recognize the crucial conflicts and orient play intervention around them.

In applying the "pure play therapy" with child patients, we address the unconscious directly; *we are in direct contact with the unconscious.* We do not take something for a "symbolic substitution" and believe that we are raising it into consciousness by interpreting it, translating it into the language of the conscious. The language of the conscious is for the child still a foreign language. The child does not *experience* in it anything concrete; he or she hears only sounds and knows only imprecisely what they clothe. To be able to cure a child of mental disorder, however, we must reach that stratum of his or her psyche in which he or she *lives*. This is the magical, the prelogical, the not yet intellectual, sometimes even ineffable language (Zulliger, 1952: 102).

All the while, Zulliger believes it to be both possible and reasonable not to limit oneself to play too rigidly with older children and to include interpretations.

Three points, in our opinion, are central to the critical assessment of these ideas. First, the attempt to define more precisely the specificity of the child's way of living and thinking is an interesting aspect of the psychoanalytic discussion of childhood. Whatever one thinks of the details, one central shortcoming is conspicuous: the development of the child is not analyzed with a view to the unfolding of the action potence of adult existence. The formation of the child's interpersonal world is largely detached from the development of ability. Interpersonal relations are thus conceptualized as outside cooperative association to achieve generalized goals. The operative features of childrens' action is almost totally ignored. This separation of interaction from abilities is equivalent to the "depedagogicization" of the processes of support and maintenance. A therapeutic process that ignores these pedagogical features promises help to children (and adults), without any guarantee. This impoverishment of the pedagogical-therapeutic treatment is, however, not coincidental, but an expression of the adjustment of children (with or without their own good intentions) to the prevailing relations, for the separation of interactions and abilities is a distinguishing feature of adjustment to existing class relations, the preparation of children for a restrictive adult existence. In this way social relations are robbed of their content and shut off from the possibilities of association on the basis of common superordinate goals. In place of cooperation and collectivity comes the separation of what is public and what is private, and of what is cognitive and what is emotional (which is, for the most part, distributed unevenly with respect to gender).

Second, a special consequence of Zulliger's views is the idea that children's imaginations are intensively stimulated by especially primitive toys. We can certainly agree with Zulliger that children's existence is much less limited, constrained, and alienated than that of adults. So there is a certain kernal of truth to what he says because societal contradictions have not yet fully penetrated into the life of the child. But it must be pointed out at the same time that children are to a large extent dependent on adults, that they can appropriate only limited segments from the wealth of societal life. For this reason we are led to the opposite conclusion that imaginative activity is stimulated and develops to a rich internal life to the extent that the child extends his or her vital relations, improves his or her comprehension of the world, and increases his or her control of reality. When Froebel emphasized the inextricability of the "inner" and the "outer" processes, he not only formulated an element of a dialectical conception of education (given the limits of his time), but also, indirectly, rejected all forms of the two-world theory of play (the free and imaginative world of the playing child here, the alienated, spontaneity-suppressing world of the working adult there).

Third, the flawed nature of Zulliger's partisanship for the (child-) subject can be seen in the fact that the affected persons are permitted only a limited voice, if any, in the matter of the problems that affect them. Whether it has to do with therapeutic knowledge about interpretations or about interventions, it is finally not verifiable by the subject because the therapeutically assumed and supported detachment of the child's life from the general societal processes of production and reproduction (and the associated development of abilities) does not demand or promote an extension of control over reality and thus cannot at all bring about a genuine psychical relief based upon the working through of developmental conflicts. Such a play therapy cannot effect a real counterbalance and thus opens the door to arbitrariness. But well-intended arbitrariness remains arbitrariness and thus can prepare the way for an authoritarian treatment.

Conclusion

I have tried to clarify the materialist understanding of play. Two points should be emphasized. First, from the fact that we have presented here various approaches, pointing out both their strengths and weaknesses, it should not be concluded that such a materialist theory of play can be obtained by the eclectic combination of these positions. Rather, intensive efforts will be required in the future to arrive at such a theory; we have intended here to make clear the main problems that will have to be considered.

Second, a Marxist theory of play needs, alongside psychology, an *independent* foundation in pedagogy. Only when this requirement is met will the real problem be given proper focus, namely, that of the relationship of the educational stages of play and instruction to the necessities of ontogenetic development, the ontogenetic developmental characteristics of the generalization of meaning, the transcendence of immediacy, and the fully developed action potence, along with its limitations specific to capitalism (cf. Braun, 1986).

12 Functions of the Private Sphere in Social Movements

Frigga Haug

The fact that we are living in the midst of a profound social crisis is so much a part of our everyday understanding (at least in the Federal Republic of Germany) that it seems hardly necessary to elaborate it further. Serious threats to human survival (nuclear war and ecological catastrophe) dangerously overshadow the economic crisis. There is mass unemployment in the First World and extreme poverty in the Third. The problems tend to be seen in terms of single issues: We have a "women's problem," a "youth problem," and the "problem of immigrant workers." These are phenomena that are found elsewhere in the world. They are becoming "normal," and their systematic nature must be understood as signaling the existence of a wider transformation in capitalist societies. The very diversity of these crises makes it difficult to understand where the solutions should be sought. The difficulty is compounded by the fact that all these crises are located at different levels, involve different actors and different arenas of action. If we are to begin with an analysis that draws its logic from the actors' possibilities for action, then we have to ask the questions that Lenin asked: What is it that the exploiters can no longer do, and what are the exploited no longer prepared to put up with?

The simple answers to these questions have always been wrong, namely, that the exploiters are no longer able to make a sufficient profit, or that the exploited are no longer prepared to work for the purposes of profit. Such analysis may reveal to us the direction in which the forces are operating, but not the friction that restrains them.

I leave it to the specialists to answer Lenin's first question, to determine the extent to which there is an economic crisis for big capital and to what extent the Keynesian policies are still capable of functioning. I will turn instead to the second question, namely, what is it that the "exploited" are no longer prepared to tolerate, and how are they fighting against it? What opportunities exist for a socialist project, and what obstacles does it face?

If we maintain that the crisis is experienced as a feeling that we can't go on like this, then it is just those things that are experienced as intolerable and

234

those problems that incite a sense of horror that should point to areas of struggle where new possibilities emerge. We should look for the new forces not only where "advances" are recorded, but, more important, where disruptions and problems are accumulating; in other words, we must look for them not in the tranquility of the graveyard, but at the centers of crises. We can fairly assume that we will encounter the right wing's new projects and proposals in these "areas of struggle." That is, every determined left-wing project will be endangered not only by traditional conservatism, but by a dynamic new policy of the right. External opponents are joined by internal ones.

In a certain sense, the left is also conservative. It is often suggested that "new social movements," particularly the women's movement, might be a source of support and renewal for a future left-wing project. Couldn't the workers' movement, which is not very powerful at the moment in the face of new technology and unemployment, acquire a new strength for a common project from the Greens or from the feminist challenge?

I do not wish to discuss the relationships among different social movements or whether the workers' movement should play a dominant or nondominant role. Rather, I want to examine a problem that is common to all movements. In times of radical change it is important to determine how far forward the bearers of possible progress are inclined to go, as opposed to giving in to regressive stability. And in what lines of advance do they see hope and utopia?

I am therefore asking both about what structures are breaking down and about the aspirations and plans of the individuals in movement. I am asking how individuals are integrating themselves into the new conditions, how they are changing, and what interventions in society they envision.

I am also concerned with what the right wing is doing to reconstruct the living conditions of workers and of women. Above all, I want to expose the conflict between those forces striving for a new form of social cooperation and those attempting to confine individuals to their private lives. Out of the results of my analysis will come proposals for cultural transformation. My focus will be on problems in the workers' and women's movements.

Socialization of Work and Privatization of Workers

Marx thought that capitalism would rush the productive forces into revolutionary change that would force work out of the narrow limits of the private and into the social sphere, until at last the final limit would be challenged, privacy in the ownership of the means of production, the very foundation of the capitalist social order. A visible sign of the socialization of work has been the bringing together of masses of workers in the factory. This has served as the starting point for the organization of a counterforce and has made factory workers into the bearers of radical change. There is no doubt that the productive forces have been developed in a revolutionary way and that social labor has expanded and become a decisive force. But to all appearances, the most recent revolution in the development of the productive forces – electronic automated production – has buried the hope of a socialist victory of the working class. Although what can be considered as social labor is encompassing an ever-broader scope, the exclusion of large segments of the population from employment makes it next to impossible for those who are employed to see the relevance to them of more progressive policies. What's more, the new machines are not bringing many individual workers together under one roof – the situation that Marx welcomed – but are giving rise once again to an isolated form of work. This is especially true in respect to the computer. Work that is segmented and isolating has a negative effect on the will for change and movement.

In the past ten years such tendencies have been accompanied by Cassandra cries that automation of capitalist production would lead to deskilling, polarization, taylorization, in short, to a complete dehumanization of working conditions. Recently we have witnessed a change of tune (Kern & Schumann, 1984). From the depths of despair we have risen to the heights of enthusiasm over the positive possibilities the new technology offers to those who have a job. The German Social Democratic Party (SPD) is presently pursuing a project of modernization that attempts to unite technological progress with "progressive" management.

We shall allow these one-sided views their historical rights and examine instead the contradictions that arise from the new developments in the forces of production and are leading to crisis; let's determine on what terrain the struggle will take place. What follows is condensed from the research work of our "project on automatization and qualification" (Projektgruppe Automation und Qualifikation [PAQ], 1975, 1978a, b, 1980, 1981a, b, 1983, 1987). By "productive forces" we mean the mode of human work in relation to nature, that is, how labor is socialized. Social formations arise such as are adequate to the productive forces, and therefore a new technology should make new formations possible. Historically, several societal formations have existed on the basis of one mode of production. Today we find the same technological basis in both capitalist and socialist countries, that is, a technology from the first industrial revolution, which accompanies the different societal formations of capitalism and socialism. (To this can be added the different kinds of societal relations that exist in Third World countries.) We have socialist societies with a technically primitive base. In terms of technical development, productivity, and so forth, capitalist societies surpass socialist ones. We have technological revolution where societal revolution is lacking and societal revolution where, from year to year, technology lags behind the plan. History does not progress in an orderly way. In the Third World, where colonial capitalism imposed itself on precapitalist societies and created societal formations subject to the opposition between East and West, we encounter social states of affairs containing unimaginable contradictions.

Whereas the productive forces are lagging behind in the few remaining socialist societies, in capitalist societies they are overdeveloped. It is this overdevelopment that determines the nature of the class struggle in capitalist societies. That's why, for the present, we can assume that further expansion of the productive forces will cause radical change at all levels. There will be a great reordering of things, out of which the ingredients of transformation will be drawn.

Automation of production and management revolutionizes the societal production process in the very place in which Marx located both the basis and the result of class domination: in the division of labor, especially the division of manual and intellectual work. The activity of automation is essentially the study of the errors of objectified regulation theory; it analyzes processes from the perspective of their future development. The radical changes demanded of the workers are in their knowledge and skills, their attitudes, and in the division of labor and forms of cooperation. The revolutionary change affects the old producers, their experience, knowledge, virtues, and way of dealing with the old relations within which the revolutionary change is pushed forward. If the production process is to function at all, both sides of it are challenged. Entrepreneurs naturally try to produce as cheaply as possible. But the cheapest option is no longer to save on labor, to intensify exploitation of workers, or to lower the costs of their training. Instead, developing the capacities of individual production workers has proved to be a good investment for the enterprise. Likewise, workers' organizations – trade unions, for example – find the productive forces to be the source of both uplift and opposition at the same time. Emancipatory demands for the development of work in relation to qualifications, training, and cooperation can be justified by reference to the functioning of the entire process; conversely, the endeavors of the entrepreneurs to win over the workers as partners in the areas of automation are incomparably more pronounced. Human engineering becomes a flourishing branch of manager training. Industrial policy becomes a central topic of sociological conferences. Moreover, the threat of unemployment makes it much easier for entrepreneurs to integrate their workers psychologically. On the battlefield thus defined, how individual workers deal with the conditions of automation becomes very important. It is here that one can see the flaws in the structure. This is where the sources of resistance and of support for a socialist project can be worked out in detail.

There is an important division between labor time and leisure time in the lives of wage laborers. Though such a division may be problematic from a conceptual point of view, it is experienced in a very practical way by individuals as a separation that runs through their lives and that they jealously guard. In this connection, the latest breakthrough in the automation of production is experienced by workers as both a danger and a liberation.

Managerial strategies in existence long before automation have often been based on the fusion and combined utilization of elements from the life of *labor* and from the domain of *leisure time*. The term "company family" [*Betriebsfamilie*] is a common articulation of this idea. Attempts are made to transfer to the enterprise, through a paternalistic, solicitous attitude, feelings and behavior patterns typical of the family, such as loyalty, confidence, devotion, that is, attitudes that cannot be bought with money. These special forms of social behavior, with the obligations they place on employees, offer capital a possibility for resolving the problems of responsibility, diligence, and optimization of the operations required by automation. For trade union struggles, the acceptance of the enterprise's point of view by employees is a major obstacle.

In one enterprise, for example, workers were regularly sent to industrial fairs. Those selected to represent their enterprise were offered an opportunity to win distinction "at home" (within their enterprise) by presenting reports and making proposals about new machines. By this means they learned to see the means of production from the viewpoint of profit making. This was made easier by the design of the fairs, in which production facilities were presented purely in terms of technical apparatus.

In an oil refinery the principle of self-evaluation was introduced as a way of imposing an alien standpoint on the workers. In a public discussion orchestrated by the head of the department, the workers were able to grade themselves on a preestablished scale, thereby also determining the amount of their wages. In observing themselves and others from the aspect of their output, they adopted the quantifying standpoint of capital. These methods of integration disorganize the old structures of worker solidarity and create a new group of solitary fighters. The old cultures of worker solidarity that made it possible, for example, to organize slowdowns are thus undermined and transformed. The practice of critical self-evaluation (stage-managed from above) is all the more effective if workers' previous opinions about each other and about themselves are integrated into the new criteria (PAQ, 1987: 153).

We also encountered simpler ways in which workers can be inveigled into adopting the entrepreneur's attitude. In 15 percent of the cases that we examined this was achieved by profit sharing (bribing). This technique (the linking up of an individual worker's *personal benefit* with *somebody else's*) has been well-known since the working class came into existence. Other workers were given some of the responsibilities of the entrepreneurs so that, having a "free hand" in the enterprise, they were in a position to reflect on profitability and what more could be done "with regard to productivity and the market" for the benefits of the enterprise. Constant monitoring of the market and estimation of the economic utilization of the instruments of production are frequent tasks of workers in automated production. The entrepreneurs we polled regarded the "favorable" standpoint as a question of character and expressed their "trust" in their subordinates by saying "one can rely on them." The language of such formulations already reveals the problem that entrepreneurs face with unreliable workers and how large an effort is required to produce the standpoint that employers favor.

Among the most important things we learned about the ways in which alien attitudes can be encouraged was the discovery of how the private sphere of individual workers is used for the private objectives of the entrepreneurs. The community of the workplace shrinks to the size of the family, whose boundaries in relation to the "external" world are defended as a private space so as to maintain the communal interior. This meant that it was not, as we had at first assumed, the *societal nature* of production that needed to be gotten hold of in order to mobilize the communal forces, but rather its *private nature.* Entrepreneurs formulate this in the following terms: "Everyone is naturally a private person and knows that everything costs money. In this way we can encourage them to reflect about saving. If they get the impression that it is *their* machine they are operating, then they will automatically want to get the most out of it" (PAQ, 1987: 154). Former smallholders, therefore, are the best workers in costly automated plants. It is typical of such people "to calculate everything with precision, to be guided by the market situation when planning the costs, because they had, themselves, been independent farmers" (PAQ, 1987: 154). In this context we see a driving force in capitalistically applied automation, which gradually eliminates the sharp division between work and leisure time that located real life in the sphere of leisure time. And conversely, the domestic standpoint enters into the realm of work.

Putting familial attitudes and habits to the service of work in the enterprise was one side on which we encountered a kind of breakdown of the boundary between "private life" and "working life." We expected, on the other side, that there would be an effect of the radical change in production and work on the general way of life. We thought that the demands posed by the productive forces would have to lead to an intolerable strain on the habits of life and thus to a crisis of individual socialization.

A whole series of work tasks now take on wider proportions and call for more intense engagement, which may become incompatible with the preservation of a regulated, self-enclosed workday and workplace. We believed that this would put a burden on family relations, especially when women work in automation. The remedy and avoidance of technical disturbances demand flexibility in relation to what has been learned and an openness in relation to new forms of learning. This applies especially to the increasingly rapid innovations in technology (PAQ, 1987: 108ff.). What changes are entailed in the demand that people continue to learn throughout the lifespan when the usual practice has been to stop learning while still young? Prior to automation, the working day was a temporally self-enclosed unit with a prescribed timetable, consisting of tasks given out, regulations about breaks, and work controlled from above. Unfilled time, unforeseen assignments, and independent control of time are, on the other hand, characteristics of automated labor that obscure the boundaries between work dictated by someone else and work according to one's own priorities. The necessary element of autonomy within the framework of paid work is a jolt to the customary idea that self-determination can only be found in hobby work. How, then, do workers experience the relationships that are affected by the demands of productions, viz., the relationship between the sexes, between work and leisure time, between learning and professional training, between self-determination and other-determination in work?

During conversations with groups of programmers on the subject of "private life," they constantly referred to the realm of work. The conversations reflected a contradiction between fascination and indifference. It is common knowledge that workers are fascinated by new means of production, and this is above all true of those who work with computers. But it is important how this fascination is expressed. Virtually all the statements referred to fascination as something that deserves contempt, as simply amounting to a striving for senseless competence. It means a stomach ache and insomnia. One forgets about food and leisure time, and the result is a kind of incompetence in private life. The threat to private life is the starting point for their reflections; the desire to protect it structures their perception of working life. Thus a marked interest in work is experienced and expressed as alienation "from oneself," a form of domination: "One always thinks about doing something new." This assertion by programmers is not in praise of human creativity; it expresses a kind of obsession: "An idea has taken hold of me." "I don't like being fascinated because then there's no room for anything else . . . " (PAQ, 1987: 156). The contradiction between the private individual and alienated societal labor is expressed as the unreasonable demands of productive forces. The conflict with the relations of production is shifted onto the machines. The workers flee the fascination and seek a center for their lives outside their profession. Programmers insist that their work becomes increasingly indifferent. Marx wrote that indifference to a particular kind of work suits a social formation in which the individual can easily move from one job to another; the specific kind of work becomes merely incidental and therefore indifferent.

The metaphor of indifference was successful in the older industrial sociology because it allowed the productive relations to be understood by their own standard as well as by the subjective standards of the workers. But in our context all this seems a bit crazy: Programmers are not indifferent to their work, an easy transfer to another job is out of the question, and the productive relations are not even in the field of vision. If the flight from fascination is not successful, the class struggle is shifted to struggle with the machine:

OTTO: Still, these things are a terrible temptation. They're perfect. They're absolute. They're complete.

INGE: It seems to me that it's a power struggle with the machine to see who's better.

OTTO: The machine is absolutely merciless, without emotions. And when the program you have made works, once it's running, it's the most objective thing you can imagine. No one can be as competent as a machine. The machine has no mercy. You put in a full stop instead of a comma, and the whole program goes out the window. And this is no small example; it's normal. Such a trifle in a gigantic system makes the whole thing collapse. (PAQ, 1987: 158)

Learning in our society is generally organized competitively. Only one can be the best. Grades are handed down from above. Dependence on superiors represents both arbitrariness and opportunity. In this connection, the programmers act surprisingly, though consistently, given the constraint of the productive relations. Next to a consciousness of competence, complaints about a lack of recognition from superiors, who are probably incompetent anyway, run through the interviews as a leitmotiv.

Programmers express sharp criticism of capitalism, but in a way that is contradictory: They do not wish to work for money alone because "that is not a concrete form of recognition." They complain about an insufficient relevance of their work to social use, and in the same sentence – "No one is interested in that" – a bridge is erected to the reestablishment of normal managerial relations. A better "style of leadership" is called for: The superiors should say a few appreciative words. Their criticism of capitalism thus becomes an acceptance of it.

The field of action is determined in a contradictory way; work requires a high degree of autonomy, but at the same time programmers have no say on the nature of tasks and no insight into what they mean. Superiors do not exercise immediate control over the work; rather, the programmers organize the tasks and time themselves. One programmer compensated at home for the lack of praise from superiors by effusively praising her son "because that's what makes a person feel worthy as a human being and motivates him for further action" (PAQ, 1987: 160).

Working life and private life are opposites in their subjective meaning: The former is experienced as heteronomous; the latter as autonomous. In their work arrangements, programmers experience a kind of self-determination within other-determination as a fascination with machines. Against the background of

such an intolerable paradox they stake out the private life that they protect
from assaults coming from the realm of work. One of the programmers goes
so far as to renounce claims to recognition for his work: "I get enough
recognition in my private life." The opposition between working life and
private life leads to a block in the ordering of the problems. The problems
of work are seen through the spectacles of the private; they are subordinated
to private life, and instead of being worked out, they are defined as less
important.

In conclusion, programmers are faced with a series of conflicts that arise
from further development of the productive forces, but against a background of
more or less the same relations of production. This moves them then into a
state of conflict between their work and private lives.

- Their programming activities demand a confident engagement in their
  work such as would be expected for those with a voice in productive relations regarding social use. Programmers do not demand such a voice;
  they protest against the engagement because their self-consciousness and
  life's focus are in the private sphere.
- That they can and must organize their own time would seem to require
  that they treat their own time as something precious, as part of the working time of society that should be filled in a worthwhile way. Such a
  conception of time is contrary to the mechanical division into paid time
  and remaining time. But programmers respond to the unreasonable demands neither by a struggle for a shortening of working time nor by an
  individual attempt to achieve real autonomy. Instead, they demand the
  right to a frictionless existence that demands as little as possible from
  them, thus saving for themselves as much energy for private life as possible.
- Their work requires that they come up with new ideas and develop new
  systems, that they be more than mere executors of tasks. Instead of questioning the superiority of their dubious "superiors," they demand superficial praise from them. They would rather not have ideas because they
  don't want to be seized by them. They oppose this being-taken-possession-
  of with a "private self," an "own self," with respect to which even their
  own ideas, thought up for alien interests, are themselves alien.

Thus all the problems that touch the boundaries of private productive relations
are structured and displaced by the programmers in terms of their private lives.
Changes in productive relations are therefore resisted not only by the interests
of the private owners of the means of production, but also by the privacy of
the producers themselves.

Female Identity and the Privatization of the Women's Movement

Insofar as the privacy of producers constitutes a barrier against the forces of
the societal sphere, for better or worse, it would seem senseless to make the
privacy of women a subject of study. Women are, in a certain sense, identical

with the everyday private sphere. Indeed, this confinement to the private sphere had a lot to do with the outbreak of the feminist movement in the 1960s and 1970s. The slogan "The private is the political" was intended to make the private sphere into an important topic of public discussion and, at the same time, to insist that the isolation of the private sphere was essential for maintaining the system as a whole. A considerable part of the feminist initiative can be described as an assault on the walls that close off private spaces from that which is public: the insistence on the importance of housework and the demand that the work of housewives be paid, attempts to socialize the education of children (in alternative care centers), and above all, the identification and publication of facts about violence in married life, the establishment of refuges for women, and attempts to have the law recognize "rape in marriage" as a criminal act.

On the theoretical plane, questions were asked about how, for example, housework could be incorporated into Marx's theory of value, that is, regarded as a form of the constant primary accumulation of capital, how subsistence production all over the world could be brought into the focus of social theory and the critique of political economy.

The attempt to raise the "women's issue" out of the isolation of the private to the public level, to expose the division of private and public life as a fertile soil for domination, did not bring women directly into the life of society, but first into the problems of state administration. Here it was learned in a practical way that the private sphere was not only a prison but also a protected area, though the state had already extensively penetrated it. Compulsory education, adoption law, and alimony, as well as marriage itself, are regulated by the state and pervade the life of women as orienting structures. Women do not become citizens of the state like men, who, on entering adult life, combine economic independence with the performance of an occupation. Women become citizens – as housewives.

Making women's problems into affairs of the state draws women deeper into these structures rather than freeing them. Nevertheless, the result is ambiguous. The effort to draw public attention to domination in the private sphere has provoked extensive discussions and aroused a consciousness of the fact that matters like life, illness, death, protection, and preservation of the environment have become marginalized as private affairs of individuals, whereas public interest is supposed to be concentrated on the production, circulation, and consumption of goods. The fact that much of this, too, is carried on by private producers for the sake of profit is, in general, accepted, since small households are accustomed to thinking and operating in private terms. (The populist monetary policy as exemplified by Margaret Thatcher's policies has made a very successful appeal to these sentiments.)

The protests of women brought seeming oppositions into new light: Their own oppression, which was made virtually permanent by preoccupation with the private, and privacy of the greater part of society were promoting class rule as a kind of general interest. It was seen as intolerable – and here, again, we return to Lenin's primary question – that nature and life, human care and happiness should figure as negligible, marginal issues. Hence the closeness and partial identity of the feminist, ecological, and peace movements. At the present time the subject of reproductive technology is bringing the women's movement together with the Green Alternatives.

Meanwhile, in most Western countries right-wing governments have taken power and the problems that the women's movement successfully made public are being returned to the domestic hearth. Funds for women's refuges have been cut, surveillance and control have been intensified, either feminist chairs at the universities are being directly abolished or courses for women are canceled as the result of budgetary restrictions. This policy of cutbacks is, of course, not proceeding smoothly. The privatization policy pursued by the Christian Democrats in the Federal Republic of Germany is meeting with opposition from women in its own ranks; black, red, and Green alliances have become possible, for example, in opposing the abortion law that the Christian Democrats want to make more rigorous.

Administrative suppression of women's demands is accompanied by calls for the preservation of the family, for devoted wives and mothers, for feminine values, for love and care, and so forth. Even the "feminization of society" is becoming a topic that can be talked about by the right, whereas only ten years ago it would have been unheard of. It would have been as scandalous then as it would be today to propose the "homosexualization" of society.

Such an "upgrading" of the value of women was a surprise for which the feminist movement was unprepared; the ground was prepared in a way for a fruitful reception of these right-wing ideas. In some sections of the feminist movement "feminine values" were also being rediscovered, appreciated, and celebrated as the voice of the future, as if they were essential properties of women and not merely social requirements. The power of motherhood was traced back to religions that revered mother goddesses as an eternal principle. There was widespread insistence on the importance of family space and work on relationships and reproduction. How could one turn a deaf ear to the enticements of the Christian Democrats?

Can one now expect resistance from those in the feminist movement – and there were many of them – who didn't particularly care about developing their "femininity," but rather aimed at the conquest of all walks of life by women? After all, not all women confine their interest primarily or exclusively to the "domain of reproduction," nor do they see it as their future. A hopeful glance at these sections of the feminist movement finds another kind of resistant alignment with the government's intentions: a deep sense of resignation and indignation, together with a defiant inclination to abandon politics and return to private life. That is, a desire for reprivatization, a desire for children, for one's own home and togetherness are again becoming dominant goals.

Our own investigation of this aspiration of women for reprivatization (Haug & Hauser, 1985) led us to the conclusion that a woman's desire to subordinate herself to a man, along with the tendency to consider politics and more far-reaching social change as being beyond her competence, was a component part of the female identity even if she was gainfully employed and still politically active. In an attempt to find out how this kind of femininity is constructed, we discovered, among other things, that many elements of family subordination derive from a resistance to the role women envisage for themselves in the social structure, rather than from adjustment and acquiescence. Resistance against their parental family drives women to found new and better families in which they see the prospect of freedom. Resistance against a situation in which others have control over their time provokes a protest against the planning of time generally, which in the long run ends with the subordination of their time structure to somebody else's. Girls resent the fact that their mothers are called upon voluntarily to renounce their own well-being for the sake of the physical and spiritual well-being of members of their family, but later on this sacrifice is what helps young women assume for themselves the role of a self-sacrificing, loving wife and mother.

Armed with such hopes and wishes, born of a robust socialization, women ultimately come to interpret society's inhospitality as a demand that can and ought to be satisfied in a small circle. But there remains a general unease, a sense of having wanted something else. This sense of frustration lingers on in them as a kind of lifelong schizophrenia; the majority of women think or feel that they are something other than what they appear to be, that they are deceiving other people, or that they are not really acknowledged for what they are. By retreating into the private sphere, they at once comfort themselves with the thought that – if not now, then surely later – they will have a different life. They hope for a kind of revelation and are assisted in this by the industry whose business it is to create illusions.

Life and Its Maintenance: Conclusions

We have seen that productive workers are paralyzed by a perspective derived from the standpoint of the private sphere, leisure time, and family, in short, from the standpoint of individuals socialized in private relations. We have seen a decline in the strength of one of the important new social movements, the feminist movement, which is doubly caught up in the threads of the private. Where, then, will the elements of transformation be found for the construction of a better society?

It seems fair to assume that the controversy over the private sphere is itself a sign, if not of a breaking, then at least of a loosening, of its fetters. The forces are distributed in a crazy manner. On the one hand, the privacy of productive workers functions as an obstacle to their exploitation in the name of profit, but it also prevents an appropriation of technology in the interests of the workers themselves. On the other hand, the privatization of women's issues occurs as an opposition to their incorporation into the state and as a protest against the inhospitality of society.

The crisis affects the sphere of labor, the spatially separated private domain, and their interconnections. The major societal questions are experienced as immediate threats to the individual. It is no longer possible to separate a sick society from a healthy private world. The crisis is articulated as a problem of our way of life. Accordingly, new social movements locate their protests in these areas and not in the domain of production, even in those cases where they are protesting against new technologies. Habermas (1985) takes this to signal the end of "a kind of utopia that had, in the past, crystallized around the potential of a society based on work." This notion subsumes for him such diverse movements as Marxism and the European workers' movements, "authoritarian corporatism in fascist Italy, in national-socialist Germany," and the "social-democratic reformism of mass democracies in the West" (p. 146). He recommends that a "communication society" be taken up as an incentive to utopias, that the communication media be used in an alternative way, and that "autonomous publics be formed by self-determined activity" (pp. 158ff.). As Habermas understands earlier social theory, its emancipatory impulses urged the abolition of heteronomous labor in favor of self-determined activity. Given the crises of the welfare state, new labor-saving technology, growing unemployment, and the new social movements at the periphery of the production process, he recommends – and this has been a widely discussed topic among sociologists in the German Federal Republic at the last three sociological conferences – that the concept of work be removed from the center of social theory, but he wants the demand for self-determined activity to be retained as "emancipation."

His argument may be satisfactory from the "standpoint of phenomena" (Marx). And the option of self-determined activity should not be left to the populism of the right wing, but retained as an indispensable element of every form of emancipation. But self-determined activity would have to be connected with "self-socialization," with a growing collective control over the conditions of the life of society. The mere "do it yourself" has in itself no goal or direction toward liberation, and there is a constant danger that others' priorities will be imposed on it. The dynamics of automation have turned everything upside down. The struggle for a decent life, as well as attempts to defend the private sphere, can be interpreted as a matter of disbanding the sphere of public work. But why should we not hold onto the Marxian principles that Habermas cites as so unconvincing? "We have come to the point where individuals must appropriate the existing totality of the productive forces in order to achieve self-assertion. . . . The acceptance of these forces is simply the development of individual abilities that correspond with the instruments of material production. Only at that level does self-determined activity overlap with material life, which corresponds to the development of the individual into a total individual and to the rejection of every natural primariness" (quoted in Habermas, 1985: 145).[1]

Marx certainly did not think that the productive forces would develop automatically and without struggle. On the level of electronic automated production, this means generalizing the ability to use these productive forces, which includes the possibility of developing them and collectively deciding how their unique features can be used to the best societal advantage. At the same time, work itself should be generalized. With everyone then working only four or five hours for the purpose of earning a living, time would be left free for sociopolitical activity, further education, and cultural production and reproduction. Overcoming the old division of labor would then be possible. Of course, the new conditions might also be used for strengthening the old divisions, while an army of housewives tries to repair the cultural damage created by specialization and unemployment and while the inflated state apparatus tries to stave off attacks on the production process by specialists and to limit and redistribute the misery of the isolated and unemployed. This, to all appearances, is the program of the new right.

We, on the other hand, should see to it that the crisis is used for a reorganization. One important political task would be to establish an alternative model of a working life. Ways should be found to promote appropriation of the new productive forces in alternative projects. An offensive utilization of the new media could help in linking up the countless projects of self-determined activity, thus creating a model for generalizing the new mode of living and working. Precisely because the crisis touches and arouses such a diverse range of people in different walks of life, it presents an opportunity for the breakthrough of a general model of a more civilized life. The question of what we want to produce and how to go about it would, however, remain a fundamental question.

With respect to our analysis of the functions of the private sphere for participants in social movements, we are led to the conclusion that their privatization not only amounts to a shackle made of old relationships, but is also a challenge to political organizations. The questions about the mode of living need a political articulation, just as the people involved need more room of their own in the political sphere.

For this we must build on the forces of self-socialization, on the aspiration and need to regulate society collectively. In our "utopia of a working society" (which Habermas imagines as coming to an end), we see, first, that the collective forces are firmly bound to the market model of capitalist socialization. In any case, they do not exist by themselves, freely available, but are bound in particular forms that, when they fall apart, are experienced as crisis. The forms we are mainly concerned with are the *factory,* in which production is carried out collectively and socially, and the *home* and *family,* in which the rest of one's life is regulated. We designate both of these places – and not just the state – as forms of communal life and their actors as embodiments of utopian hopes. The new productive forces are subverting these places, destroying the forms, and creating insecurity for the actors. We need new forms of common life and work. We are now offered the opportunity to overcome (*aufheben*) the separation of work from leisure time and of men from women in such a way that a collective regulation of life can be attained in all areas of life.

From the viewpoint of the reproduction of society, the questions of the production of the means of life and the production of life itself are both central. That the production and maintenance of life, which are treated as marginal in the capitalist mode of production, are experienced as a state of crisis cannot, to my mind, be taken to mean that matters of production are becoming marginal. It seems, rather, that the point has been reached at which the effects of the capitalist mode of production have become intolerable and destructive in all areas of life and, consequently, "individuals must appropriate the existing totality of the productive forces in order to achieve self-determination." At the level of electronic automated production this means a new model of civilization, according to which time for work, cultural-social reproduction, and political activities must be regulated in new ways. The regulation of societal needs can no longer be done behind our backs and in second place to production for profit.

We have linked the crises in the Western industrialized countries to the determining role of the productive forces, to the electronic automated mode of production. We have seen that their appropriation is both determined and hindered by the privacy of the producers. The economic crisis is also being experienced as a crisis in the way of life. Here women are affected doubly. In industrial societies they are the ones regarded as being responsible for the "way of life" in the broadest sense of the term. The private sector, the private sphere of the family, would be inconceivable if it were not inhabited by women. Women experience the crisis as a threat to the private sphere. Even the feminist movement, for all its effort to cross the boundaries of the private in order to enter the public domain, is ill prepared when it comes to dealing with the penetration of the crisis into the private sphere.

Concerning the old controversy over whether the workers' and women's questions are linked together or stand opposed to each other, our conclusion is that they are on the same agenda. The catastrophic logic of the capitalist mode of production threatens the survival of humankind and, at the same time, creates the conditions in which the full participation of women in regulating all aspects of societal life becomes a necessity. There must be a radical change in what we consider to be essential and peripheral in capitalist-structured societies.

Contrary to Habermas, how society is determined through work will remain the central question for as long as work remains one of its defining elements. To that extent, the socialist project, too, remains on the agenda, and working people must play an essential role in changing the old societal relations. The claim that the "measure of general emancipation" is the "degree of women's emancipation" (Marx & Engels, 1845/1970b: 207) takes on a new and tangible meaning in present historical context. The women's issue is therefore not just a question of concern to women. It is increasingly clear today that it bears on the very survival of humankind.

Notes

1 Habermas cites Marx from the *German Ideology* (Marx & Engels, 1846/1969) without mentioning the page and with some highly idiosyncratic editing. Regardless of philological imprecision, which leaves the impression that the sentences Habermas quotes can go together and still make sense, Habermas's reading of Marx omits the following elements: the relation of the individual's development to subsistence; the unconditional dependence of the individual's development on the development of the instruments of production (an aspect that needs to be emphasized in the age of electronic automated production, about which Habermas is explicitly writing; see Volker Braun, "Der Grosse Frieden"); the possibility which the new forces of production offer for the development of the proletariat itself (an aspect which Gramsci further elaborated for worker-intellectuals); the necessity of a social revolution so as to make such a development possible; and, lastly, the role of modern communication which Habermas himself presents as an alternative.

Bibliography

Adorno, T. W., Albert, H., Dahrendorf, R., Habermas, J., Pilot, H., & Popper, K. R. (1969). *Der Positivismusstreit in der deutschen Soziologie.* Neuwied/Berlin: Luchterhand.

Ajzen, I., & Fishbein, M. (1977). Attitude and behavior relations: A theoretical research analysis and review of empirical research. *Psychological Bulletin, 84*, 888–918.

(1980). *Understanding attitudes and predicting social behavior.* Englewood Cliffs, NJ: Prentice-Hall.

Albert, K. (1971). Konstruktivismus oder Realismus? Bemerkungen zu Holzkamps dialektischer Ueberwindung der modernen Wissenschaftslehre. *Zeitschrift für Sozialpsychologie, 2*, 5–23.

Allport, G. W. (1935). Attitudes. In C. A. Murchison (Ed.), *Handbook of social psychology* (pp. 798–844). Worcester, MA.: Clark University Press.

Aronfreed, J. (1968). *Conduct and conscience: The socialization of internalized control over behavior.* New York: Academic Press.

Autorenkollektiv am Psychologischen Institut der Freien Universität Berlin. (1971). *Sozialistische Projektarbeit im Berliner Schülerladen Rote Freiheit. Analysen, Dokumente, Protokolle.* Frankfurt/M.: Fischer.

Bader, K. (1985). *Viel Frust und wenig Hilfe: Die Entmystifizierung sozialer Arbeit.* Weinheim: Beltz.

Bain, R. (1927/1928). An attitude on attitude research. *American Journal of Sociology, 33*, 940–957.

Bannister, D. (1960). Conceptual structure in thought disordered schizophrenics. *Journal of Mental Science, 106*, 1230–1249.

Baritz, L. (1960). *The servants of power. A history of the use of social sciences in American industry.* Middletown, CT.: Wesleyan University Press.

Bateson, G., Jackson, D. D., Haley, J., Weakland, J. H., & Wynne, L. C. (1969). *Schizophrenie und Familie.* Frankfurt/M.: Suhrkamp.

Beech, H. R., & Liddell, A. (1974). Decision-making, mood states and ritualistic behaviour among obsessional patients. In H. R. Beech (Ed.), *Obsessional states* (pp. 143–160). London: Methuen.

Bindra, D. (1959). *Motivation: a systematic reinterpretation.* New York: Ronald Press.

Blochmann, E. (Ed.). (undated). *Fröbels Theorie des Spiels I.* Weinheim: Beltz.

Blumer, H. (1939). An appraisal of Thomas and Znaniecki's "The Polish Peasant in Europe and America." *Social Science Research Council Bulletin, 44*, 69–81.

(1955/1956). Attitudes and the social act. *Social Problems, 3*, 59–65.

Boetel, H., Gerhardt, R., & Scheffler, W. (1978). Aufarbeitung der Störungsgenese und ausgewählter Therapieschwierigkeiten im konkreten Einzelfall auf Basis kritisch-psychologischer Konflikttheorie. Unpublished diploma thesis, Psychologisches Institut, Freie Universität Berlin (West).

251

Bogardus, E. S. (1924/1925). Measuring social distances. *Journal of Applied Psychology, 9*, 299–308.

Bosch, G. (1978). Arbeitsplatzverlust. *Die sozialen Folgen einer Betriebsstillegung.* Frankfurt/M.: Campus.

Brannon, R. (1976.) Attitudes and the prediction of behavior. In B. Seidenbert & A. Snadowsky (Eds.), *Social psychology. An introduction* (pp. 145–198). New York: Free Press.

Braun, K.-H. (1979). *Kritik des Freudo-Marxismus. Zur marxistischen Aufhebung der Psychoanalyse.* Cologne: Pahl-Rugenstein.

Braun, K.-H. (1986). Umrisse einer pädagogischen Theorie des Spiels. *Behindertenpädagogik, 3,* 242–255.

Brendler, G. (1983). Martin Luther. Ein politisches Porträt aus marxistischer Sicht. *Blätter für deutsche und internationale Politik, 10,* 1348–1362.

Bruschlinski, A. W., & Tichomirow, O. K. (1975). *Zur Psychologie des Denkens.* Berlin/GDR: Deutscher Verlag der Wissenschaften.

Buytendijk, F. J. J. (1934). *Wesen und Sinn des Spiels.* Berlin: Wolff.

Campbell, D. T. (1963). Social attitudes and other acquired behavioral dispositions. In S. Koch (Ed.). (1959–1963). *Psychology: A study of a science* (Vols. 1–6). Study II: Empirical substructure and relations with other sciences. (Vol. 6, pp. 94–172). New York: McGraw-Hill.

Chance, M. R. A. (1962). An interpretation of some agonistic postures: The role of "cut-off" acts and postures. *Symposia of the Zoological Society of London, 8,* 71–89.

Cialdini, R. B., Petty, R. E., & Cacioppo, J. T. (1981). Attitude and attitude change. *Annual Review of Psychology, 32,* 357–404.

Cornforth, M. (1975). *Materialism and the dialectical method.* New York: International.

Davids, A. (1974). *Children in conflict: A casebook.* New York, London, Sydney, Toronto: Wiley.

DeFleur, M. L., & Westie, F. R. (1963/1964). Attitude as a scientific concept. *Social Forces, 42,* 17–31.

Delius, J. D. (1970). Irrelevant behaviour, information processing and arousal homeostasis. *Psychologische Forschung, 33,* 165–188.

Dell, P., Bonvallet, M., & Hugelin, A. (1961). Mechanisms of reticular de-activization. In G. E. W. Wolstenholme & M. O'Connor (Eds.), *Ciba Foundation Symposium on the Nature of Sleep* (pp. 86–102). London: Churchill.

Dewey, J. (1922). *Human nature and conduct.* New York: Carlton.

Dreier, O. (1980). *Familiäres Sein und familiäres Bewusstsein: Therapeutische Analyse einer Arbeiterfamilie.* Frankfurt/M.: Campus.

(1984). Probleme der Entwicklung psychotherapeutischer Arbeit. In K.-H. Braun & G. Gekeler (Eds.), *Objektive und subjektive Widersprüche in der Sozialarbeit* (pp. 137–150). Marburg: Verlag Arbeiterbewegung und Gesellschaftswissenschaft.

(1985a). Zum Verhältnis von psychologischer Therapie und Diagnostik. In K.-H. Braun & K. Holzkamp (Eds.), *Subjektivität als Problem psychologischer Methodik. 3. Internationaler Kongress Kritische Psychologie Marburg 1984* (pp. 232–246). Frankfurt/M.: Campus.

(1985b). Psychotherapy on the basis of Critical Psychology. In J. J. Sanchez-Sosa (Ed.), *Health and clinical psychology* (pp. 549–556). Amsterdam: North Holland.

(1985c). Grundfragen der Psychotherapie in der Psychoanalyse und in der Kritischen Psychologie. In K.-H. Braun, O. Dreier, W. Hollitscher, K. Holzkamp, M. Markard, G. Minz, & K. Wetzel, *Geschichte und Kritik der Psychoanalyse. Bericht von der 3. internationalen Ferienuniversität Kritische Psychologie, 25. Februar bis 2. März 1985 in Innsbruck* (pp. 127–152). Marburg: Verlag Arbeiterbewegung und Gesellschaftswissenschaft.

(1986a). Persönlichkeit und Individualität in psychologischer Theorie und klinischer Praxis. In H. Flessner (Ed.), *Marxistische Persönlichkeitstheorie. Marxistische Studien: Vol. 10* (pp. 256–277). Frankfurt/M.: Institut für Marxistische Studien und Forschungen.

(1987a). Zur Funktionsbestimmung von Supervision in der therapeutischen Arbeit. In W.

Maiers & M. Markard (Eds.), *Kritische Psychologie als Subjektwissenschaft. Klaus Holzkamp zum 60. Geburtstag.* Frankfurt/M.: Campus.

(1987b). Der Psychologe als Subjekt therapeutischer Praxis. In J. Dehler & K. Wetzel (Eds.), *Zum Verhältnis von Theorie und Praxis in der Psychologie. Bericht von der 4. Internationalen Ferienuniversität Kritische Psychologie, 5.-10. Oktober 1987 in Fulda* (pp. 113–138). Marburg: Verlag Arbeiterbewegung und Gesellschaftswissenschaft.

(1988a). Denkweisen über Therapie. *Forum Kritische Psychologie, 22,* 42–67.

(1988b). Zur Sozialpsychologie der Therapie von Uebergewichtigen. Bemerkungen zum Aufsatz von Haisch & Haisch. *Zeitschrift für Sozialpsychologie, 19*(4), 287–295.

(1988c). Der Psychologie als Subjekt therapeutischer Praxis. In J. Dehler & K. Wetzel (Eds.), *Zum Verhältnis von Theorie und Praxis in der Psychologie.* Marburg: Verlag der Arbeiterbewegung und Gesellschaftswissenschaft.

(in press). Private thinking: Towards a theory of therapeutic action in context. In S. Chaiklin & J. Lave (Eds.), *Understanding practice: Perspectives on activity and context.* New York: Cambridge University Press.

Ehrlich, H. J. (1969). Attitudes, behavior, and the intervening variable. *The American Sociologist, 4,* 29–34.

Elfferding, W. (1983). Staat, Klassen, Kommunismus. Zur Diskussion über Ideologie und Staat. *Forum Kritische Psychologie, 11,* 76–93.

Eliasson, R., & Nygren, P. (1983). *Närstudier i psykoterapi.* Stockholm: Prisma.

Elkonin, D. (1965). *Zur Psychologie des Vorschulalters.* Berlin/GDR: Volk & Wissen.

Engels, F. (1963). Zur Kritik des sozialdemokratischen Programmentwurfs 1891. In *Marx/Engels, Werke* (Vol. 22, pp. 225–240). Berlin/GDR: Dietz. (Original work published 1890)

(1968a). Vorbemerkung zum zweiten Abdruck (1870): "Der deutsche Bauernkrieg." In *Marx/Engles, Werke* (Vol. 16, pp. 393–400). Berlin/GDR: Dietz. (Original work published 1870)

(1968b). Dialektik der Natur. Notizen und Fragmente. In *Marx/Engels, Werke* (Vol. 20, pp. 456–568). Berlin/GDR: Dietz. (Original work published 1925)

(1970). Antwort an Herrn Paul Ernst, 5. Okt. 1890. In *Marx/Engels, Werke* (Vol. 22, pp. 80–85). Berlin/GDR: Dietz. (Original work published 1890)

(1971). Der Status quo in Deutschland. In *Marx/Engels, Werke* (Vol. 4, pp. 40–57). Berlin/GDR: Dietz. (Original work published 1847)

Epstein, S. (1972). The nature of anxiety with emphasis upon its relationship to expectancy. In C. D. Spielberger (Ed.), *Anxiety. Current trends in theory and research* (Vol. 2, pp. 291–337). New York, San Francisco, London: Academic Press.

Esser, A. (1987). Familie: Ein kybernetisches Problem? *Forum Kritische Psychologie, 19,* 116–131.

Fanter, W. (1978). Zur Bedeutung der Emotionen im Therapieprozess. Unpublished diploma thesis, Psychologisches Institut, Freie Universität Berlin (West).

Faris, E. (1928). Attitudes and behavior. *American Journal of Sociology, 34,* 271–281.

(1931). The concept of social attitudes. In K. Young, (Ed.), *Social attitudes* (pp. 3–16). New York: Holt.

Feuser, G. (1984a). *Gemeinsame Erziehung behinderter und nichtbehinderter Kinder im Kindertagesheim. Zwischenbericht.* Bremen: Diakonisches Werk.

(1984b). Gemeinsame Erziehung behinderter und nichtbehinderter Kinder (Integration) als Regelfall?! In *Protokoll der Fachtagung der GEW Hessen "Gemeinsam lernen. Integration behinderter Schüler"* (pp. 7–56). Kassel: Gewerkschaft Erziehung Wissenschaft.

(1984c). Die Grundschule – Schule für alle Schüler!? *Demokratische Erziehung, 5,* 30–33.

Fiedler, P. (Ed.). (1981). *Psychotherapieziel Selbstbehandlung: Grundlagen kooperativer Psychotherapie.* Weinheim: Edition Psychologie.

Fisch, R., & Daniel, H. D. (1982). Research and publication trends in experimental social psychology: 1971–1980. A thematic analysis of *The Journal of Experimental Social Psychology,*

The European Journal of Social Psychology, and the *Zeitschrift für Sozialpsychologie. European Journal of Social Psychology, 12,* 395–412.

Fleming, D. (1967). Attitude: The history of a concept. *Perspectives in American History, 1,* 287–365.

Flitner, A. (1982). *Spielen-Lernen.* Munich: Piper.

Freud, A. (1968). *Wege und Irrwege der Kinderentwicklung.* Bern, Stuttgart: Huber, Klett.

(1980). *Einführung in die Technik der Kinderanalyse.* Munich: Kindler.

Freud, S. (1975). *Beyond the pleasure principle.* J. Strachey (Trans.). New York: Norton. (Original work published 1920)

(1967). Ueber eine Weltanschauung. Neue Folgen der Vorlesungen zur Einführung in die Psychoanalyse. XXXV. Vorlesung. In *Gesammelte Werke,* Vol. 15, (pp. 170–197). (4th ed.). Frankfurt/M.: Fischer. (Original work published 1933) (Engl. edition: The question of a Weltanschauung. New introductory lectures on psycho-analysis. Lecture XXXV. In J. Strachey [Ed. and Trans.], *The standard edition of the complete psychological works of Sigmund Freud,* Vol. 21, pp. 158–182, London: Hogarth, 1963.)

(1968). Die Zukunft einer Illusion. In *Gesammelte Werke.* (Vol. 14, pp. 325–380). (4th edition). Frankfurt/M.: Fischer. (Original work published 1927) (Engl. ed.: The future of an illusion. In J. Strachey [Ed. and Trans.]. *The standard edition of the complete psychological works of Sigmund Freud.* [Vol. 21, pp. 5–56]. London: Hogarth, 1961.)

Froebel, F. (1965). Ueber Wesen und Begriff der Erziehung. In J. Scheveling (Ed.). *Friedrich Froebel, Ausgewählte pädagogische Schriften.* Paderborn: Schoningh.

Furth, P. (1980). Negative Dialektik und materialistische Theorie der Dialektik. Einleitende Bemerkungen zur Dialektikauffassung in Westdeutschland. In P. Furth (Ed.), *Arbeit und Reflexion. Zur materialistischen Theorie der Dialektik: Perspektiven der Hegelschen "Logik"* (pp. 15–68). Cologne: Pahl-Rugenstein.

Gibson, J. J. (1979). *The ecological approach to visual perception.* Boston: Houghton-Mifflin.

Goldstick, D. (1980). The Leninist theory of perception. *Dialogue: Canadian Philosophical Review, 19,* 1–19.

Gramsci, A. (1967). *Philosophie der Praxis. Eine Auswahl* (C. Riechers, Ed., with a foreword by W. Abendroth). Frankfurt/M.: Fischer.

Groos, K. (1899). *Die Spiele des Menschen.* Jena: Fischer.

Gross, H., & Harbach, I. (1978). Ursachen, Funktionszusammenhänge und Folgen einer depressiven Störung. Aufarbeitung eines konkreten Therapiefalles. Unpublished diploma thesis, Psychologisches Institut, Freie Universität Berlin (West).

Groves, P. M., & Thompson, R. F. (1970). Habituation: A dual process theory. *Psychological Review, 77,* 419–450.

Gruen, A. (1984). *Der Verrat am Selbst. Die Angst vor Autonomie bei Mann und Frau.* Munich: Causa.

Günther, K.-H., Hofmann, F., & Hohendorfer, G. (1973). *Geschichte der Erziehung.* Berlin/GDR: Volk & Wissen.

Habermas, J. (1968). *Erkenntnis und Interesse.* Frankfurt/M.: Suhrkamp.

(1985). *Die Neue Unübersichtlichkeit. Kleine politische Schriften V.* Frankfurt/M.: Suhrkamp.

Haug, F., & K. Hauser (1985). Probleme mit weiblicher Identität. In Kritische Psychologie der Frauen, Vol. 1. *Argument-Sonderband* (AS Special Issue), *117,* 14–64. West Berlin: Argument.

Haug, W. F. (1983). Hält das ideologische Subjekt Einzug in die Kritische Psychologie? *Forum Kritische Psychologie, 11,* 24–55.

Helbig, N. (1986). *Psychiatriereform und politisch-ökonomische Strukturkrise in der Bundesrepublik Deutschland.* Marburg: Verlag Arbeiterbewegung und Gesellschaftswissenschaft.

Herkommer, S., Bischoff, J., & Maldaner, K. (1984). *Alltag, Bewusstsein, Klassen.* Hamburg: Verlag für das Studium der Arbeiterbewegung.

Hildebrand-Nilshon, M. & Rückriem, G. (Eds.). (1988). *Proceedings of the 1st International Congress on Activity Theory* (4 Vols.). West Berlin: Systemdruck.

Hilgard, E. R. (1970). Allgemeines über Lerntheorien. In E. R. Hilgard & G. H. Bower, *Theorien des Lernens* (pp. 16–29). Stuttgart: Klett.

Hoff, E.-H., Lappe, L., & Lempert, W. (Eds.). (1985). *Arbeitsbiographie und Persönlichkeitsentwicklung.* Bern: Huber.

Holland, H. C. (1974). Displacement activity as a form of abnormal behaviour in animals. In H. R. Beech (Ed.), *Obsessional States* (pp. 161–173). London: Methuen.

Holzkamp, K. (1964). *Theorie und Experiment in der Psychologie. Eine grundlagenkritische Untersuchung* (2nd ed., suppl. with a postscript 1981). West Berlin: de Gruyter.

(1968). *Wissenschaft als Handlung. Versuch einer neuen Grundlegung der Wissenschaftslehre.* West Berlin: de Gruyter.

(1972a). *Kritische Psychologie. Vorbereitende Arbeiten.* Frankfurt/M.: Fischer.

(1972b). Zum Problem der Relevanz psychologischer Forschung für die Praxis. In K. Holzkamp, *Kritische Psychologie. Vorbereitende Arbeiten* (pp. 9–34). Frankfurt/M.: Fischer. (Reprinted from *Psychologische Rundschau*, 1970, *21*, 1–22.)

(1972c). Wissenschaftstheoretische Voraussetzungen kritisch-emanzipatorischer Psychologie I: Der Rückzug der modernen Wissenschaftslehre. In K. Holzkamp, *Kritische Psychologie. Vorbereitende Arbeiten* (pp. 75–98). Frankfurt/ M.: Fischer. (Reprinted from *Zeitschrift für Sozialpsychologie, 1*, 1970, 5–21).

(1972d). Wissenschaftstheoretische Voraussetzungen kritisch-emanzipatorischer Psychologie II: Die kritisch-emanzipatorische Wendung des Konstruktivismus. In K. Holzkamp, *Kritische Psychologie. Vorbereitende Arbeiten* (pp. 99–146). Frankfurt/M.: Fischer. (Reprinted from *Zeitschrift für Sozialpsychologie, 1*, 1970, 109–141).

(1972e). "Kritischer Rationalismus" als blinder Kritizismus. In K. Holzkamp, *Kritische Psychologie. Vorbereitende Arbeiten* (pp. 173–205). Frankfurt/M.: Fischer. (Reprinted from *Zeitschrift für Sozialpsychologie, 2*, 1971, 248–270).

(1972f). Konventualismus und Konstruktivismus. In K. Holzkamp, *Kritische Psychologie. Vorbereitende Arbeiten* (pp. 147–171). Frankfurt/M.: Fischer. (Reprinted from *Zeitschrift für Sozialpsychologie, 2*, 1971, 24–39.)

(1972g). Die Beziehung zwischen gesellschaftlicher Relevanz und wissenschaftlichem Erkenntnisgehalt psychologischer Forschung. (Kritisch-historische Analyse der vorstehenden Aufsätze). In K. Holzkamp, *Kritische Psychologie. Vorbereitende Arbeiten* (pp. 207–288). Frankfurt/M.: Fischer.

(1973). *Sinnliche Erkenntnis – Historischer Ursprung und gesellschaftliche Funktion der Wahrnehmung.* Frankfurt/M.: Campus.

(1977). Die Ueberwindung der wissenschaftlichen Beliebigkeit psychologischer Theorien durch die Kritische Theorie. *Zeitschrift für Sozialpsychologie, 8*, 1977, 1–22, 78–97). (Reprinted in K. Holzkamp [1978], *Gesellschaftlichkeit des Individuums. Aufsätze 1974–1977* [pp. 129–201]. Cologne: Pahl-Rugenstein.)

(1978). Das Marxische "Kapital" als Grundlage der Verwissenschaftlichung psychologischer Forschung. In K. Holzkamp, *Gesellschaftlichkeit des Individuums. Aufsätze 1974–1977* (pp. 245–255). Cologne: Pahl-Rugenstein. (Original paper published 1976).

(1979). Zur kritisch-psychologischen Theorie der Subjektivität I. Das Verhältnis von Subjektivität und Gesellschaftlichkeit in der traditionellen Sozialwissenschaft und im Wissenschaftlichen Sozialismus. *Forum Kritische Psychologie, 4*, 10–54.

(1983). *Grundlegung der Psychologie.* Frankfurt/M.: Campus.

(1984). Kritische Psychologie und phänomenologische Psychologie. Der Weg der Kritischen Psychologie zur Subjektwissenschaft. *Forum Kritische Psychologie, 14*, 5–55.

(1985). "Persönlichkeit" – Zur Funktionskritik eines Begriffs. In Herrmann, T., & Lantermann, E. D. (Eds.), *Persönlichkeit. Ein Handbuch in Schlüsselbegriffen* (pp. 92–101). Munich, Vienna, Baltimore: Urban & Schwarzenberg.

(1986). Die Verkennung von Handlungsbegründungen als empirische Zusammenhangsannahmen in sozialpsychologischen Theorien: Methodologische Fehlorientierung infolge von Begriffsverwirrung. *Zeitschrift für Sozialpsychologie, 17,* 216–238. (Reprinted in *Forum Kritische Psychologie, 19,* 1987, 23–58).

Holzkamp, K., & Holzkamp-Osterkamp, U. (1977). Psychologische Therapie als Weg von der blinden Reaktion zur bewussten Antwort auf klassenspezifische Lebensbedingungen in der bürgerlichen Gesellschaft – am Beispiel eines "Examensfalles" von Manfred Kappeler. In Kappeler, M., Holzkamp, K., & Holzkamp-Osterkamp, U. (Eds.), *Psychologische Therapie und politisches Handeln* (pp. 148–293). Frankfurt/M.: Campus.

Holzkamp-Osterkamp, U. (1972). Zum Verhältnis von produktiver und individueller Konsumtion in seiner Bedeutung für die Sozialisationsforschung. In *Ringvorlesung WS 1971/72 des Psychologischen Instituts der Freien Universität Berlin* (pp. 102–110). West Berlin: Ressort Dokumentation Psychologisches Institut FU Berlin.

(1975). *Grundlagen der psychologischen Motivationsforschung 1.* Frankfurt/M.: Campus.

(1976). *Motivationsforschung 2. Die Besonderheit menschlicher Bedürfnisse – Problematik und Erkenntniswert der Psychoanalyse.* Frankfurt/M.: Campus.

(1978). Erkenntnis, Emotionalität, Handlungsfähigkeit. *Forum Kritische Psychologie, 3,* 13–90.

(1983). Ideologismus als Konsequenz des Oekonomismus. Zur Kritik am Projekt Ideologietheorie (PIT). *Forum Kritische Psychologie, 11,* 7–23.

(1984). Förderung von "Ausländerfeindlichkeit" zur Durchsetzung kapitalistischer Verwertungsinteressen. *Forum Kritische Psychologie, 14,* 110–127.

Holzkamp, K., & Schurig, V. (1973). Zur Einführung in A. N. Leontjews "Probleme der Entwicklung des Psychischen." In A. N. Leontyev, *Probleme der Entwicklung des Psychischen* (pp. xi–lii). Frankfurt/M.: Campus.

Jäger, M. (1977). Wissenschaftstheoretische Kennzeichnung der funktionalhistorischen Vorgehensweise als Ueberwindung der Beschränktheit der traditionellen psychologischen Wissenschaftspraxis. In K. H. Braun & K. Holzkamp (Eds.), *Kritische Psychologie. Bericht über den 1. Internationalen Kongress Kritische Psychologie vom 13.–15. Mai 1977* (Vol. 1, pp. 122–139). Cologne: Pahl-Rugenstein.

Jäger, M., Keiler, P., Maschewsky, W., & Schneider, U. (1978). *Subjektivität als Methodenproblem.* Frankfurt/M.: Campus.

Jantzen, W. (1980). *Grundriss einer allgemeinen Psychopathologie und Psychotherapie.* Cologne: Pahl-Rugenstein.

Katz, D., & Stotland, A. (1959). A preliminary statement to a theory of attitude structure and change. In S. Koch (Ed.). (1959–1963). *Psychology: A study of a science* (Vols. 1–6). Study I: Conceptual and systematic (Vol. 3, pp. 423–475). New York: McGraw-Hill.

Keiler, P. (1977). Zur Problematik des Verhältnisses zwischen historischer Analyse und traditioneller empirischer Forschung in der Psychologie. In K. H. Braun & K. Holzkamp, *Kritische Psychologie. Bericht über den 1. Internationalen Kongress Kritische Psychologie vom 13.–15. Mai 1977* (Vol. 1, pp. 158–175). Cologne: Pahl-Rugenstein.

(1985). Zur Problematik der Tätigkeitskonzeption Leontjews. *Forum Kritische Psychologie, 15,* 133–139.

Kelly, G. A. (1955). *The psychology of personal constructs.* (2 Vols.). New York: Norton.

Kern, H., & Schumann, M. (1984). *Das Ende der Arbeitsteilung. Rationalisierung in der industriellen Produktion.* Munich: Beck.

Kessen, W., & Mandler, G. (1961). Anxiety, pain, and the inhibition of distress. *Psychological Review, 68,* 396–404.

Klafki, W. (1964). *Das pädagogische Problem des Elementaren und die Theorie der kategorialen Bildung.* Weinheim/West Berlin: Beltz.

Koch, S. (1959). Epilogue. In S. Koch (Ed.). (1959–1963). *Psychology: A study of a science* (Vols. 1–6). Study I: Conceptual and systematic (Vol. 3, pp. 729–788). New York: McGraw-Hill.

Köhler, W. (1947). *Gestalt psychology.* New York: Liveright.

Kritische Psychologie. (1970). [Reader with contributions by T. W. Adorno, K. Holzkamp, et al.]. Bochum: Fachschaft Psychologie.

Lazarus, R. S. (1966). *Psychological stress and the coping process.* New York: McGraw-Hill.

——— (1977). Cognitive and coping processes in emotion. In A. Monat & R. S. Lazarus, *Stress and coping. An anthology* (pp. 145–159). New York: Columbia University Press.

Lazarus, R. S., & Averill, J. R. (1972). Emotion and cognition: With special reference to anxiety. In C. D. Spielberger (Ed.), *Anxiety. Current trends in theory and research* (Vol. 2, pp. 242–283). New York, San Francisco, London: Academic Press.

Lazarus, R. S., Averill, J. R., & Opton, E. M. (1973). Ansatz zu einer kognitiven Gefühlstheorie. In N. Birbaumer (Ed.), *Neuropsychologie der Angst* (pp. 158–183). Munich, Berlin, Vienna: Urban & Schwarzenberg.

Leiser, E. (1977). Zum gegenwärtigen Stand der methodologischen Explikation des historischen Verfahrens der Kritischen Psychologie: ungeklärte Probleme, Lösungsansätze und zukünftige Forschungsaufgaben. In K. H. Braun & K. Holzkamp, *Kritische Psychologie. Bericht über den 1. Internationalen Kongress Kritische Psychologie vom 13.–15. Mai 1977* (Vol. 1, pp. 140–149). Cologne: Pahl-Rugenstein.

Leontyev, A. N. (1971). *Probleme der Entwicklung des Psychischen.* Berlin/GDR: Volk und Wissen. (West German ed. 1973. Frankfurt/M.: Campus)

Lerner, M. (1979). Surplus powerlessness. *Social Policy* (January/February), 19–27.

Lewin, K. (1920). *Die Sozialisierung des Taylorsystems. Eine grundsätzliche Untersuchung zur Arbeits- und Berufspsychologie.* Berlin: Verlag Gesellschaft und Erziehung.

——— (1931). *Die psychologische Situation bei Lohn und Strafe.* Leipzig: Hirzel.

——— (1969). *Grundlage der topologischen Psychologie.* Bern, Stuttgart: Huber. (Original work [Engl.] published 1936.)

——— (1981). Der Uebergang von der aristotelischen zur galileischen Denkweise in Biologie und Psychologie. In Kurt Lewin, *Werkausgabe* (Vol. 1, pp. 223–278). Bern/Stuttgart: Huber/Klett-Cotta. (Original work published 1931).

Liebknecht, K. (1958). *Spartakusbriefe.* (Institut für Marxismus-Leninismus beim ZK der SED, Ed.). Berlin/GDR: Dietz.

Lipps, T. (1902). *Vom Fühlen, Wollen und Denken.* Leipzig: Barth.

Maier, N. R. F. (1965). *Psychology in industry* (3rd ed.). Boston: Houghton Mifflin.

Maiers, W. (1979). Wissenschaftskritik als Erkenntniskritik. Zur Grundlegung differentieller Beurteilung des Erkenntnisgehalts traditioneller Psychologie in kritisch-psychologischen Gegenstandsanalysen. *Forum Kritische Psychologie, 5,* 47–128.

——— (1985). Menschliche Subjektivität und Natur. Zum wissenschaftlichen Humanismus in den Ansätzen A. N. Leontjews und der Kritischen Psychologie. *Forum Kritische Psychologie, 15,* 114–128.

Maiers, W., & Markard, M. (1977). Kritische Psychologie als marxistische Subjektwissenschaft. Fazit einer Entwicklung anlässlich des ersten "Internationalen Kongresses Kritische Psychologie." *Sozialistische Politik, 41,* 136–156.

Mandler, G. (1964). The interruption of behavior. In D. Levine (Ed.), *Nebraska Symposium on Motivation* (Vol. 12, pp. 163–219). Lincoln: University of Nebraska Press.

——— (1972). Helplessness. Theory and research in anxiety. In Spielberger, C. D. (Ed.). *Anxiety. Current trends in theory and research* (Vol. 2, pp. 359–374). New York, San Francisco, London: Academic Press.

Mandler, G., & Sarason, S. B. (1952). A study of anxiety and learning. *Journal of Abnormal and Social Psychology, 47,* 561–565.

Mandler, G., & Watson, D. L. (1966). Anxiety and the interruption of behavior. In C. D. Spielberger (Ed.), *Anxiety and behavior* (pp. 263–288). New York, London: Academic Press.

Markard, M. (1984). *Einstellung – Kritik eines sozialpsychologischen Grundkonzepts.* Frankfurt/M.: Campus.

Marx, K. (1965). Brief an P. W. Annenkow [December 1846]. In *Marx/Engels, Werke* (Vol. 27, 451–463). Berlin/GDR: Dietz. (Original work published 1846)

(1968). Ueber P. J. Proudhon. Brief an J. B. v. Schweitzer. In *Marx/Engels, Werke* (Vol. 16, pp. 25–32). Berlin/GDR: Dietz. (Original work published 1870)

(1969a). Thesen über Feuerbach. In *Marx/Engels, Werke* (Vol. 3: 5–7). Berlin/GDR: Dietz. (Original work published 1845)

(1969b). Das Kapital. Kritik der politischen Oekonomie. In *Marx/Engels, Werke* (Vols. 23–25). Berlin/GDR: Dietz. (Original work published 1867)

(1970a). Zur Kritik der Hegelschen Rechtsphilosophie. In *Marx/Engels, Werke* (Vol. 1: 203–333). Berlin/GDR: Dietz. (Original work published 1843)

(1970b). Zur Kritik der Hegelschen Rechtsphilosophie. Einleitung. In *Marx/Engels, Werke* (Vol. 1: 378–391). Berlin/GDR: Dietz. (Original work published 1844)

(1971a). Der Kommunismus des "Rheinischen Beobachters." In *Marx/Engels, Werke* (Vol. 4: 191–203). Berlin/GDR: Dietz. (Original work published 1847)

(1971b). Einleitung [zur Kritik der Politischen Oekonomie, 1857]. In *Marx/Engels, Werke* (Vol. 13, pp. 613–642). Berlin/GDR: Dietz. (Original work published 1857)

(1974). *Grundrisse der Kritik der Politischen Oekonomie* (Rohentwurf 1857–1858. Berlin/GDR: Dietz.

(1981). Oekonomisch-philosophische Manuskripte aus dem Jahre 1844. In *Marx/Engels, Werke* (Suppl. Vol. 1, pp. 465–588). Berlin/GDR: Dietz. (Original work published 1844)

Marx, K., & Engels, F. (1969). Die deutsche Ideologie. In *Marx/Engels, Werke* (Vol. 3, pp. 9–530). Berlin/GDR: Dietz. (Original work published 1845–6)

(1970a). *The German ideology.* New York: International. (Original work published 1845–6)

(1970b). Die heilige Familie oder Kritik der kritischen Kritik. Gegen Bruno Bauer und Konsorten. In *Marx/Engels, Werke* (Vol. 2, pp. 3–223). Berlin/GDR: Dietz. (Original work published 1845)

Maschewsky, W. (1977). *Das Experiment in der Psychologie.* Frankfurt/M.: Campus.

Maslow, A. H. (1972). *Eupsychian management: A journal* (12th ed.). Homewood, IL: Irwin and the Dorsey Press.

Mattes, P. (1985). Die Psychologiekritik der Studentenbewegung. In M. G. Ash & U. Geuter (Eds.), *Geschichte der deutschen Psychologie im 20. Jahrhundert. Ein Ueberblick* (pp. 286–313). Opladen: Westdeutscher Verlag.

Mellett, P. G. (1974). The clinical problem. In H. R. Beech (Ed.), *Obsessional states* (pp. 55–94). London: Methuen.

Messmann, A., & Rückriem, G. (1978). Zum Verständnis der menschlichen Natur in der Auffassung des Psychischen bei A. N. Leontjew. In G. Rückriem, F. Tomberg, & W. Volpert (Eds.), *Historischer Materialismus und menschliche Natur* (pp. 80–133). Cologne: Pahl-Rugenstein.

Meyer, M. (1921). *The psychology of the other one.* Columbia: Missouri Bookstore.

Minz, G. (1983). Als Erzogene erziehen. Zum besonderen Interesse von Linken an Alice Miller. *Forum Kritische Psychologie, 11,* 126–143.

Moscovici, S. (1972). Society and theory in social psychology. In J. Israel & H. Tajfel (Eds.), *The context of social psychology: A critical assessment* (pp. 17–68). London: Academic Press.

Murphy, G., & Likert, R. (1967). *Public opinion and the individual.* New York: Russell and Russell. (Original work published 1938).

Murphy, G., & Murphy, L. B. (1931). *Experimental social psychology.* New York: Harper.

Nisbett, R. E., & Schachter, S. (1966). Cognitive manipulation of pain. *Journal of Experimental Social Psychology, 2,* 227–236.

Peitsch, H. (1983). Deutschlands Gedächtnis an seine dunkelste Zeit. Zur Funktion der Autobiographik in den Westzonen Deutschlands und den Westsektoren von Berlin 1945–1949. Habilitationsschrift, Freie Universität Berlin (West).

Peitsch, H., Kühnl, R., & Osterkamp, U. (1985). Methoden der Medienanalyse am Beispiel von Selbstzeugnissen über den Faschismus in den Massenmedien der Nachkriegszeit. In K.-H. Braun & K. Holzkamp (Eds.), *Subjektivität als Problem psychologischer Methodik. 3. Internationaler Kongress Kritische Psychologie Marburg 1984* (pp. 294–314). Frankfurt/M.: Campus.

Perls, F. S. (1976). *Gestalt-Therapie in Aktion*. Stuttgart: Klett.

Piaget, J. (1975). Nachahmung, Spiel und Traum. *Gesammelte Werke*, Vol. 5. Stuttgart: Klett.

Pompeiano, O. (1965). Ascending and descending influences of somatic afferent volleys in unrestrained cats: Supraspinal inhibitory control of spinal reflexes during natural and reflex-induced sleep. In M. Jouvet (Ed.), *Aspects anatomo-fonctionnels de la physiologie du sommeil* (pp. 309–395). Paris: Centre Nationale des Recherches Scientifiques.

Pribram, K. H. (1963). Reinforcement revisited: A structural view. In M. R. Jones (Ed.), *Nebraska Symposion on Motivation* (Vol. 11, pp. 113–159). Lincoln: University of Nebraska Press.

(1967a). Emotion: Steps toward a neuropsychological theory. In D. C. Glass (Ed.), *Neurophysiology and emotion* (pp. 3–40). Proceedings of a conference under the auspices of Russell Sage Foundation and the Rockefeller University. New York: The Rockefeller Press.

(1967b). The new neurology and the biology of emotion: A structural approach. *American Psychologist, 22*, 1329–1336.

Projektgruppe Automation und Qualifikation. (1975). Automation in der BRD. *Argument-Sonderband* (AS Special Issue) 7. West Berlin: Argument.

(1978a). Entwicklung der Arbeitstätigkeiten und die Methode ihrer Erfassung. *Argument-Sonderband* (AS Special Issue) *19*. West Berlin: Argument.

(1978b.) Theorien über Automationsarbeit. *Argument-Sonderband* (AS Special Issue) *31*. West Berlin: Argument.

(1980). Automationsarbeit: Empirische Untersuchungen 1. *Argument-Sonderband* (AS Special Issue) *43*. West Berlin: Argument.

(1981a). Automationsarbeit: Empisrische Untersuchungen 2. *Argument-Sonderband* (AS Special Issue) *55*. West Berlin: Argument.

(1981b). Automationsarbeit: Empirische Untersuchungen 3. *Argument-Sonderband* (AS Special Issue) *67*. West Berlin: Argument.

(1983). Zerreissproben. Automation im Arbeiterleben. Empirische Untersuchungen 4. *Argument-Sonderband* (AS Special Issue) *79*. West Berlin: Argument.

(1987). *Automation im Widerspruch. Ein Handbuch*. West Berlin: Argument.

Psychologie als historische Wissenschaft. (1972). Geschichte der psychologischen Theorien und der Berufspraxis von Psychologen mit dem Ziel der Entwicklung einer kritischen Psychologie. *Pressedienst Wissenschaft 8*. West Berlin: Freie Universität Berlin.

Redeker, H. (1963). Beobachtung oder Praxis. Ueber Wesen und Funktion der Kunst. *Deutsche Zeitschrift für Philosophie, 11* (7), 805–825.

Reed, G. F. (1968). Some formal qualities of obsessional thinking. *Psychiatria Clinica, 1*, 382–392.

(1969). "Under-inclusion": A characteristic of obsessional personality disorder. (Pts. 1 and 2). *British Journal of Psychiatry, 115*, 781–785; 787–790.

Rehm, J. (1986). Theoretische und methodologische Probleme bei der Erforschung von Vorurteilen. Pt. I: Vorurteil und Realität – Ist das traditionelle Forschungsprogramm der Vorurteilsforschung gescheitert? Part II: Vorurteile und menschliche Konstruktion der Realität – Neue Erkenntnisse zu alten Phänomenen? *Zeitschrift für Sozialpsychologie, 17*, 18–30; 74–86.

Reich, W. (1933). *Charakteranalyse. Technik und Grundlagen für Studierende und praktizierende Analytiker*. Vienna: Author.

Richter, H. E. (1981a). *Alle redeten vom Frieden. Versuch einer paradoxen Intervention.* Reinbek: Rowohlt.

(1981b). Spiegel-Gespräch: "Wir leben im kollektiven Verfolgungswahn." *Der Spiegel, 44* (October 26), 39–46.

(1982). *Zur Psychologie des Friedens.* Reinbek: Rowohlt.

Roitbak, A. I. (1960). Electrical phenomena in cerebral cortex during extinction of orientation and conditioned reflexes. Moscow Colloquium. *Electroencephalography and Clinical Neurophysiology, 13,* (Suppl.), 91–100.

Rokeach, M. (1968). Attitude change and behavioral change. In M. Rokeach, *Beliefs, attitudes, and values* (pp. 133–155). San Francisco: Jossey-Bass. (Reprinted from *Public Opinion Quarterly, 30,* 1966/1967, 529–550).

(1980). Some unresolved issues in theories of beliefs, attitudes, and values. In M. M. Page (Ed.), *Nebraska Symposium on Motivation,* Vol. 27, Beliefs, Attitudes, and Values (pp. 261–304). Lincoln/London: University of Nebraska Press.

Rubinstein, S. L. (1961). *Sein und Bewusstsein.* Berlin/GDR: Akademie.

Rubinstein, S. L. (1968). *Grundlagen der allgemeinen Psychologie* (6th ed.). Berlin/GDR: Volk und Wissen.

Schachter, S. (1966). The interaction of cognitive and physiological determinants of emotional states. In C. D. Spielberger (ed.). *Anxiety and behavior.* New York: Academic Press.

Schachter, S., & Singer, J. E. (1962). Cognitive, social, and physiological determinants of emotional state. *Psychological Review, 69,* 379–399.

Schiffman, S. S., Reynolds, M. L., & Young, F. W. (1981). *Introduction to multidimensional scaling. Theory, methods, and applications.* New York: Academic Press.

Schurig, V. (1976). *Die Entstehung des Bewusstseins.* Frankfurt/M.: Campus.

Searles, H. F. (1961). Anxiety concerning change, as seen in the psychotherapy of schizophrenic patients – with particular reference to the sense of personal identity. *International Journal of Psychoanalysis, 42,* 74–85.

Seidel, R. (1976). *Denken – Psychologische Analyse der Entstehung und Lösung von Problemen.* Frankfurt/M.: Campus

Seligman, M. E. P. (1975). *Helplessness.* San Francisco: Freeman.

Selsam, H., & Martel, H. (1963). *Reader in Marxist philosophy.* New York: International.

Simonow, P. W. (1975). *Widerspiegelungstheorie und Psychophysiologie der Emotionen.* Berlin/GDR: Volk & Wissen.

Skinner, B. F. (1956). A case history in scientific method. *American Psychologist, 11,* 221–233.

Smith, M. B. (1980). Attitudes, values, and selfhood. In M. M. Page (Ed.), *Nebraska Symposium on Motivation 1979,* Vol. 27, Beliefs, Attitudes, and Values (pp. 305–350). Lincoln/London: University of Nebraska Press.

Sokolov, E. N. (1960). Neuronal models of orienting reflex. In Brazier, M. A. B. (Ed.), *The central nervous system and behavior* (pp. 187–276). New York: Josiah Macy Jr. Foundation.

(1963). *Perception and the conditioned reflex.* Oxford: Pergamon Press.

Solomon, R. L. (1977). An opponent process theory of motivation. The affective dynamics of drug addiction. In J. D. Maser & M. E. P. Seligman (Eds.), *Psychopathology: Experimental models* (pp. 66–103). San Francisco: Freeman.

Spielberger, C. D. (1966). The effects of anxiety on complex learning and academic achievement. In C. D. Spielberger (Ed.), *Anxiety and behavior* (pp. 361–398). New York, London: Academic Press.

Staeuble, I. (1985). Zur Einheit von historischer Erkenntniskritik und Weiterentwicklung – Versuch der Reformulierung einer Aufgabenstellung. In K.-H. Braun & K. Holzkamp (Eds.), *Subjektivität als Problem psychologischer Methodik. 3. Internationaler Kongress Kritische Psychologie Marburg 1984* (pp. 318–321). Frankfurt/M.: Campus.

Szymanski, J. S. (1929). *Zur Denkpsychologie. Die Begriffsgefühle und das Evidenzerleben. Das Denken durch Bilder.* Vienna, Leipzig: Perles.

Tarter, D. E. (1970). Attitudes: The mental myth. *The American Sociologist, 5,* 276–278.

Thomas, W. I., & Znaniecki, F. (1958). *The Polish peasant in Europe and America.* (5 Vols.) New York: Dover Publications. (Original work published 1918–1920).

Thurstone, L. L. (1967a). Attitudes can be measured. In M. Fishbein (Ed.), *Readings in attitude theory and measurement* (pp. 77–89). New York: Wiley. (Reprinted from *American Journal of Sociology, 33,* 1928, 529–554).

(1967b). The measurement of social attitudes. In M. Fishbein (Ed.), *Readings in attitude theory and measurement* (pp. 14–25). (Reprinted from *Journal of Abnormal and Social Psychology, 26,* 1931, 249–269).

Volkelt, J. (1922). *Die Gefühlsgewissheit. Eine erkenntnistheoretische Untersuchung.* Munich: Beck'sche Verlagsbuchhandlung.

Vygotsky, L. S. (1980). Das Spiel und seine Bedeutung in der psychischen Entwicklung des Kindes. In D. Elkonin, *Psychologie des Spiels* (Appendix, pp. 441–465). Cologne: Pahl-Rugenstein.

Waelder, R. (1973). Die psychoanalytische Theorie des Spiels. In A. Flitner (Ed.), *Das Kinderspiel* (pp. 50–62). Munich: Piper.

Watson, J. B. (1924). *Psychology from the standpoint of a behaviorist.* Philadelphia: Lippincott.

Wicker, A. W. (1969). Attitudes vs. actions: The relationship of verbal and overt behavioral responses to attitude objects. *Journal of Social Issues, 25,* 41–78.

Wilhelm, R. (1983). "Staat jenseits der Klassen?" Zur Kritik der Staatsauffassung des PIT. *Forum Kritische Psychologie, 11,* 56–75.

Wolf, F. O. (1976). Psychologie oder kritische Psychologie? Metakritische Bemerkungen zu einer Kontroverse über den Gegenstand der Psychologie. In G. L. Eberlein & R. Pieper (Eds.), *Psychologie – Wissenschaft ohne Gegenstand?* (pp. 199–223). Frankfurt/M.: Campus.

Woodworth, R. S. (1918). *Dynamic psychology.* New York: Columbia University Press.

Wundt, W. (1896). *Grundrisse der Psychologie.* (11th ed. 1913). Leipzig: Kröner.

Zulliger, H. (1952). *Heilende Kräfte im kindlichen Spiel.* Stuttgart: Klett.

(1957). *Bausteine zur Kinderpsychotherapie und Kindertiefenpsychologie.* Bern, Stuttgart: Huber, Klett.

Index

263